HIGH POINTS
OF
MEDIEVAL
CULTURE

JAMES J. WALSH

Essay Index Reprint Series

 BOOKS FOR LIBRARIES PRESS
FREEPORT, NEW YORK

First Published 1937
Reprinted 1969

CB
351
.W3
1969

STANDARD BOOK NUMBER

8369-0057-X

LIBRARY OF CONGRESS CATALOG CARD NUMBER

69-18940

PRINTED IN THE UNITED STATES OF AMERICA

PREFACE BY THE GENERAL EDITOR

MORE intimately than any other English-speaking author Dr. Walsh has become identified in our minds with the study and interpretation of the culture of the Middle Ages. Equally alert in his contact with the world about him, he has further understood how to make his knowledge available to the time in which he lives. His work, therefore, has exercised a predominant influence in revealing anew this period which stands unique in the history of the world.

We are all aware of the interest taken by men of learning and of science in the discoveries made in this field within our own generation; of the personal researches frequently carried out by them; and in general of the changed attitude toward everything pertaining to medieval life on the part of scholars and thinkers.

This knowledge, however, has percolated, but slowly, down to the general public and into the journalistic literature of our day. To aid in hastening that process, not merely by way of factual information but also by pointing out the larger good to be derived from it, the present volume has been written. It will be of interest to all classes and go far to promote a more comprehensive understanding of the relation of the Middle Ages to education and intellectual development, no less than to art, architecture, and the true amenities of human life.

It has been the merit of the modern historian, archaeologist, and general seeker after artistic treasures of whatever kind to rediscover much of the lost culture of the Middle Ages. Yet while each has thus contributed his own special share to making them better known, Dr. Walsh has understood how to combine into a single unified work what is most valuable in the findings of all. He has skimmed for us the cream of his own rich information, consistently accumulated through the course of a long lifetime, and has presented it in this book. A separate volume will be required to deal with the science and scientific aspects of the same period, a subject from which we have definitely prescinded here for that very reason.

Our modern discovery of the Middle Ages, after the long period of intervening darkness that obscured them, was of necessity a gradual process. To begin with, there were landmarks that could never be wholly lost to sight, however dimly they might be limned for the men of that day on the dull gray band of their horizon line — promontories and mountaintops that stood out stark and bold, as undeniable realities which deluge and earthquake never could obliterate. Such were Dante, Aquinas, Francis of Assisi, and farther away in the remote distance, Benedict, Gregory the Great, Charlemagne, Alfred the Great, and a host of others whom mankind would never forget.

Then, as the darkness lifted and the mist withdrew, the last wraiths drifted and hung about the graceful Gothic spires, that rose like dreams of beauty against the blue of the enduring skies.

Yet these were but obvious rediscoveries, while many of the subjects dealt with in this book remained as hidden as before, and still remain so for the men and women of a mechanized age, prone to think only in terms of material things. But the fact is — a fact the author never fails to insist upon — that much on which we pride ourselves as most typically modern is in reality strictly medieval.

True, we must not make the mistake of recognizing only the good that existed in the Middle Ages. Men and women, then as now, were creatures of flesh and blood, as well as gifted with immortal souls. They were tempted, as we all are, to allow temporal interests to dominate their aspirations after higher things. Shadows, often deep and dark, lay across those times. But, surprising as it may seem, no one could well have dealt with them more severely than the Holy See itself in the background painted by it in the Encyclical *Rite Expiatis*, St. Francis yesterday and today. Saints were needed, then as now, to lift men up from the mire and set their feet again, sure and safe, upon the upward road, their faces turned unflinchingly upon the vision of that only Good and True and Beautiful which knows no bounds. And yet it was this after which the Middle Ages sought, and from this they drew their keen appreciation of all that in turn is good and true and beautiful in nature and in art. Here, then, is the secret of their greatness. Their failure, when it occurred, lay in abandoning this course. To them then, as to our own modern world, might be applied the powerful but no less tender words of the Prophet Isaias, representing God's complaint to ungrateful Israel:

> The ox knoweth his owner
> and the ass his master's crib,
>> but Israel hath not known me
>> and my people hath not understood.[1]

Surely, the Middle Ages never failed so greatly as we. For that reason, too, the world knew more true contentment, joy, and happiness. England was *merry* England only then. In proportion as men deny their Creator they will find that their own creations turn against them. Their very inventions, intended for their material service, turn to their destruction. The word of the Lord cannot be made void:

---

[1] Isa. 1:3.

> And his zeal will take armor,
> and he will arm the creature for the revenge
>   of his enemies;
> and he will sharpen his severe wrath for
>   a spear,
> and the whole world shall fight with him
>   against the unwise.[2]

The Middle Ages had happily learned the lessons of true wisdom. Hence arose not merely their satisfaction in life but also their joy in creating beautiful things, to which the author never tires of reverting. It was the period when for the first time in history — and for the last time since then — the artisan came into his own, and both he and his handiwork were truly honored. Hence the wealth of artistic production to which this book refers and the unexampled skill to which even the humblest craftsman could attain.

At the same time, intellectual culture in the schools was far from unknown, and it is precisely in this regard that the reader will find perhaps the most astonishing revelations he may meet with in the present book.

But it is not the purpose of this preface to forestall what the author himself has to say. With the shadows and weaknesses of the Middle Ages he is not concerned. As this title clearly indicates, he has the more grateful task of dwelling only upon the true and beautiful, understanding that from these the good is not dissociated.

JOSEPH HUSSLEIN, S.J., PH.D.,
General Editor, Science and Culture Series.

St. Louis University,
October 22, 1937.

---

[2] Wisd. 5:21.

CONTENTS

HIGH POINTS OF MEDIEVAL CULTURE

I

MEN OF THE EARLY MIDDLE AGES

JOHN FISKE, the well-known New England historical writer, in the introduction to his volume *The Beginnings of New England,* has a passage in which he pays a high tribute to the men of the earlier Middle Ages.

"When we think," he says, "of all the work big with promise of the future that went on in those centuries which modern writers in their ignorance used once to set apart and stigmatize as the 'dark ages'; when we consider how the seeds of what is noblest in modern life were then painfully sown upon the soil which imperial Rome had prepared; when we think of the various works of a Gregory, a Benedict, a Boniface, an Alfred, a Charlemagne, we feel that there is a sense in which the most brilliant achievements of pagan antiquity are dwarfed in comparison with these."

The five men whose names are here recalled will admirably serve as an illustration of the contributions made by the men of the early Middle Ages toward the progress of mankind and the conservation of the treasures of culture. About each of them many books have deservedly been written. A few paragraphs must here suffice to convey some general conception of their work, and show why succeeding generations have vied with each other in honoring their memory. But they are far, as shall be seen, from exhausting the honor roll of the illustrious men and women of those days.

The first of the five great names to be mentioned by the New England historian is that of *Gregory,* surnamed *the Great* (550–604). An immense influence was exercised by this

1

brilliant pontiff which still continues in many ways down to the present time.

Gregory belonged to one of the old patrician families, and after a large experience in life entered a monastery in Rome which he himself had founded. During his early youth he had devoted himself to the study of what was then known as the *trivium*, consisting of logic, grammar, and rhetoric. Later he took up the study of law, and finally entered the imperial service. When about thirty-five years of age he was appointed *praetor urbanus*, city magistrate, by Emperor Justin II, but a few years later resigned from this career and embraced the monastic life. Again his talents were recognized and made use of when he was sent to Constantinople by Pope Pelagius II, as *apocrisiarius* or papal legate. Thenceforth his career was definitely ecclesiastical and his service was demanded for many purposes.

At the age of about fifty Gregory was elected pope. His first care was for the restoration of monastic discipline. His attention was next turned to the enforcement of celibacy among the clergy. He then, in a masterly way, took up the question of the liturgy. He himself, it is said, personally arranged the Gregorian chant which has been preserved in the Church ever since, and during our own age has been revived in a special way, manifesting after the lapse of so many centuries the musical genius of its inventor.

Gregory further developed a great spirit of missionary zeal for the propagation of Christianity. Significant of this was the familiar incident with regard to the Anglo-Saxon youths whom he saw offered for sale in the Roman market place. "Not Angles but angels!" was his now classical exclamation. At the time he made this play of words on their angelic looks, he was not as yet pope. But he at once ordered the purchase of the boys and gave them the freedom of Christ that they might become missionaries to their own people. In fact, he himself pleaded to be allowed to go as a missionary to those regions. But his presence in Rome was too important and he was not permitted to leave. Being elected pope he sent missionaries to many other places besides England, and his knowledge of men and experience in life enabled him to choose apostolic laborers who were likely to be successful.

Of his works it may be said quite literally that there was nothing he touched which he did not adorn. His achievements, because of their importance, continue to make themselves felt down to our own modern days. They demonstrate beyond all doubt the genius of the man who amid the discouraging conditions of his time was able deeply to impress his name on human life and thought.

Gregory is a type of the men who guided the destiny of the Church at the beginning of the Middle Ages. Many of these leaders were of high natural ability. Not a few possessed the gift of genius, but this was joined in them with a spirit of self-forgetfulness and readiness to labor for others. They thus realized in their own person that definition of a saint which happily describes him as a man who thinks first of others.

Hard upon the name of Gregory in Fiske's eulogium follows that of *Benedict* (480–543), although in point of time he actually preceded the former. Both men lived in the trying period of the barbarian invasions. They accomplished their work at a time when the influence they exerted was sadly needed. The Romans, at this period, had degenerated to such a degree that almost no interest in intellectual or spiritual pursuits remained among them. Then it was that these two descendants of ancient Roman families arose to teach their people how well worth while was the life of the spirit and how little lasting satisfaction came with mere life of the body. It is from Gregory that we have the account of the life of St. Benedict, and above all of St. Benedict's sister, St. Scholastica. Had Gregory done nothing else than that he would have deserved our lasting gratitude.

Benedict, the founder of the Benedictines, is one of those many interesting souls who are caught up by the idea of retirement from the world and its distractions desiring thus to develop unhindered what is best in man. Quickly drawing others to them they are soon surrounded by an almost incredible number of followers.

Men like St. Dominic, of Spain, St. Francis of Assisi or Gerard Groote, founder of the Brethren of the Common Life, were striking examples of this in the later Middle Ages. So too, in the days of the Renaissance, Ignatius Loyola, in the eighteenth century, Alphonsus Liguori, and in the nineteenth, Rosmini, forsook the world only to become great leaders of men in the cause of God. The life of St. Benedict shows very clearly how souls are attracted by the spirit of discipleship toward leaders truly possessed of unselfish ideals.

Benedict was born of a well-to-do Roman patrician family. A life of pleasure and gaiety spread out before him had he cared to yield himself up to its enticements. But disillusioned with the world, he preferred the quest of intellectual and spiritual good. He retired to a cave and there devoted himself to prayer and intimate communion with the spirit world. Before long others came to him, asking to share his solitude with him in a common effort after a new life. Very soon the necessity arose of organizing a community in which the daily life might be so regularized that all could devote a reasonable length of time to the various phases of community affairs.

Only a few years before the birth of Benedict the invasion of the barbarians had brought about the fall of the Roman empire. The Romans themselves had been sinking gradually into decadence, so that almost nothing of the intellectual and spiritual life remained in the social order. Divorce had become easy and frequent, marriage was often childless, men and women were preoccupied with things of the body and not of the mind and soul. Such a life could not satisfy earnest men. This, therefore, accounts in no small measure for the eager flocking of disciples to Benedict in his monastic retreat.

The saint himself devoted much thoughtful study to solving the question as to the best way of governing this monastic establishment. Out of his prayer and deliberation grew his famous Rule of the Benedictines, looked upon as one of the supremely great constitutions drawn up for the government of men. It has served the purpose of making millions of souls happier than they would otherwise have been, while it has rendered their lives of the truest usefulness to mankind. Quickly the sons of Benedict destroyed the blight of slavery that had degraded the agricultural laborer and bettered his condition, while they saved the great literary treasures of the classical world.

Benedict divided the duties of the day into prayer and labor. The latter was to be mental and manual. He further decided how the hours should be filled with adoration, as well as with intellectual and physical occupation. He understood men as few have done before or since, and as a consequence his name still remains in benediction after fifteen hundred years.

Those among the members of the Order who were gifted with the necessary talent were afforded an opportunity for mental education. The greater part of their time was spent in copying precious manuscripts both for their own monastic libraries and for exchange with other monasteries. Thus the intellectual life was kept from perishing and the classics saved from utter disappearance during the darkest portion of the Middle Ages. It was the time when control of the social order fell into the hands of the barbarian invader and the Church was needed alike to save and to preserve civilization.

The organization of manual labor was extremely important, not only because it lifted the stigma which had so long been connected with it in the minds of the Romans, but from another standpoint as well. The Benedictine monasteries, namely, became real schools of agriculture, in which the improvement of crops and of stock, together with the development of farming in a progressive way was the aim of the monks. As the number of tenants grew who in time came to occupy the farms attached to the monasteries, the knowledge gained by the agricultural experience of the monks was widely diffused. The monks not only laid down the principles of agriculture but they exemplified them in practice, laboring with their own hands.

Benedictine monasteries soon spread all over Europe and proved to be centers of learning no less than schools of life for those who were brought in contact with them. So Augustine, when sent to England, made his monasteries schools and took up in them the teaching of the classics. This became the custom in most of the Benedictine foundations. Their intimate relation to education thus gave them a place of great influence in the world of the earlier Middle Ages.

What Benedict did for the men, his sister Scholastica did for the women. Brother and sister were very closely allied to each other in disposition and affectionately united in fraternal bonds. The convents of the Benedictine nuns spread as fast and as far as the monasteries of the Benedictine monks. The days of the sisters were taken up with many of the same tasks that engaged the attention of their monastic brothers. They occupied themselves with the making of beautiful objects for the service of the Church. Fine linens and embroideries came from their skillful hands. But they were no less provided with manual labor in their gardens. Here, too, like the brethren of Benedict, they saw to it that their tenants were duly trained in farming methods so that in a real sense of the word their institutions represented agricultural schools.

The intellectual life of these Benedictine convents is gloriously demonstrated by the fact that in the tenth century, often considered the darkest hundred years in the Middle Ages, a Benedictine nun in one of the convents along the Rhine wrote a series of dramas, based on a classic model and highly admired today, that she might help to provide appropriate reading matter for the monks and nuns of her time. Two centuries later a Benedictine abbess of one of the convents in the same neighborhood wrote the most important book on science composed in the twelfth century. Her work has been the subject of intensive study in modern times, with the result that the more we learn to know about her the higher grows our estimation of her information on the physical sciences.[1]

Benedict created an institution which at once took up the work of saving, for subsequent generations, the classic literature of the past. At the same time he provided a magnificent opportunity for the cultivation of the intellectual and spiritual life by the men of his age. The appreciation in which the Benedictines came to be held by all classes of people will probably be best understood from the statistics of the order. According to reliable authority they already had, at the beginning of the fourteenth century, several thousand monasteries scattered throughout the world. Up to that period they had given the Church 24 popes, 200 cardinals, 7,000 archbishops, 15,000 bishops, and — what they rightfully consider their greatest glory — over 1,500 canonized saints. It was not uncommon for men and women of the highest rank to abandon their worldly honors and assume the garb of a humble religious. Into the Benedictine membership have been received 20 emperors, 10 empresses, 47 kings, and 50 queens.

The religious Order, thus instituted, welcomed all classes of the population and afforded to all those who came to it opportunities for happiness far higher, even in this life, than could be obtained in any other way. Even the average length of life among its members was much longer than the general average for humanity at that time.

The Benedictines are proud to be just what the rule of St. Benedict made them nearly fifteen hundred years ago. One of the great constitutions of the world's history, as we have said, this rule has been the subject of deep study and hearty admiration on the part of many scholars ever since it was promulgated. It is particularly so in our own time. Here, quite literally, is a constitution which enables those who faithfully observe its rule of life "to form a more perfect union, estab-

---

[1] The references here are to Hroswitha and Hildegarde (see Chapter XII).

lish justice, insure domestic tranquillity . . . promote the general welfare, and provide the blessings of liberty for themselves and those who come after them." How appropriate, indeed, is the word *order* to describe this mode of life which represents one of the triumphs of human intelligence. It redeems man's tendency to selfishness and demonstrates that it is possible for men to live in peace and quiet, devoted to the things of the intellect and of the spirit, while richly developing their human personality.

Today, a millennium and a half after Benedict began his work on Monte Cassino, that work still lives on. Next to the Church the Order of St. Benedict represents the oldest institution in Western history. When we recall how many human foundations of all kinds have disappeared in the course of history, the persistence of this religious Order seems to indicate that it is more than merely human in its establishment — an institution that represents the intervention of divine power on earth.

This brings us to the third outstanding name to be considered here. It is that of *Boniface,* born probably about the year 675 and known to the world as the Apostle of Germany. More than any other man he was instrumental in the conversion of the Germanic people. Descended from a noble Anglo-Saxon family, his name, Boniface, most familiar to us now, is probably only a free Latin translation of his Saxon name, Wynfrith.

A brilliant secular career had been intended for him, but he preferred the religious state and became noted for his piety and learning. After making his profession as a member of the Benedictine Order he was placed in charge of a monastic school, giving at the same time great promise as a preacher. Yet with every prospect of a notable career and possessing the high esteem of the people of his own country, he resolved to dedicate himself to the conversion of the Germans. The permission to do so was finally granted him.

For some forty years he devoted himself to this missionary

work with most remarkable success in the conversion of souls. Among his memorable achievements is the foundation of the abbey of Fulda shortly before the middle of the eighth century. He was made bishop by Pope Gregory II and later archbishop of Mainz by Pope Gregory III.

Boniface became a martyr to his zeal during a missionary tour east of the Zuyder Zee. He had resigned his archbishopric in order to give himself to missionary work among the fierce and barbarous tribes who still inhabited certain sections of Germany where Christianity, with its civilizing power, had not yet achieved its final conquest. His martyrdom took place at Dokkum, in Friesland. He was here slain with fifty-two of his companions by the pagan idolaters in the year 754. Soon after his death his tomb, in the monastery of Fulda, became a sanctuary to which the faithful thronged in crowds, especially on the day of his feast and during its octave.

Fulda itself was one of the great Benedictine abbeys which were to become centers of intellectual life and which mightily contributed to transform the face of Germany after the conversion of the native population. Great success crowned the agricultural works of the monks at Fulda, and small colonies were gradually established at different places to become in turn the centers of civil communities and villages. Thus, in course of time, the abbey rose to a commanding position in the German empire, and came in particular to be the monastic refuge of members of the nobility among the Germans when, in the old-time phrase, they wanted "to fashion their souls."

Fulda, moreover, was one of the abbeys that devoted itself above all to the intellectual and artistic life. Architecture, sculpture, and painting were zealously cultivated here. Even during the time of Charlemagne and Alcuin, and still more under Rabanus Maurus, it became the chief nursery of civilization and learning in Germany, celebrated throughout Europe. Secular students were admitted to the classes as well as ecclesiastics. The curriculum embraced the subjects usually taught during the Middle Ages, namely: the seven liberal arts

— rhetoric, grammar, logic, arithmetic, astronomy, mathematics, music — as well as theology and the German languages. Among their renowned pupils was Rabanus Maurus, the well-known disciple of Alcuin, who later taught philosophy, theology, and poetry at Paris and afterward became archbishop of Mainz. Then there were Rudolphus Fuldensis, the distinguished scholar, and Walafried Strabo, with a European reputation.

Unfortunately the greater part of the library of this old monastery, which was one of the largest in Germany, disappeared during the looting of the abbey by the Hessians in 1631 and has not since been discovered. Fulda suffered very much during the wars that were brought about through the so-called Reformation movement in Germany. The world in consequence must mourn the loss of a great many precious bibliographic treasures.

The fourth figure crowned with world renown is that of *Charlemagne* (742–814).

Charlemagne, or Charles the Great, is one of the few men with whose name the title "Great" has become so intimately associated that most people are unaware of the incorporated epithet. All of his long life he was engaged in wars upon the barbarous people of his time, until he succeeded in bringing a large part of western Europe under his sway. For the protection of his kingdom he erected on the border districts the so-called Marks or Margravates. At the close of his reign his dominions extended from the river Ebro in Spain to the Raba in Austria, and from the Eider in Germany to the Garigliano in southern Italy. His residence, whenever his wars permitted him to be at home, was at Aix-la-Chapelle. It thus came to be the capital of his empire.

In the intervals of his wars Charlemagne found time to devote himself to the arts of peace and attracted to his court such distinguished scholars as Alcuin, Eginhard (or Einhart), and Warnefried. It seems probable, however, that Charlemagne himself never learned the art of writing. For a great many people, therefore, to whom reading and writing represent the basis of education, it must surely seem impossible that Charlemagne could ever have independently conceived the idea that education would better the barbarous conditions he beheld about him. He must have followed, as they may conceive, the suggestion of monkish advisers, who had their own personal ends in the matter, and so may have encouraged education as a panacea. In Charlemagne's time, however, writing was something the nobility did not learn — often for the simple reason that they had clerks on whom they depended for that sort of thing. With typewriters as a common possession, we can readily conceive a time when people generally will give up writing, though they may still make their marks with a pen in some distinctive way. Charlemagne had secretaries to do his writing, but his interest in education was a thing apart from that, and it is astonishing to see the zeal for intellectual pursuits which as a consequence developed during his reign.

Eginhard, who wrote a life of Charlemagne, tells us that the emperor "was ever learning and fond of learning; no subject came amiss to him; everything, from the most commonplace, everyday occurrences to the profoundest philosophical and theological inquiries, interested him. He wanted to know the price of commodities; he understood the stocking and planting of farms, the erection of houses, the building of churches and palaces and bridges and fortresses; and he was no less familiar with the construction of ships and canals. He was interested in the course of the stars, the text of the Scriptures, the equipment of schools."

And then, too, the great emperor had a sense of humor. Though his biographer says that he was very much interested in "the hair-splitting subtleties of metaphysics," yet he was also attracted by "the sallies of wit." His intellectual interest never flagged. Eginhard tells us that he devoted himself to knowing something about "the unknown depths of theology; the origins of law; the reason of usage in the manner and life of nations; their traditions in poetry, legend, and song; the mysterious framework of liturgical forms; musical notation; the Gregorian chant; the etymology of words; the study of languages; the flection of verbs; and many more topics." But what must startle our modern complacency, his biographer goes on to say that Charlemagne spoke Latin as fluently as German and had a fair knowledge of Greek. This latter he would probably have derived from the Irish monks and their disciples who at one time or another had been at Charlemagne's court. Above all, Eginhard says that "he spent much time in labor with Alcuin in the study of rhetoric, dialectics, and astronomy; learned arithmetic, and with eager curiosity and intelligent scrutiny applied himself to the investigation of the motions of the heavenly bodies."

This practically implies the study of the seven liberal arts as they constituted the basis of education for nearly a thousand years after that time. Charlemagne's schools further introduced Scholasticism.

There can, then, be no doubt, after this long category of intellectual interests, that in founding schools Charlemagne knew exactly what he desired to see established. He must have organized education in a very fundamental fashion, and yet with a development that assured the broadest kind of intellectual interests. As for his people, it can be readily understood that when their sovereign was as much interested in the things of the mind as they knew him to be, he would find many imitators among his subjects. His own example would count for very much in lifting up his people from merely bodily interests to mental striving. Besides, Charlemagne used all the weight of his influence to have young men among the nobility devote themselves to education. For this purpose he held out to them inducements of every kind, making them understand that nothing would secure his favor more surely than successful devotion to study.

Eginhard tells a story in this regard which of itself suffices to indicate how deeply Charlemagne was interested in the

spread of learning and how true it was that he would endure
no lack of compliance in the matter of education. We shall
quote at length a passage from his biographer:

"After a long absence the most victorious Charles returned
into Gaul, and caused the children, whom he had left with
Clement as his pupils, to be brought before him. He required
them to be examined, and was amazed at the commendable
progress of the poorer class of children, whose written produc-
tions were most creditable to them. On the other hand, those
of illustrious parentage showed very poor specimens of their
skill. He then set the good scholars on his right, and the bad
on his left, saying to the former: 'I praise you much, dear children, for your excellent efforts, and desire you to continue so
that you may attain unto perfection; then I intend to give you
rich bishoprics, or splendid abbeys, and shall ever regard you as
persons of merit.' Then he turned in anger to those on his left,
who trembled at his frowns and the sound of his voice, which
resembled the roll of thunder, as he cried out to them: 'Look
here, ye scions of the best nobility, ye pampered ones, who,
trusting to your birth or fortune, have disobeyed me, and instead
of studying, as you were bound and I expected you to do, have
wasted your time in idleness, on play, luxury, or unprofitable
occupation.' He then took his accustomed oath, and with up-
lifted head and arm, said in a voice of thunder: 'By the king
of heaven, let others admire you as much as they please; as
for me, I set little store by your birth or beauty; understand
ye and remember it well, that unless you give heed speedily to
amend your past negligence by diligent study, you will never
obtain anything from Charles.' "

The fifth name mentioned in our historic role of honor is
that of *King Alfred* (849–901). Like Charles he has been
deservedly surnamed "the Great," for the variety of his
achievements as monarch, warrior, and scholar. He is without
question one of the most notable men that Britain ever produced, and usually is spoken of as king of England. In reality
he was the fifth and youngest son of Ethelwulf, king of the
West Saxons, whom he succeeded to the throne. Before assum-
ing the crown he had fought successfully against the Danes
and against his brother, King Ethelred. When he became king

himself he took up the heavy task of securing peace for his people by confining the Danes within their territory in England. His organization of a fleet makes him in a certain sense the founder of the English navy and under him the Saxons gained a decided naval advantage over the Vikings. He further reorganized the military service of his kingdom so as always to be prepared against an invasion of the Danes. With the successful enforcement of peace achieved, he next turned to the cultivation of letters for himself and his subjects, and to the introduction of judicial and educational reforms. He compiled a code of laws which secured justice for his people, rebuilt the schools which had been destroyed at the time of the invasion by the Danes, and above all devoted himself to the reconstruction of the monasteries. In addition he invited to his court the scholars of his time.

Alfred was himself a scholar, and indeed a man of wide learning. He was particularly anxious that his people should have the opportunity to read some of the great books in their own tongue. He therefore set himself the task of rendering into Saxon the ecclesiastical history of England, which had been written by Venerable Bede in the preceding century. After that he translated the *Epitome of Universal History* of Orosius. But his favorite reading was the *Consolations of Philosophy* by Boethius. In order that his countrymen might share his own enthusiasm for this work, it too was given them in their own tongue. Another of his translations was the *Dialogues* of Pope Gregory the Great.

Alfred is undoubtedly one of the most notable monarchs of history. When, moreover, it is realized that he was born in the year 849 and died in 901 — that is, at scarcely more than fifty years of age — it is easy to understand how packed with activity his life must have been and what a store of energy he had. No wonder a number of legends gathered round his name. There is no satisfactory authority to support these, but Alfred needs no addition to his actual achievements to make him forever famous.

It might easily be imagined that a king who devoted himself to study and who set himself the time-consuming task of translating favorite authors into his native Anglo-Saxon in order to afford his people an opportunity to read them without difficulty, could not have been a very successful ruler. As a matter of fact, Alfred was one of the greatest rulers of all times. His earlier life had been spent in wars with the Danes. Many times in danger of death, he at last succeeded in rousing the courage of his people. In a decisive battle they defeated the invaders, leaving so many of the enemy dead upon the battleground that the place still goes by the name of Slaughter Ford. But the conquered Danes acquired respect for the religion of their conquerors — for so the minds of men run — became converts to Christianity and settled down to become peaceful English subjects.

With his country at peace Alfred was able to take up the difficult problems of the civil lives of his people. War had brought in its train, as ever, the frustration of civil laws. The country was in a sad state of disorder and confusion. Alfred therefore took the matter in hand and very soon accomplished thoroughgoing reforms. He found that a number of the magistrates throughout the country, owing to the unsettled state of affairs brought about by war, had been very unjust in their decisions, to the great detriment of respect for law and justice. The poor, particularly, suffered at their hands and justice was extremely difficult to obtain. While the attention of the king was concentrated on the war these magistrates had fallen into the habit of taking bribes and of rendering their decisions in favor of wealthy suitors. Alfred made it his personal duty to probe thoroughly every injustice, punishing severely the guilty magistrates, and casting out of office every dishonest judge. He then proceeded to introduce new legislation that would act mainly for the benefit of the poor.

Fortunately he was seconded in this by his Witenagemot, the body of Anglo-Saxon councillors which constituted the highest court of judicature in the kingdom. The results were marvelous. Not only were good laws enacted, but they were enforced so well that an old Saxon chronicler says: "Golden bracelets could be hung up by the roadside and no one dared to touch them." More than that, we are told a young woman might walk from one end of England to the other, "handsome herself and handsomely gowned," and she would not be molested in any way. It was a golden age of peace and happiness for Alfred's subjects, for their scholar king could rule as well as study or fight. They knew that he ever had at heart their best interests and was ready to devote his time to the solution of their problems.

Above all, as might be expected, Alfred was very much interested in education. He founded schools for both rich and poor throughout all of England. One of these schools was built at Oxford. Hence arises the old English tradition that Alfred was the founder of Oxford. The university, however, was established quite independently of Alfred's school, which had been seriously disturbed by the Normans.

Alfred, moreover, was interested as much in the comfort of his subjects as in the development of their intelligence. He thus devoted himself assiduously to the less exalted but very necessary problems of better housing and better furniture for his people. In these matters he created a tradition in English life which meant very much for the happiness of his people.

In his educational work he received valuable assistance from three great scholars, all of them monks — Asser, from Wales, afterward the biographer of Alfred; John, from the great Benedictine monastery of Corbie in Saxony; and Grimbald, from the college of St. Omer in France. There were further a group of learned Saxons who by Alfred's invitation came to live at court. With their help he organized schools and provided them with books and masters.

Like Charlemagne, Alfred was well aware how invaluable the monks were to him for this great task of educating his people. Both of these monarchs had among their dearest friends monastic scholars whom they learned to appreciate ever more and more. It is no wonder, then, if we hear that just as Alfred divided his time into three eights, giving eight hours to prayer and study, eight hours to business, and eight to meals and sleep and recreation, so also he divided his revenues in the same manner. One share was for the expenses of his court, servants, and public buildings; a second was given to convents, monasteries, and schools; and a third was distributed in charity.

Is it any wonder, then, that his people called him Alfred the Great? Surely no monarch has ever been more worthy of such distinction. His final words were to his son. They were words of good advice, counseling him how to care for his people. But what is most worthy of note in them is that his very last thoughts were given to certain slaves captured in battle and sold into captivity. These Alfred had freed and he now feared lest any policy of his son should take away their liberty. Here, then, was the last admonition of a great soul: "For God's love, my son, and for the advantage of my soul, I will that they be masters of their own freedom and their own will; and in the name of the living God I entreat that no man disturb them; that they should be as free as their own thoughts to serve what lord they please."

These five men — Benedict (480–543), Gregory (550–604), Boniface (675–754), Charlemagne (742–814), and Alfred (849–901) — who lived just about a generation apart from each other, provide the best possible evidence for the existence of a never-ceasing interest in education and in the development of intellectual life during even that period often called "the benighted part" of the Middle Ages. They are also witness to the existence of a succession of supremely great leaders who fostered this tradition. As the memory of these men has lived for over a thousand years, amid the stress and strain of the countless vicissitudes through which human life has passed during all these centuries, their fame is likely now to be immune against the tooth of time. Men will never fail to look up to them as leaders of mankind. They faithfully represent the aspirations of our race after all that is best. Their sublime purpose was to make those around them share in the beneficent developments wherewith they generously enriched the world. Their names are household words for scholars of every nation, while they are respected no less by the great multitudes who in all lands have learned to read the printed page. Three of them have been accorded the honors of sainthood by the people who knew them best, and this privilege has been confirmed by the Church which valued their services so highly. The title of saint, more than anything else, implies that they were men who nobly forgot about themselves and thought of others. As a result they accomplished wonders for mankind. Such men are never willingly forgotten.

II

THE IRISH CHAPTER

THE first phase of the intellectual life and cultural achievement of the Middle Ages is seldom accorded the position it deserves in history. While Roman decadence and in-wandering barbarians accomplished the destruction of the old Graeco-Roman civilization, a vigorous people in the distant west of Europe, possessed of a deep and broad natural culture, were giving expression to their genius in marvelous ways. They had not come under the Roman domination and remained unaffected by the social confusion and disturbed conditions which might have dragged them down with the rest of the civilized world. Instead, they developed an intellectual life which was to make itself felt very deeply over most of Europe during the next two centuries. These people were the Irish on their tight little island out in the Atlantic.

During the second and third centuries of our era before the introduction of Christianity into their country, the Irish achieved fame as warriors but also as bards and musicians. They were then busy creating a series of sagas or epic poems as well as building up the beginnings of a folklore rich in mystical ideas. They further originated a popular music that was destined to have deep influence over all the surrounding nations for centuries to come, and indeed down to our own time. Many of the national and popular airs of other countries are Irish in origin.

Uninfluenced by Greek and Roman writers, Irish bards gave birth to a great literature of their own. The description of the lives and activities of the native islanders led to the creation in their literature of numerous types of men and women whose careers were as poignantly full of life, of its joys and woes, its humanities, its strivings and its aspirations, as were those of the characters of Homer. With the modern revival of the knowledge of Irish (Gaelic) literature, the names of these heroes and heroines have become more widely familiar. Deirdre, for instance, is the Irish Helen whose transcendent beauty brought only sadness and misfortune in its train to those who loved her and whom she loved. Emer was the Irish Andromache, long courted and striven for in the journeys and feats which she set for her lover. In the midst of the dangers he incurred for her sake, she gloried in him and watched over him until he went out to meet his fate. Cuhulain is the Irish Achilles, famous at once for his prowess in arms and the depth of his friendship. When he has slain his best friend, he proves as susceptible to grief and shows himself as unrestrainedly demonstrative of it as ever the original Achilles or any of his fellow chieftains at the siege of Troy.

These great sagas of Irish literature furnish a definite demonstration of the literary genius of the Irish and above all of the height and depth of their poetic inspirations. Their originality is all the more striking because they had been utterly unaffected by the literature of other peoples. During the past generation, particularly since the days of Standish O'Grady, distinguished French and German scholars have called these Gaelic literary remains to the attention of the literary world. Not only have they devoted themselves to the study of the old Irish [Gaelic] literature, but they have been enthusiastic in their admiration of it. Not a few of them have been ready to proclaim that the Irish, in the second and third centuries of our era, composed a series of epics which for poignancy of human interest, for feeling, acumen, and lofty characterization, can well rank with the masterpieces of literature.

These great Irish poems display a profound knowledge of the human heart and well merit for their makers that best of designations for a poet, "the seer" — the man, namely, who sees far beyond the vision of those around him, so that they are glad to see with his eyes in order to be able to share in his vision.

Expressions such as these are usually looked upon as pious exaggerations prompted by national feeling. But during the twentieth century the place of Celtic literature in Europe, and the cultural influence of the Celts in the earlier Middle Ages, have come to be profoundly appreciated. German and French scholars are agreed in reversing the commonly accepted historical version as to the place of the Celts in the culture of Europe. Almost needless to say, when Germans and French agree there is certain to be some foundation for their findings. The Celts, formerly regarded as rather ferocious barbarians, are now looked up to as possessed of many cultural qualities which made them capable of being the schoolmasters of other countries in which they found a home.

The French for over a thousand years have traced the origin of their own literature and culture back to the Romans, and even beyond them to the Greeks. Troy was looked upon as the source of France's culture and many documents were supposed to corroborate this opinion. But all this has been changed mainly by the discoveries and researches made during the twentieth century. Professor Gerig of the Celtic department of Columbia University, in an address before the American Irish Historical Society,[1] mentioned four works that are mainly responsible for this change of opinion. They represent monumental contributions to the solution of the Celtic problem on the continent of Europe. These four works were, d'Arbois de Jubainville's well-known *Course of Celtic Literature,* which was published in eight volumes during the last decade of the nineteenth century; Professor Camille Jullian's *History of Gaul* in three volumes, the publication of which was completed just as the war began — its author's untimely death in 1933 being a sad blow to French scholarship; the

---

[1] January, 1934. See the *Transactions of the Society.*

three-volume *Manual of Pre-Historic Celtic and Gallo-Roman Archaeology* on which Joseph Dechelette, a retired French business man, spent some ten years; and lastly the work of M. Henri Hubert, in two volumes, *The Celts and Celtic Expansion,* which appeared quite recently in France.

These books make it very clear that the Gauls, and especially the Irish, were the teachers of the continent of Europe. Schools in which Latin and Greek were taught by the Irish monks flourished throughout Gaul, and one at least situated near Lyons, became so famous that Roman patrician families sent their sons to be educated there. When the Celts in Ireland became Christians, they made a heroic effort to bring Christianity and civilization and culture to their brother Celts on the continent.

It is not surprising to find that the Irish monks came to be so highly esteemed that when Charlemagne decided to revise education in France he invited Alcuin to come to his court for that purpose. Alcuin is usually said to have been an Englishman. This, however, is not entirely certain, and there is no doubt that he was educated at the great monastic school of Clonmacnoise in Ireland. His reorganization of the French schools, then, followed the model of the Irish schools. He was the founder of the great Palace School of Charlemagne which is usually considered to be the precursor of the University of Paris and thereby, in a certain sense at least, may be regarded as the precursor of modern educational institutions.

Alcuin's greatest work, however, was not accomplished as an educator but as a scholarly auxiliary of other scholars. When he was made Bishop of Tours he devoted himself to the organization of the *scriptorium,* or writing room there, which really became, as Professor Gerig suggests, a medieval publishing center. Professor E. K. Rand of Harvard has written a work in two volumes on the *scriptorium* at Tours. Alcuin set the example and furnished the incentive for the organization of *scriptoria* at Cologne, at St. Gall in Switzerland, at Bobbio in Italy, and even at Monte Cassino in the southern part of Italy. In the last-named place a number of Irish monks were engaged as well as at several other places on the continent. Thus at Würtzburg and Milan prominent places in the monastic communities were occupied by Irish monks. In all of these *scriptoria* uniform styles of writing developed known as the Uncial and Caroline minuscule, that is, the larger capital letters and the smaller letters. This form of writing was imitated by the early printers of books in the incunabula period when the modes of our modern Roman and Italic letters were being stabilized.[2]

It was these people, profoundly susceptible to culture, whom Patrick converted to Christianity during the first half of the fifth century. They remain still a martial people, readier almost to fight than to do anything else, but after the coming of Christianity their warlike spirit was sublimated into the lofty purpose to bring to all the rest of the world and especially to those nearest to them the advantages which they knew could be enjoyed through Christianity alone.

Above all, the intellectual genius of the Irish people was deeply touched, and they devoted themselves now to education instead of to war. As a result Ireland became "the island

---

[2] While the French in the twentieth century were remaking the history of the Celts in Europe and their place in the story of culture, the Irish were gathering materials which were of great significance as demonstrating the influence of Ireland in the culture of the Middle Ages. A great impetus to the development and interpretation of Irish archaeology was given by the researchers in connection with the Harvard University archaeological missions to Ireland. The second one, particularly, revealed the island as a veritable mine of hitherto unrevealed archaeological treasures. They found Ireland rich in monuments dating back to the Bronze Age, and have further unearthed evidence that the first immigrants to Ireland arrived there about 7,000 years ago, having probably come from the continent by land bridges then existing. The interest taken by Irish scholars was mainly responsible for the success of the first important Celtic Congress held at Dinard in Brittany, September 4 to 9, 1933. The Germans are now beginning to place the Irish as much in their debt as the French previously had done. There appeared recently at Halle in Germany the first *fasciculus* of a *Lexicon of the Irish Language* which bears the secondary title, *A Concise Dictionary of Early Irish, with Definitions in German and English*. The editor is Dr. Hans Hessen who has obtained the collaboration of Irish, German, and other scholars. When completed this lexicon will comprise a thousand pages.

of saints and of scholars" — a designation that is not Irish in origin but was accorded them by the outlanders. Throughout the fifth century the Irish themselves flocked from all over the island to the score or more of institutions of higher learning that were founded by these recently converted Christians. In the following century, as more of these institutions of learning came into existence, students came to them from all the neighboring countries. From England and Wales as well as Scotland, from Iberia in Gaul and from distant parts of the Mediterranean littoral, from the south of France and from Italy, from many parts of the East and especially from Egypt these student wanderers came and seem to have influenced Irish art rather deeply.

During the period extending from the sixth to the ninth century Ireland was the great leader of the Western world in education. Mrs. John Richard Green, wife of the author of the well-known *History of the English People,* and the daughter of the English litterateur Stopford Brooke, in her volume *The Irish Nationality* (p. 53),[3] has an enthusiastic paragraph on the wandering of the Irish scholars and the many schools founded by them. The story is told of Irish monks landing at Marseilles and finding that everybody who had anything to offer the people hawked it about the streets. Following this example they bravely set forth and proclaimed that they had education for sale. When someone demanded the price of it, they replied that it would be sold for only the pleasure of being allowed to impart it. With that in mind Mrs. Green's passage is all the more interesting:

"They [the Irish missionaries] passed through England to northern France and the Netherlands; across the Gaulish sea and by the Loire to middle France; by the Rhine and the way of Luxeuil they entered Switzerland; and eastward they reached out to the Elbe and the Danube, sending missionaries to Old Saxony, Thuringia, Bavaria, Salzburg and Carinthia; southwards they crossed the Alps into Italy, to Lucca, Fiesole, Rome, the

---

[3] Home University Library. Quoted here by permission of Henry Holt and Company, publishers.

hills of Naples, and Tarentum. Their monasteries formed rest houses for travelers through France and Germany. Europe itself was too narrow for their ardour, and they journeyed to Jerusalem, settled in Carthage, and sailed to the discovery of Iceland. No church of any land has so noble a record in the astonishing work of its teachers, as they wandered over the ruined provinces of the empire among the pagan tribes of the invaders. In the Highlands they taught the Picts to compose hymns in their own tongue; in a monastery founded by them in Yorkshire was trained the first English poet in the new England; at St. Gall they drew up a Latin-German dictionary for the Germans of the Upper Rhine and Switzerland, and even devised new German words to express the new ideas of Christian civilization; near Florence one of their saints taught the natives how to turn the course of a river. *Probably in the seventh and eighth centuries no one in western Europe spoke Greek who was not Irish or taught by an Irishman.* No land ever sent out such impassioned teachers of learning, and Charles the Great and his successors set them at the head of the chief schools throughout Europe."

An excellent idea of the education that might be secured under favorable circumstances in Ireland in the sixth century is conveyed by the details given with regard to the education of Columcille, the Irish missionary who holds a place in the hearts of Irishmen almost equal to that of Patrick himself. He was born in Donegal, in 521, and was a descendant of Hyneill. This means that he came from one of the most famous families in Ireland, descendants of "Niall of the nine hostages." He belonged, therefore, to the royal family of Ireland, and every possible opportunity for education was afforded him. During the early Middle Ages children were wont to be sent away from home for education when they had reached about the age of seven. At that age therefore, Columcille, "the dove of the Church," as his name signifies in Irish, was sent to the school of St. Finnian at Moville on Lough Foyle. St. Finnian was himself of Irish royal blood. As a young man he had spent some seven years in Rome studying the languages, particularly Latin and Greek, but also

Hebrew, for it was the custom among the Christian scholars of that time to learn the original language of the Old Testament.

After having spent some seven years at Moville, Columcille, just as adolescence was bringing its development, was sent to the Leinster school of bards where he was trained by an old Irish poet, Gemman. Here the sagas of Ireland, the old legends, and the Druidical lore of the Irish were taught him. Then for some years he was at Aranmore, the college founded on the largest of the Aran islands, some thirty miles off the coast of Galway. In this school, founded by St. Enda, the poetry and the mysticism of the ancient Irish were sedulously cultivated. From here Columcille transferred to the College of Clonard on the Boyne where another St. Finnen or Finnian was teaching, and where, according to a tradition that seems well grounded, there were gathered some 3,000 pupils from every part of Europe. This St. Finnian is even more famous than Finnen or Finnian of Moville, and his school was one of the great European institutions of that time. Not content, however, with even all this, Columcille went for some time to Glasnevin near Dublin. Only then did he consider himself properly equipped to be a missionary of Christianity and culture to those in the darkness of paganism in western Europe.

In spite of his education Columcille had a temper of his own, as many another scholar or even a saint may have had in spite of his mystical development. Through an unfortunate display of lack of judgment in an important matter he became responsible for a furious battle between two Irish factions in which thousands of lives were lost. In remorse for his fault he set himself the penance of leaving Ireland, never to set eyes on it again. That was the severest penance he could well have inflicted on himself. In conformity with it he passed over to the island of Iona, off the Scotch coast and just out of view of the beloved shores of his native country. There he founded a monastery that became famous as the home of a school and a fruitful center from which missionaries went out to convert first the Scotch and then later the English.

St. Augustine (Austin of the English) is sometimes spoken of "as the apostle of England," but he did not land on the coast of Kent until the year after Columcille's death. For years before that time Irish missionaries had been at Lindisfarne, in Northumbria, and indeed throughout the whole northern part of England. Hence, as the Anglican bishop historians of England declare, it is one of Columcille's monks, St. Aidan, who was the real apostle of England, leaving to Augustine the prestige of being the apostle of Kent. The education offered by St. Columcille was to be a burning light in the darkness of the barbarism of those days and through his disciples was to be diffused throughout Europe where it was to mean very much for civilization. Iona proved to be an abundant breeding place for missionaries of faith and culture.

The first notable contribution of this cultured people, so intent on the uplift of mind and heart, was the invention of rhyme in poetry. As Douglas Hyde in his *Literary History of Ireland* said:

"It is a tremendous claim to make for the Celt that he taught Europe to rhyme; it is a claim in comparison with which if it could be substantiated everything else that he has done in literature pales into insignificance. Yet it has been made for him by some of the foremost European scholars. The great Zeuss himself is emphatic on the point."

Zeuss who is acknowledged to be the greatest Gaelic scholar of modern times and whose special studies in philology gave him an indisputable right to an opinion on the subject, declared that the form of Celtic poetry was more ornate than the poetic form of any other nation. So it was, "that at the very time the Roman Empire was destined to ruin, the Celtic forms — at first in part, afterwards entire — passed over not only into the songs of the Latins but also into those of other nations and remained in them." Constantine Negra, the distinguished European scholar, concludes that the Celtic poets, through the rules of their assonance and its development, were the inventors of rhyme.

When it is realized what poetry would lack with the loss of rhyme, and how the music of verse becomes through rhyme a marvelous wedding of sense and sound, it is easy to understand the exquisite importance of this Irish contribution to literature. There are some magnificent examples of very early rhyme among the Irish. Such, for instance, is "Patrick's Hymn," the oldest Christian verse in the Gaelic tongue, which has been translated into the meter of the original. Critics find in it something of the simplicity and directness of St. Francis of Assisi's "Hymn to the Creatures," combined with that naïveté so characteristic of Irish poetry. It was probably written during the early part of the second half of the fifth century:

THE DEER'S CRY

I bind me today,

I

God's might to direct me,
God's power to protect me,
God's wisdom for learning,
God's eye for discerning,
God's ear for my hearing,
God's word for my clearing.

II

God's hand for my cover,
God's path to pass over,
God's buckler to guard me,
God's army to ward me,
  Against snares of the devil,
  Against vice's temptation,
  Against wrong inclination,
  Against men who plot evil,
  Anear or afar, with many or few.

III

Christ near,
Christ here,

Christ be with me,
Christ beneath me,
Christ within me,
Christ behind me,
Christ be o'er me,
Christ before me.

IV

Christ in the left and the right,
Christ hither and thither,
Christ in the sight, ·
   Of each eye that shall seek me,
   In each ear that shall hear,
   In each mouth that shall speak me —
Christ not the less
In each heart I address.
I bind me today on the Triune — I call,
With faith in the Trinity — Unity — God over all.

It is not surprising that the Irish should have invented rhyme in poetry, thus adding music to verse, because the Gaels have been famous for many centuries for their devotion to music and their marvelous success in expressing the deepest feelings by means of simple successions of single notes. Dr. P. W. Joyce, president of the Royal Society of Antiquaries of Ireland, in his volume *Old Irish Folk Music and Song*,[4] gives proof that over 5,000 different Irish airs have been published. Not a few of these are found among the popular music of other countries, but the origin of them can be traced back to Ireland. Some of the most frequently heard melodies in a number of other countries were adopted, or only slightly adapted, from Irish airs. Perhaps the best exemplification of this for Americans is the fact that both "Yankee Doodle" and "Dixie" are old Irish airs, heard in Ireland long before they became popular over here. There have been any number of serious studies of Irish music made since the first, that of John Scotus Erigena, "John the Scot Erin-born," who wrote a treatise on music in the ninth century. In our day Dr.

[4] Dublin, 1909.

Petri's *Ancient Music of Ireland;* Dr. Grattan Flood's *History of Irish Music;* and *The Music of Ireland* by Francis O'Neill of Chicago, show how much there is available for those who desire information.

Giraldus Cambrensis, Gerald Barry, or Gerald the Welshman, who visited Ireland during the twelfth century and left us an account of his experiences there, was enthusiastic about the music of the Irish. Yet much of this developed during precisely that early medieval period. He said:

"The skill of the Irish in music is incomparably superior to that of any other nation. For them modulations are not slow and morose, as in the instruments of Britain to which we are habituated, but the sounds are rapid and precipitate, yet sweet and pleasant. . . . Such agreeable swiftness, such unequal parity, such discordant concord . . . so delicately pleasant, so softly soothing that it is manifest the perfection of their art lies in concealing art."

Above all the Irish were ingeniously inventive in their creation of musical instruments. Grattan Flood, in his article on Irish music in the volume *The Glories of Ireland,*[5] records that a thousand years ago a whole series of musical instruments existed in Ireland which enabled the Irish to express every mood and tense of feeling by musical sounds. There were the bagpipe, the flute and the pipe, the horn and bass horn, the trumpet and the pipe, the cymbal and the castanet, and the fiddle. The harp is above all the Irish musical instrument, and our modern piano was developed in Italy out of the harp.

The Irish devoted themselves wholeheartedly and very successfully to other phases of artistic expression besides poetry and music. During the eighth and ninth centuries they interested themselves particularly in the making of beautiful books. As a result of their ardent enthusiasm for the production of volumes of the Scripture that would in some way be worthy of the inspired writings, the Irish have left us some

---

[5] Washington, 1914.

of the most beautiful books that ever were made. Mr. Louis Ely O'Carroll, in his article on "Irish Manuscripts" in the volume just mentioned cites the *Book of Kells* as "the all surpassing masterpiece of Celtic illuminative art and the most beautiful book in the world." Describing the marvels of its art, he said:

"Into its pages are woven such a wealth of ornament, such an ecstasy of art and such a miracle of design that the book is today not only one of Ireland's greatest glories but one of the world's wonders. . . . The *Book of Kells* is the Mecca of the illuminative artist but it is the despair of the copyist. The patience and skill of the olden scribe have baffled the imitator; for on examination with a magnifying glass it has been found that in a space of a quarter of an inch there are no fewer than 158 interlacements of a ribbon pattern of white lines edged by black ones on a black ground."

What Sir Edward Sullivan says at the beginning of his introduction to the *Book of Kells*,[6] may seem the language of an overardent enthusiast, but it sums up the qualities of this great illuminated manuscript volume so well that every serious student of the early Middle Ages ought to know his words:

"Its weird and commanding beauty; its subdued and goldless colouring; the baffling intricacy of its fearless designs; the clean, unwavering sweep of rounded spiral; the creeping undulations of serpentine forms, that writhe in artistic profusion throughout the mazes of its decorations; the strong and legible minuscule of its text; the quaintness of its striking portraiture; the unwearied reverence and patient labour that brought it into being; all of which combined go to make up the *Book of Kells*, have raised this ancient Irish volume to a position of abiding pre-eminence amongst the illuminated manuscripts of the world."

There were other early volumes of great charm besides the *Book of Kells*, which was produced probably in the eighth century. Almost a rival in beauty was the *Book of Durrow*, a fragment of the Gospels with illuminations in a similar

---

[6] London, 1914.

style of art. The *Book of Armagh* is much less elaborately illuminated than the *Book of Kells*, but some of its illuminations compare in richness even with that supreme example of Irish bookmaking. Both of these volumes may be seen in Trinity College Library, Dublin, alongside the *Book of Kells*. There are also three beautiful examples of Irish manuscript, or of manuscripts executed under Irish influence, to be seen in England. These are the "Gospels of McBurnam," now in the Archbishop's library at Lambeth, England; the "Gospels of St. Chad," in the cathedral library at Litchfield; and the "Gospels of Lindisfarne," or of St. Cuthbert, hailed as "the glory of the British Museum." The Gospels of Lindisfarne were produced by the monks of Iona where St. Columcille founded his great school of religion and art. This manuscript is second only to the *Book of Kells*. As O'Carroll says, "In its glory of illuminative design and from its distinctive scheme of colors the tones of which are light and bright and gay, it forms a contrast to the quieter shades and the solemn dignity of the more famous volume."

Were it not for these specimens of Irish bookmaking, no tradition, however authoritative, would bring modern scholars to accept the idea that the Irish of the seventh and eighth centuries had the genius to execute, while the people around them had the taste to appreciate, such marvelous examples of the bookmaking art.

The same thing is true with regard to the jewelry of the Irish, which came to a climax of artistic excellence about a century later than the art of bookmaking. Ireland had a very limited store of gold and yet appreciated the precious metal very much. Hence it was used, not for personal adornment, but for the manufacture of the sacred vessels of the altar and for distinctive jewels for their rulers. Save for such actual original specimens as the Cross of Cong, the Chalice of Ardagh, and the Brooch of Tara, no one would believe that examples of artistry so exquisite could have come from the hands of Irish artist-artisans of the ninth century. It is possible to gather a sheaf of highest praises for the artistic excellence of these works. I may cite here the judgment of Miss Margaret Stokes, of the distinguished family of Irish antiquarians. In her little volume, *Early Christian Art in Ireland,* one of the series of art handbooks written for the South Kensington Museum of London and as such entirely dependable, she says of the Chalice of Ardagh:

"The Irish chalice combines classic beauty of form with the most exquisite examples of almost every variety of Celtic ornamentation."

There follows an elaborate description of the ornamentation of the chalice which makes it very clear that these handicraftsmen of the Ireland of the early Middle Ages were artists in the fullest sense of the word. The exquisite taste possessed by them is well exemplified in a series of specimens of *orfevrerie* that have never been excelled. Similar appreciations by competent art critics might be cited regarding the Cross of Cong and the Brooch of Tara.

The third mode of fine artistic expression on the part of the Irish, after the making of beautiful books and jewelry, was that of the sculptured crosses, which are so prominent a feature of the Irish remains from the Middle Ages. The round tower and the high cross are the two most characteristic Irish archeological remains. The high cross, as it was called, from a dozen to a score or more feet in height, made after the Irish fashion in the form of what is often called in modern times the Celtic cross, is to be seen in many parts of Ireland. It was sculptured very beautifully and the subjects for illustration were taken from the Scripture. The fall of man, Daniel in the lions' den, the three Hebrew children in the Babylonian furnace, and the adoration of the Magi are favorite subjects. Until comparatively recent years it was not realized how beautiful, in the sense of being eminently artistic, the sculptures on these crosses were. They are very striking examples of Irish power of artistic achievement. This is not the conclusion of enthusiastic Irishmen, naturally partial toward these relics of old Ireland, but of capable modern critics.

Miss Stokes, in her manual prepared for the South Kensington Museum, offers a comparison between the crosses made in other countries about this time, the tenth century, and those of Ireland. Her critical appreciation is very much in favor of the Irish sculptors of that time. The crosses represent, she says, "a style which overspread the three countries, Ireland, England and Scotland, in the ninth and tenth centuries, and which attained a more beautiful result in Ireland because in the hands of men possessed of a fine artistic instinct."

Arthur Kingsley Porter, professor of fine arts at Harvard University at the time of his tragic death, wrote a book on *The Crosses and Culture of Ireland,* published in 1931 by the Yale University Press. It consists of a series of lectures delivered at the Metropolitan Museum of Art in New York. Porter was an archeologist with an international reputation. His volume, issued under the patronage of such distinguished institutions as Harvard, Yale, and the Metropolitan Museum, can be taken as unquestionably authoritative. In full detail he describes some three hundred Irish crosses, linking them with the other relics of Ireland's artistic and cultural golden age. It has long been recognized, he says, that Ireland from the sixth to the ninth centuries stood at the head of European culture. From the material gathered by him he shows that in "the tenth century Ireland produced a sculpture which is not only immeasurably in advance of anything done in all the rest of Europe but is among the remarkable manifestations of medieval art." That sculpture of medieval Ireland was particularly exemplified in the Irish high crosses.

In my volume *The World's Debt to the Irish*[7] there is a chapter on "The Round Tower and the High Cross," in which these two very prominent features of Irish life are discussed with the special purpose of assigning their place in history.

---

[7] Boston, 1926.

The Irish round tower has sometimes been claimed for distant antiquity, and is said to go back to a period long before Christ. It has also been attributed to the Danes, a mistake due to the word *Danaans*, who belonged to early Irish legendary lore. In fact, however, these round towers were bell towers attached to churches, and hence came their association with high crosses, which are to be found particularly in churchyards. The Irish crosses are so beautiful that it is no wonder our generation is endeavoring to imitate them. When well designed and erected in the cemeteries of our day they form striking monuments which invariably attract attention. Professor Porter has a large number of illustrations of the sculpture of these crosses in his volume, which make it possible to appreciate properly the really artistic elements in them.

This period of Irish medieval achievement, unsurpassed in many features, has been only too little known. The presumption has been that nothing good could have come out of Ireland at that time, and above all that there could be no question of the magnificent chapter of accomplishment in the arts and crafts which actually developed. The people were supposed to be barbarous, given to fighting and quarreling among themselves, quite incapable of producing things so beautiful that they are among the most precious treasures of subsequent civilization and models of the highest artistic ability. The revelation of the achievement of the Irish, made as the result of comparatively recent research, is an earnest of other phases of early medieval accomplishment that will surely come to light as the result of further investigations. There was probably a series of very interesting cultures among the different peoples of Europe. Merovingian and Carlovingian art demonstrate this, and the whole story of the early Middle Ages remains yet to be written.

III

MONASTIC SCHOOLS — BEC

AFTER the Irish schools, so many of which were founded on the continent, came the monastery schools, especially those of the Benedictines. These monastic schools multiplied in number and soon exerted wide and deep influence throughout Europe. At the climax of their development, which was reached in the tenth and eleventh centuries, they were the most prominent teaching institutions in civilized countries, and accomplished their purpose very successfully. The supreme culmination of their influence was attained toward the end of the twelfth century. At that time the members of religious Orders were gradually being displaced as teachers by the secular clergy. At the same time the cathedral schools, later to develop into the universities, came into existence in the various diocesan cities. They were conducted under the rectorship of the chancellor of the cathedral and the administration of the bishop of the diocese.

The monastic schools left behind them enduring monuments of their achievements. In particular, the monks devoted themselves to the multiplication of books in the *scriptoria* of the monasteries, thus saving from destruction the classics and the works of the Fathers of the Church, as well as those of Boethius, Aëtius, the first great Christian physician, Alexander of Tralles, and many other important writers of the early Middle Ages. Had it not been for these efforts the loss of all this literature would almost inevitably have resulted from the profound neglect of education during the period of the transmigration of nations and the invasions of the barbarians.

The knowledge of what was actually accomplished in the monasteries, even during the centuries considered the darkest of the dark ages, has gradually accumulated as the result of actual acquaintance with their activities. It thus is coming to replace the old prejudiced assumptions. Nearly a century ago scholarly students of the Middle Ages came to recognize the fact that most of what was said in deprecation of the medieval period was due to a lack of knowledge on the part of men who spoke so glibly of "the dark ages." A strong reaction has set in against all this in intellectual circles. Mrs. Jameson, whose deep interest in art naturally made her sympathetic toward the Middle Ages, declared about the middle of the nineteenth century:

"We are outliving the gross prejudices which once represented the life of the cloister as being from first to last a life of laziness and imposture. We know that but for the monks the light of liberty and literature and science had been forever extinguished; that for six centuries there existed for the thoughtful, the gentle, the inquiring, the devout spirit, no peace, no security, no home, but the cloister."

Dean Maitland, the well-known English historical writer, was the first to point out in his volume *The Dark Ages,* how utterly without foundation were many of the aspersions cast upon the medieval monks. His admiration for the Benedictines, founded on direct knowledge of their work, was lofty and sincere. So far from laziness and selfishness ruling their lives, they were devoted to hard manual toil and alert to intellectual interests. "The Benedictines," he wrote, "were the first agriculturalists who brought intellectual resources, calculations and science to bear on the cultivation of the soil. They are the first to whom we owe experimental farming."

This newer view of monastic achievement, so startling even to most scholars in Maitland's time, has now come to be the generally accepted opinion, never better phrased than by Maitland himself. When superficial students of history declared that the monks greedily grabbed up whatever land they could — and always the best — Maitland did not hesitate to declare that it was they who had made the land so valuable, often lifting it up out of conditions that made agriculture on it seem practically impossible:

"It was, as we ought most gratefully to acknowledge, a most happy thing for the world that they did not confine themselves to the possession of such small estates as they cultivated with their own hands. The extraordinary benefit which they conferred on society by cultivating waste places, places chosen because they were waste and solitary and such as could be recalled only by the incessant labor of those who were willing to work hard and live hard on lands often given because they were not worth keeping, lands which for a long while left their cultivators half starved and dependent on the charity of those who admired what we must too often call their fanatical zeal — even the extraordinary benefit, I say, which they conferred on mankind by this clearing and cultivation was small in comparison with the advantages derived from them by society after they had become large proprietors, landlords with more benevolence, and farmers with more intelligence and capital than any others."

Probably the most valuable contribution that the monks made to education, and especially to the popular education of the early Middle Ages, was to rescue manual labor from the contempt into which it had fallen. The Romans had all such work done for them by slaves; the barbarians had it done for them by their women. Benedict ordained in his Rule that a certain number of hours each day should be spent by the monks in manual labor. This lifted up labor to a new level and made it respected. As men of all classes, from peasant to prince, including the nobility and sons of the better-to-do classes, applied for entrance into the Benedictine monasteries, they took upon themselves the fulfillment of this Rule of the community. As a result, manual labor became a precious factor in human life.

Often the monasteries were so situated that it was necessary for the monks not merely to supply provisions for the community, when these were needed, but to be self-supporting in every way. They had, therefore, to organize for the production not only of foodstuffs but of all other materials required for the welfare of the house. In the course of this organization they established industries and above all set up what in our time we would call agricultural schools.

As the monasteries increased in importance they often came to be surrounded by tenants who held and worked the monastery lands. These found that life could be happy indeed under the conditions which prevailed in connection with the monastery. Just at the turn of the century, Dr. Henry Goodell, president of the Massachusetts Agricultural College, in an address at the summer meeting of the Massachusetts State Board of Agriculture, told the story of "The Influence of the Monks in Agriculture." He was probably in a better position to judge of the place of the monks and what the monasteries meant for the development of scientific agriculture than anyone else in this country at the time. His words are a precious testimony to the fact that while we are accustomed to think of agricultural schools as comparatively modern foundations, they came into existence nearly fifteen hundred years ago in connection with the monasteries. He did not hesitate to say that the monks, who were the subjects of so much deprecation and the favorite epithet for whom has so often been that of "lazy," were really magnificent exemplars of what can be done to accomplish that extremely important task, so valuable for mankind, of making two blades of grass grow where only one grew before. He said:

"Agriculture was sunk to a low ebb [as a result of the incursions of the barbarians and the Roman contempt for labor]. Marshes covered once fertile fields and the men who should have tilled the land spurned the plow as degrading. The monks left their cells and their prayers to dig ditches and plough fields. The effort was magical. Men once more turned back to a noble but despised industry, and peace and plenty supplanted war and poverty. So well recognized were the blessings they brought that an old German proverb among the peasants runs, 'it is good to live under the crozier,' that is, it is a happy lot to hold your farm from an abbot or abbess — both of them carried the crozier — for you could be quite sure not only of fair treatment but above all of sympathetic co-operation in the accomplishment of all the tasks that fall to the farmer, and that so often require trained intelligence of a high order for success."

Dr. Goodell continues:

"The monks ennobled manual labor which in a degenerate and Roman world had been performed exclusively by slaves and among the barbarians by women. For the monks it is no exaggeration to say that the cultivation of the soil was like an immense alms spread over a whole country. The abbots and superiors set the example and stripping off their sacerdotal robes toiled as common laborers."

The story is told that when a papal messenger came in haste to consult the Abbot Equutius on important matters relating to the Church, he was not to be found anywhere in the monastery, but was finally located in the valley cutting hay. No wonder that President Goodell should say:

"Under such guidance and such example the monks upheld and taught everywhere the dignity of labor, first by consecrating to agriculture the energy and intelligent activity of freemen, often of high birth and clothed with a double authority of the priesthood and of hereditary nobility, and second by associating under the Benedictine habit sons of kings, princes, and nobles, with the rudest labors of peasants and serfs."

The old tradition with regard to the laziness of monks was never better nullified than through the immense number of manuscript books which the members of religious Orders wrote and which the *scriptoria* of the monasteries multiplied almost beyond belief. Many, even educated men, are inclined to think that the manuscript materials of the Middle Ages are nearly exhausted, in the sense that most of the books have been properly edited and printed, so as to be readily available for those who wish to consult them. This is far from being the case: an immense number of manuscripts is still waiting to be edited for proper presentation to the modern world of scholarship. Literally, there are many thousands of such manuscripts that remain to be studied. All the European libraries of any importance contain such materials in abundance, and there will be plenty of occupation for scholars over many years in collating and editing them.

A definite persuasion exists in the minds of many that the physical sciences were almost entirely neglected during the Middle Ages, and that this was an unfortunate condition of affairs because it failed to encourage the development of an extremely important quality of the many-sided mind of man.

Professor Lynn Thorndike of Columbia, whose two-volume work on *The History of Magic and Experimental Science Down to the Thirteenth Century*[1] deservedly brought him a reputation for broad medieval scholarship, presented a striking contradiction on this subject at the joint session of the History of Science Society and the scientific session of the American Historical Association, in Boston, December, 1930. He had published in *Isis*,[2] the quarterly organ of the history of Science Society, and of the International Committee of the History of Science, a "Prospectus for a Corpus of Medieval Scientific Literature in Latin." In this he proposed the publication of a series of works which had been written in the Middle Ages and which are not now readily available for consultation by writers on the history of science. "Ignorance of the medieval contribution and background," he added, "has long been a weak point of scientists and historians of science." He felt that it was extremely important to obtain this material since it would notably modify the attitude of mind among modern scholars. Of the numerous scientific, medical, and surgical works in medieval Latin he says:

"Many authors and treatises are at present quite unknown, but will be turned up sooner or later in manuscript form. A second very large group are known and some manuscripts of their work have been located and perhaps somewhat studied, but

[1] The Macmillan Company, New York, 1923.
[2] October, 1930.

they have never been printed. A third group are in type as incunabula and other early editions which are almost equally rare and inaccessible, especially in America."

Even many of the works which were printed in the early Renaissance time were often quite carelessly printed from a single late and inferior manuscript of the treatise in question. Occasionally, too, the editors took unwarrantable liberties with the language and perverted the thought of the author. As Professor Thorndike says: "Revised editions of such works must be issued, based upon careful collation with the earliest and best manuscripts." The revision of these works would mean much for the proper presentation of medieval scientific truth to our generation. It would correct ever so many false notions. Almost needless to say, this would require immense labor and would take a very long time, but it would be well worth the while. It would be a real contribution to true and accurate scholarship, properly orienting the minds of the learned with regard to the Middle Ages.

Much has already been accomplished in the publication of such works as Migne's *Patrologia,* and in German works on the history of philosophy, the history of the mathematical sciences, and the history of medicine. Important proposals to carry on further works of this nature have been made. Thorndike's idea is not to run counter to these in any way but to take only the works on medieval science that are not readily available. The editing would require almost endless patience and labor, but would be amply rewarded because of the immense amount of material which would thus for the first time be rendered available for scholars.

Professor Thorndike calculated that it would probably take some 200 years to bring this work to even a reasonable completion. He thought that perhaps it would still be in process in the year of our Lord 2130, "just as the *Acta Sanctorum,* of which the first volume was published by the Jesuit, Bollandus, in 1643, is still in process today, while the *Histoire Littéraire de la France,* initiated in 1733 by the Congregation of

St. Maur, has so far covered its material only to the fourteenth century." Almost needless to say the American audience quite gasped at the thought of beginning a task in historical scholarship that might not be completed for more than two hundred years.

The list of some 250 books enumerated by Thorndike, which he believes would have to be edited for this purpose, may be regarded as a mere beginning of the enterprise. Anyone who knows Thorndike's own scholarly work will understand what he implies by calling attention to the many medieval source materials of all kinds that need to be revealed before we can know the thoughts of medieval scholars on scientific subjects. We are only just beginning to learn something about that topic. Perhaps in another two hundred years we may know a great deal more, though very probably even at that date we shall still be on the trail of manuscript materials of great value for the proper understanding of science in the Middle Ages. The monastic schools were hives of industry, and in spite of all the losses that have been incurred through the vicissitudes of the past thousand years, there are still preserved immense treasures of medieval knowledge to bear testimony to their indefatigable labors.

Take two of these monastic schools, Bec, founded in the first half of the eleventh century, and Cluny, founded early in the tenth! The men connected with them deeply influenced the Europe of their time. Bec was begun by a Norman knight, Herluin, who gave up life at court in order to devote himself to the life of the spirit. The abbey was built on the banks of the Bec (a Northman's name for a brook) and was very modest in its beginnings. But it quickly attracted attention when Lanfranc, who had been giving lectures at the school of Avranches, gave up his career as a teacher to become a monk at Bec. Within a few years he opened a school in the monastery and pupils flocked to him from all over western Europe attracted by his scholarly exposition of the Christian philosophy of life. Many of the pupils who came developed a monastic vocation, so that a new and larger monastery was built a bit removed from the water. In the course of time Lanfranc became the prior of the monastery and to a great extent replaced the abbot founder, now advanced in years, in shaping the policy and directing the affairs of the institution. He came to be looked upon as one of the greatest of the churchmen of that time.

In 1066 Lanfranc was chosen abbot of Caen. The place of prior at Bec was taken by a much younger man, Anselm, destined to become even more famous than his predecessor. Anselm became the most important teacher at Bec and his famous lectures attracted still more pupils to the monastery. When the abbot founder, Herluin, died in 1078, Anselm succeeded him as second abbot of Bec. The abbey continued in existence down to its dissolution at the time of the French Revolution. Its long list of abbots includes many of the most distinguished names in French history. These demonstrate that Bec continued to be for nearly 800 years a center of influence and education, though in the later centuries it no longer had a prestige comparable to that acquired in the eleventh and twelfth centuries. Unfortunately it suffered much at the time of the Hundred Years' War between France and England, and fared still worse during the religious wars in the Huguenot days. But during the long years of its existence it proved a harbor of refuge for many thousands of men who found peace and happiness within its walls, and an opportunity for the development of the mind and the cultivation of the spirit.

In what have been called the golden days of the first century of its existence, the abbey of Bec gave three archbishops to Canterbury — Lanfranc, Anselm, and Theobald. After the ruling duke of Normandy had won the battle of Hastings and become king of England, as William the Conqueror, in 1066, the Norman rulers naturally favored as primates in their English dominion the men who had achieved distinction in Normandy. Though foreigners by birth, these three archbishops from Bec proved valiant upholders of the rights of the Church in England. They showed themselves ready no less to suffer valiantly in defense of the rights of the Church when Norman monarchs would have infringed on traditional customs and privileges.

The life of Lanfranc provides the best evidence as to the interest of the men of western Europe in education at the beginning of the second millennium of Christianity, just when, according to old-fashioned tradition, the "dark ages" were darkest. Lanfranc's parents were probably only good middle-class people. Both his father and mother died while he was still quite young. In spite of the serious handicap to success in life that circumstances of this kind almost inevitably create, Lanfranc was afforded the advantage of a liberal education in his native town of Pavia and afterward practiced law there with distinguished success. But this practice seems to have rather troubled his conscience, as it did that of St. Francis de Sales half a millennium later. Besides, Lanfranc aspired to be a teacher. To achieve his desire he left his native land and became a professor at the school of Avranches in Normandy. Here his lectures soon came to attract attention far and wide throughout France.

In the midst of his success he gave up teaching to become a monk in the abbey of Bec, and after a few years opened there the school which attracted students from many parts of the continent. Some of those rose to high rank in the Church in after life. Pope Alexander II, usually considered one of the greater popes of the time, and Anselm, Lanfranc's successor as prior of Bec and subsequently as archbishop of Canterbury, are the most distinguished of his pupils. Lanfranc came to be looked upon as one of the most illuminating teachers of philosophy and theology in his time. He was often invited to make an exposition of Catholic doctrine for ecclesiastical councils in many parts of the country.

John Richard Green, the historian of the English people, thus gives his own view on Lanfranc's work at Bec:

"His teaching raised Bec in a few years into the most famous school of Christendom. It was, in fact, the first wave of the intellectual movement which was spreading from Italy to the ruder countries of the West. The whole mental activity of the time seemed concentrated in the group of scholars who gathered around him; the fabric of the common law and of medieval Scholasticism, with the philosophical skepticism which first awoke under its influence, all trace their origin to Bec."

The year following the conquest of England, Lanfranc was chosen archbishop of Rouen, but pleaded to be allowed to continue his work in the monastery of St. Stephen at Caen, of which he had been made abbot. When some three years later, however, Stigand, the archbishop of Canterbury, was removed from office by a council at Winchester for various acts unbecoming a bishop, Lanfranc was appointed his successor. Once more he would have refused the episcopacy, preferring the quiet and the opportunity for study provided by his abbey. At last, however, he yielded to the solicitations of ecclesiastical friends and above all to the advice of Abbot Herluin of Bec, whose opinion he had learned to value very highly.

Lanfranc proved to be one of the great archbishops of the primatial see of Canterbury, but neither his dignity in the hierarchy nor his long friendship with the duke saved him from friction with the new English monarchs. He had shown thoroughgoing independence of character in his relations with the ruling monarch of Normandy as is demonstrated by various incidents that are related of him. This was not diminished but emphasized while he was archbishop. He had almost ceaseless conflicts with the second son of the Conqueror, the red-headed William Rufus, whom Lanfranc crowned at Westminster less than three weeks after the Conqueror's death. He succeeded, however, in valiantly maintaining the rights and privileges of the Church.

While Lanfranc was an Italian by birth, his long years of teaching in France followed by his English experience served to make him a man of catholic interests.

"He proved to be in every capacity, as scholar, as author, as politician, and as churchman, a man of sound sense, rare tact, and singular ability which marked him as a great man among his contemporaries and gained for him a memory that remains vivid even down to our own day eight hundred years later."

More distinguished even than Lanfranc and doubtless owing most of his highly developed intellect and his fine administrative capacity to his experience at Bec as prior and afterwards as abbot, Anselm may be taken as a typical representative not only of Bec but also of other Benedictine schools of the time. His writings on philosophy and theology have continued to interest scholars down to our own day, and editions of them in several languages have been issued even in the twentieth century. He was proclaimed a Doctor of the Universal Church by Pope Clement XI, in 1720, and has come to be recognized as one of the founders of Scholasticism — the philosophy of the Schoolmen. His ontological argument for the existence of God has been the subject of strenuous discussion on the part of scholarly men in nearly every generation since his time.

While this argument was rejected by St. Thomas Aquinas and by the Dominican schools of philosophy and theology generally, it was not rejected by all the Schoolmen, for the great Franciscan scholars of the precious thirteenth century, Alexander of Hales and Duns Scotus, accepted it. Rejected by Kant seven centuries later, it was in turn very strenuously defended by Hegel, for whom the argument had something approaching a fascination. It is surprising enough to find the two German philosophers, who have been the leaders of modern non-Catholic philosophic thought not only in Germany but in most of the countries which accepted the Reformation, thus disputing over the philosophic teaching of a man who received his education in a Benedictine monastery about the middle of the eleventh century. It is still stranger to find that in the United States in the nineteenth century two of our own thoughtful philosophers, Orestes A. Brownson and Thomas Davidson, were very much taken by Anselm's argument, and considered it a marvelous revelation of the power of human reasoning.[3]

Like Lanfranc, Anselm was an Italian. He was born at Aosta in northern Italy. His experience at Bec, as prior and abbot, formed his character and enabled him to demonstrate his high administrative abilities when chosen archbishop of Canterbury. He became thoroughly English in his interests and has been looked upon as a representative English churchman. Freeman, the English historian, who was probably better acquainted with this period of English history than any other, said of Anselm in his *History of the Norman Conquest :*[4]

"Stranger as he was Anselm has won his place among the noblest worthies of our island. It was something to be the model of all ecclesiastical perfection; it was something to be the creator of the theology of Christendom, but it was something higher still to be the very embodiment of righteousness and mercy, to be handed down in the annals of humanity as the man who saved the hunted hare and stood up for the holiness of Aelfheah."

Anselm's proclamation as a Doctor of the Church means that everything he wrote has been submitted to the most careful scrutiny and that he has been found to be thoroughly in accord with the doctrines of the Catholic Church. Unfortunately his life as archbishop of Canterbury was seriously disturbed by the necessity of defending the rights of his Church against the kings of England who were invading ecclesiastical privileges. In spite of the preoccupation of mind caused by the continued difficulties with the king's ministers, he continued to write. He did not systematize his philosophy and theology as did his great successors in their books of Sentences and Summas, but he covered the whole field of Catholic theology. "There are few pages of our theology that

---

[3] Curiously enough the simple form of Anselm's ontological argument, *Deus potest esse, ergo est* (God can be, therefore He is), is to be found in the lists of theses defended in the colonial colleges in America on Commencement Day as a test of scholarship for the degree of bachelor of arts.

[4] Vol. IV, p. 444.

have not been illustrated by the labors of Anselm."[5] Of him, too, it has been said, "Whatever he touched he failed not to adorn." He has written on the most difficult theological subjects, on the Holy Spirit, the Holy Trinity, and the Atonement. That much disputed topic of free will, and above all the question of predestination in relation to it, he treated very fully. It has often been said that he anticipated later controversies on these subjects and worked out solutions of the main problems connected with them.

Anselm's work, *Cur Deus Homo,* "Why God Became Man," is a classic in the best sense of the word. Professor G. E. B. Saintsbury of Edinburgh University, whose wide experience in the field of criticism makes his opinion of special value, did not hesitate to class the *Cur Deus Homo* among the great books of the world even in the matter of its style. In his volume *The Flourishing of Romance and the Rise of Allegory*[6] he makes the following interesting allusion to it:

"The influence of form which the best Latin hymns of the Middle Ages exercised in poetry, the influence in vocabulary and in logical arrangement which Scholasticism exerted in prose, are beyond dispute: and even those who will not pardon literature whatever its historic and educative importance may be for being something less than masterly in itself will find it difficult to maintain the exclusion of the *Cur Deus Homo* and impossible to refuse admission to the *Dies Irae.*"

For Saintsbury these two great works, one of them a masterpiece in Latin rhymed poetry, the other an equally great masterpiece in philosophic prose, are considered to be outstanding in their respective classes and furnish striking examples of the power of expression in medieval Latin which these authors in the tenth and eleventh centuries had acquired.

Anselm was the forerunner of Scholasticism, of which Professor Saintsbury writes:

---

[5] *Catholic Encyclopedia,* Vol. I, p. 549.
[6] New York, 1897.

"The claim for it of a far-reaching educative influence in mere language, in mere system of arrangement and expression, will remain valid. If at the outset of the career of modern languages, men had thought with the looseness of modern thought, had indulged in the haphazard slovenliness of modern logic, had popularized theology and vulgarized rhetoric as we have seen both popularized and vulgarized since, we should indeed have been in evil case."

Lanfranc and Anselm are but two noteworthy exemplifications of the Benedictine education of those days. Both of them were profound thinkers, thoroughly capable of expressing their thoughts, though they lived at a time when it used to be said that thinking and style were largely lacking in the education of the day. Their careers are a demonstration that the education thus afforded was indeed liberal in the sense that it freed the mind from the shackles of thinking in the formulas of other men. Whatever lack of information there may have been in that education owing to the circumstances of the times, it not only taught them to think for themselves but they were proudest of the fact that it trained them above all to use their will power to the most decided advantage. Huxley in his address on "A Liberal Education and Where to Find It" rightly remarks: "That man, I think, has had a liberal education who has been so trained in youth that his body is the ready servant of his will . . . whose passions are trained to come to heel by a vigorous will, the servant of a tender conscience." Would that everything that Huxley wrote were as full of common sense as that.

IV

MONASTIC SCHOOLS — CLUNY

THE culmination of monastic influence in Europe came with the foundation of the monastery of Cluny, at the beginning of the tenth century. The broad attention that this monastic establishment attracted over most of Europe for hundreds of years thereafter makes it of signal importance in the history of education. Unfortunately Cluny suffered severely during the religious wars of the sixteenth century, when many of its precious treasures of books and manuscripts were destroyed. It met with still greater havoc at the French Revolution in 1790 and the suppression which followed it. But with the increase of interest in medieval history, aroused in our time, the ruins of Cluny have proved a magnet to attract attention to this spot, where during two full centuries had existed one of the most important seats of culture in the world. In particular the Medieval Academy of America became the promoter of a series of archaeological explorations and excavations at the site of the old monastery, representing such an important landmark in the history of civilization.

The buildings themselves amply illustrate the genius for construction and the fine taste in ornamentation which developed at that time. There has probably never been a more beautiful architectural development than that of Cluny, and the tragedy of it is that these rare edifices should have been blown to pieces for no other reason than to provide materials for the erection of a set of breeding stables and quarters for army grooms.

The abbey church of Cluny was planned and erected on a

scale worthy of the greatness of the religious community and its affiliates which it so well represented. It is not surprising to learn, then, that it was looked upon as one of the wonders of the earlier Middle Ages. The church was altogether over 555 feet in length and continued to be the largest church in Christendom until the completion of St. Peter's in Rome, in Michelangelo's time, about the middle of the sixteenth century. The edifice consisted of a nave with double side aisles, a chevet of five apsidal chapels, and a narthex or antechurch. The construction of the building was begun in 1089 and was finished for consecration by Pope Innocent II some forty years later. Including the church, the conventual buildings covered an area of twenty-five acres. It was an extremely impressive group and showed clearly how well these medieval monks were able to solve the most difficult problems in architectural engineering.

During most of the later Middle Ages, the library of Cluny contained the richest and most important collection of books in France and throughout all Europe, probably only surpassed by the collection at Rome. It was the storehouse of a very large number of valuable manuscripts. Unfortunately, when the abbey was sacked by the Huguenots, in 1562, many of these priceless treasures perished and others were dispersed. Of those left at Cluny in charge of the monks who came back after the invasion of their monastery, some were burned by the revolutionary republican mob at the time of the suppression in 1790, and others were stored away precariously enough in the town hall of Cluny. These were eventually transferred to the Bibliothéque Nationale in Paris. The monastery itself gradually fell to ruin.

The monastic rules of Cluny show how deep was the interest of the community in the intellectual life. According to rule there was a time appointed for private reading every day, from the fourth to the sixth hour. Besides this, on Sundays and holydays of obligation — and the latter, be it remembered, were some fifty in number during the year — the monks

were free to read between offices and meals. Most of them
were ardent in their readiness to follow the rule. According to
the regulations of St. Benedict each monk was expected to
finish, that is, exhaustively to study, one book during Lent.
In addition to this private reading, there was public reading in the church, the refectory, and the chapter house. Reading in the refectory during meals might seem to many people
in our time as scarcely likely to be productive of much intellectual interest, but those of us who at some time or other
have shared in the experience of listening to reading at mealtime know how much it may mean for acquaintance with
valuable books, especially because of the discussion that it
arouses among the hearers afterward.

At Cluny, perhaps even more than at Bec, the monks were
interested not only in theological studies but also in the
classics and literature. The Latin classics were the subjects
of special devotion and a great many copies of them were
made in the *scriptoria*. Otherwise so many of them would not
have been preserved. The production of religious literature at
Cluny was interesting because it served to show how thoroughly these monastic students had secured command over
the Latin language and what important contributions they
made to the practical use of it. This was true not only as
regards the refinements of Latin serviceable for subtle distinctions in the study of Scholastic philosophy, but also in
the rhythmic use of the language for that beautiful rhymed
verse in which so many of the great hymns of the Middle
Ages were written.

It was at Cluny that Bernard of Morlaix wrote his supreme
religious poem, *De contemptu mundi,* often proclaimed one of
the greatest hymns ever written. Under the title "Jerusalem
the Golden" it has been a favorite hymn in modern times.
Reverend Dr. John Mason Neale said of it: "It is the most
lovely, as the *Dies Irae* is the most sublime and the *Stabat
Mater* the most pathetic of medieval poems." Its extremely
difficult rhyme scheme and meter. Latin hexameters with

double internal rhymes, and lines rhyming in pairs besides, would seem to have put almost insurmountable obstacles in the way of expressing great thoughts in such involved literary techniques. It would seem as though this extreme difficulty put in the way of expression must inevitably have made the verse stilted and lacking in unction, and yet it is marvelous to find how profoundly this hymn has appealed to humanity all down the ages. Its 3,000 lines are a monument to the monastic knowledge of Latin as a living language. Professor F. A. March has suggested that these rhymed Latin hymns represented the genuine poetry of the Latin language, the classical Latin poetry having borrowed so much from its Greek models as to have impaired its originality. The philosophic disputations and the hymns are two demonstrations from opposite poles of how thoroughly the Latin language had been kept a living tongue by these medieval monks.

Cluny developed music worthy of the great institution that it was and influenced deeply the practice of plain chant during the later Middle Ages. Many hymns were written at Cluny only less charming in literary quality than that which is attributed to Bernard of Morlaix. These hymns were given a musical setting worthy of them. In all the arts as well as in the crafts Cluny achieved admirable results. Even if the great monastery itself did not always supply the artists and the architects who were responsible for the gorgeous edifices that the abbey and the church became, and even if some of these men were invited from distant monasteries, which is by no means certain, it was surely the taste of the monks that dictated the construction and decoration, and it was their thorough appreciation of the artistic that encouraged the making of so many beautiful things.

St. Bernard, the great founder of the Cistercians, whose rule was so much more austere and rigorous than that of other religious orders, and who seems to have hesitated to allow his monks even the pleasure there is in the things of beauty created by monastic artistry for use in divine service, declared that the monks of Cluny violated their rule of poverty in their possession of the treasures made for monastic purposes — vestments, sacraments, sacred vessels, altar furniture, illuminated missals, and the like. He suggested that much of Cluny's art was meaningless extravagance. Those who know even a little about the fine art objects designed for Cluny, rejoice that the monks devoted themselves to the making of things worthy as far as possible of the God they worshiped. As Joan Evans said in her *Monastic Life at Cluny*,[1] when summing up the significance of Cluny's architecture and the marvelous development of the arts and crafts in the service of religion which they brought about: "Beautiful and splendid they were, but with a beauty and a splendor made spiritual with their intellectual significance."

Cluny, which has been hailed as the major monument of that great period of Romanesque architecture which developed in the eleventh and twelfth centuries, is considered to be of such importance as an illustration of the achievements of this period that, as has been said, the Medieval Academy of America granted funds for the excavation of the ruins. This work was actually begun in 1928 in anticipation of the 850th anniversary in 1939 of the beginning of the great church by the abbot, St. Hugh.

With this new study of the ruins came a recognition of the magnificence and significance of the abbey buildings, particularly the church which is a masterpiece of early medieval architecture. It was quite literally one of the great buildings of the world. The middle portion of the church consisted of a bouquet of majestic towers, a triumph of esthetic and architectural engineering. These, as we have said, were blown up to provide material for a military stable and the grooms' quarters. We talk in bitter deprecation of the Vandals and their destructiveness, but modern vandalism in connection with war and religious intolerance has destroyed more beautiful buildings than all the Vandals of history.

---

[1] Oxford University Press, 1931.

Since the celebration of the millennium of Cluny, at the beginning of our century, a number of articles have been written dealing with the monastery. Its significance as a foster mother of art and education has come to be recognized. Interesting materials have been made available which show the character of the great Burgundian abbey and what its influence was during the period just before and after the end of the first thousand years of Christianity. It has often been said that men were anticipating the end of the world at the accomplishment of the thousandth year after Christ and that this preoccupation of mind greatly hampered mental activity of all kinds, literary, artistic, philosophic, and scientific. Only a little knowledge of Cluny is necessary to make it clear that this idea had little or no influence on the men of the time. During the successive generations of that tenth century the monastery developed a thoroughgoing intellectual life and a far-reaching influence that gave it great prestige throughout Europe.

The easiest way to appreciate the role that Cluny played in civilization and Christianity at that time is to take note of the careers of some of its best known abbots. One of the greatest of these is Odilon, whose personality made itself felt far beyond the monastery and its dependencies. To Odilon we owe the establishment of the Truce of God. This was a formal engagement entered into by the nobles of a large part of Europe under which they pledged themselves not to engage in warfare on Friday, Saturday, and Sunday of each week. Friday as the day on which the Son of God died for men, Saturday as His Mother's day, and Sunday, the Lord's day on which He rested after the creation, seemed specially meant for peace. This left only four days out of the seven for their quarrels and did away with a large percentage of the wars, almost as common then as in our own time. It was no easy matter to win the wills of warlike men of that time to an agreement of this kind. No doubt many in our time would be glad to have the old abbot's secret as to how to suppress even this much of human quarrelsomeness.

It was because these warlike nobles had learned to respect and reverence the abbot of Cluny for what he had done for others, forgetful of himself, that they were willing to make the sacrifice of their inclinations to war and moderate their hostile susceptibilities. During a famine Odilon is said to have once sold the sacred vessels of the monastery in order to relieve more effectively the sufferings of the people of the neighborhood. He was noted for his calmness of judgment and the readiness with which he forgave injuries and above all insults to himself. At a time when the poor met with little mercy from their overlords and only the shortest of shrift in punishment was shown them, his friends often said to Odilon that he was too easy in his judgment of his feudatories. Odilon's reply was that he would much rather be damned for having shown too much mercy, than for having exhibited too great hardness of heart.

It is not surprising to find that the churchmen of that time turned with confidence to Cluny to select from among its monks those whose qualities of mind and heart and soul should best fit them to rule over the Church. So from Cluny, during the flourishing period of its existence, came a series of popes who accomplished wonderful things for Christianity and the Church. One of the monks of Cluny who was elected pope was the great Gregory VII [Hildebrand], whom Catholics have loved for the enemies he made as well as for the reforms he effected and for the prestige he brought to the Church. Not long after Gregory came Pope Urban II, who inaugurated the Crusades which changed the course of human history and the face of Europe. Then there were the Popes Pascal II and Calixtus II, men who stand out prominently among the greater pontiffs of the period.

In trying times, when men of genius and character were needed as rulers, Cluny was able to supply them. The monastery was looked upon as the center of Christianity after Rome itself, and there were not a few men of that day who felt that the Burgundian abbey was almost of greater significance for the Church at that period than the old Roman capital which had gradually degenerated and lost so much of its prestige. Cluny continued under a succession of great abbots to be one of the mainstays of the papacy and the Church, but at the same time the chief center of culture and education in Europe.

No wonder that with this Europe-wide prestige, Cluny grew in the number of its monks as well as in the influence it exerted. Peter the Venerable, as he is affectionately called, became abbot at the end of the twelfth century and had some two thousand houses of his Order under his obedience. In all of these the intellectual life was deeply cultivated and the monks were, according to their tastes and their talents, occupied with philosophy, medicine, mathematics, and music, though all of them according to rule were bound to the recital of the office for four or five hours of the day, and to a certain number of hours of manual labor, except on Sundays and festival days. Peter, the ninth abbot, who ruled from 1122 to 1126, lifted the Order up to its highest plane of influence and prosperity. It had affiliates all over the world. There were no less than thirty-five in England at the time of the dissolution under Henry VIII, and three in Scotland. The vast majority of the men in these monasteries were living lives of peace and happiness in the proper exercise of mind and body that brought with it real satisfaction in life.

In the light of these facts it is easy to understand the remark of Sir James Stephen, regius professor of modern history at Cambridge in the days when the earliest recognition of the true place of the monks in the Middle Ages was coming home to serious students. Referring to the Benedictines he declared:

"The greatness of the Benedictines did not, however, consist either in their agricultural skill, their prodigies of architecture, or their priceless libraries, but in their parentage of countless men and women illustrious for active piety, for wisdom in the government of mankind, for profound learning, and for that contemplative spirit which discovers within the soul itself things beyond the limits of the perceptible creation."

After the end of the tenth century the place of the monks in education was gradually assumed by the diocesan authorities, and the development of the more formal educational institutions, the universities, took place. Many cathedral schools were founded, some of which developed into universities. Miss Joan Evans, sometime librarian of St. Hugh's College, Oxford, in her *Life in Medieval France*,[2] describes the passage of education in the eleventh century out of the hands of the monks into those of the secular clergy.

In France there were cathedral schools at Chartres, Laon, Auxerre, Sens, Rouen, and Clermont, as well as at Notre Dame in Paris. On the façades of these cathedrals are to be found sculptured figures of the seven liberal arts, making it clear that the cathedral authorities proposed to do what we would call "college work" in connection with the cathedral establishment. The canons of the cathedrals, in addition to their duty of chanting the office in the choir, assumed the obligation of teaching, and enthusiastic devotion to their work soon created prestige for them and brought pupils from the older schools.

As is usually true of educational institutions, the cathedral schools owed their rise to the prominence of their masters and the important role which they came to play in education. The recognition of the ability and the capacity for mental training of their teachers was the principal factor in their success. Such men as Fulbert of Chartres and Gilbert de la Porrée, not to mention other contemporary masters, came to be known far and wide throughout France, some indeed throughout Europe. Their names became celebrated in the mouths of their pupils, and distinguished teachers were elevated by their ecclesiastical superiors to prominent positions

---

[2] Oxford University Press, 1925.

in the hierarchy. Fulbert became bishop of Chartres in 1006 and was looked upon as the direct heir of the learning and educational traditions of Gerbert, that distinguished French scholar, who at the turn of the millennium was elevated to the papacy under the name of Silvester II (999–1003). Gerbert's educational prestige led to his selection as abbot of Bobbio and then as archbishop of Rheims, where he acquired new fame. Later he was elected to the archbishopric of Ravenna and subsequently to the papacy. It is not surprising that out of cathedral schools, whose teachers were so distinguished, the universities of the later Middle Ages took their rise and came to be educational institutions of high rank.

Bec and Cluny represented the culmination of the Benedictine schools. After the Crusades a new manifestation of the spirit of Christianity made itself felt. New groups of men were raised up to continue the good work that had been carried on so successfully for nearly 700 years by the Benedictines. The mendicant friars, the Franciscans and Dominicans, came to take the place in education that had previously been held by the sons of St. Benedict. These new organizations very soon developed a group of distinguished teachers and thinkers whose work attracted many thousands of students to the universities. They worked out the significance of life, and the relations of man to himself and his fellow man, in terms that gave intellectual satisfaction and that have continued ever since to provide a way of life for scholarly men. Such teachers as Aquinas, Roger Bacon, Albertus Magnus, and Alexander of Hales, helped men to probe the mystery of life to the bottom as well as it has ever been done, and their solution of its problems represents even to our day the best expression of the meaning of existence.

"In an age of oligarchical tyranny," wrote Sir James Stephen, "the mendicant friars were the protectors of the weak; in an age of ignorance, the instructors of mankind; and in an age of profligacy, the stern vindicators of the holiness of the sacerdotal character and the virtues of domestic life."

Here we have from the pen of one who knew whereof he wrote, and had no reason for partiality in their regard, a judicial opinion as to the Franciscans and Dominicans when they came to be prominent in education, and showed themselves great educators in the days of the universities. A new era in education was beginning and new leaders were needed for it. The authors of the volume, *Schools and Teaching in the Renaissance of the Twelfth Century,* said:

"Monasticism and its schools lost in the twelfth century its contact with the times, its spirit of initiative, and the feeling of progress which passed into other hands. . . . The young generation, the new classes of society, did not go to them any more. When in the year 1200 the king of France recognized officially the rights and privileges of the university teachers and scholars studying in Paris, this first charter of a European university constituted only the institutional ratification and the administrative stabilization of a secular intellectual life in the old episcopal school of Paris."[3]

---

[3] *La Renaissance du XIIᵉ Siècle, Les Ecoles et L'Enseignement,* by G. Paré, A. Brunet, P. Tremblay (Ottawa, Inst. d'Études Mediévales, 1933).

V

MEDIEVAL CATHEDRALS AND THEIR TREASURES

THE supreme triumph of the Middle Ages was the designing and erection of the great Gothic churches which fortunately remain as the most notable monuments of the time. They are the wonderful stone books in which can be read, as nowhere else, the minds of the men who lived in that period. They demonstrate in their structure, and above all in their ornamentation, the artistic genius of their generations and the training in excellent taste of the men and women of that precious day, so little understood. The people spent many hours, surely as a rule over one hundred every year — counting their Sunday and holyday gatherings — in the interior of these churches. They were thus brought intimately in contact with artistic objects of all kinds, until, if they had any touch of esthetic feeling, they could not help being deeply affected by the charm of the monuments of art they everywhere saw around them.

To get close to the meaning of these churches is to secure the best possible comprehension of the Middle Ages. The impulse to build these great monuments of their faith seems to have come as the result of inspiration received in connection with the Crusades, which proved such a mental stimulus for western Europe. According to tradition, either in the East or in some part of southern Italy which still retained stimulating remnants of the culture of the old Greeks, some of the Crusaders on their way home from the Holy Land saw the pointed arch, the essence of Gothic building, and realized how effective it would be for their native countries. Recent writers have rejected this origin. But in any event the unselfish sacrifice of many of these men in the effort to free the blessed soil which their Redeemer once had trod, attuned their minds to mighty works of faith and worship. The life experience crowded into those crusading years lifted them up to thoughts of high achievement in the service of religion. The result of it all was a series of the most beautiful churches ever erected.

The descendants of the Northmen who had taken possession of the northern coast of France and the territory called after them ever since, Normandy, came to be particularly interested in this pointed-arch architecture, which could be used to produce such impressive and devotional structures. A whole series of these Gothic cathedrals was begun in the twelfth century, and when finished, deeply impressed all who saw them. Soon all the civilized world of the time was following the example of these Normans. Gothic structures were arising all over Europe.

For more than seven centuries now these edifices have stood as monuments and witnesses not only to the constructive genius but also the artistic taste of the medieval people. They may be seen at Rouen and Rheims, as well as at Amiens and Beauvais, at Paris, Bourges, and Chartres. There are not a few of them in Spain, some in Italy, and a number can be found in Germany. They continue until the present time to be probably the most impressive architectural triumphs in the world. Everywhere Gothic churches were erected. In Spain, especially during the reign of Ferdinand III, the royal cousin germane of St. Louis of France, who himself is known as St. Ferdinand, the building of churches was much encouraged. The Spaniards demonstrated their constructive genius in the new art. The cathedral-building impulse crossed the channel to become the creator of such memorable cathedrals as those of Canterbury and Salisbury, Ely and Peterborough, Winchester and Lincoln, York and

Durham. The Teutons caught the enthusiasm, and even in parts of Germany where no stone was available Gothic churches were built in brick that are a revelation of the architectural spirit then abroad.

The name *Gothic* was invented for them as an opprobrious epithet by the men of the Renaissance in order to characterize them as barbaric. These men ascribed them to a degraded taste in architecture on the part of their ancestors, the Goths of the early Middle Ages. Blinded by their classical and humanistic studies they could see only the rationalized harmony of the classical architecture of the Greeks and the Romans, and were quite convinced that any structural achievement which departed far from these models was lacking entirely in artistic taste. It is not less than amusing now to pick up the first edition of the *Encyclopaedia Britannica*, published in Edinburgh, 1771, and read the article on architecture. Just four lines are devoted to Gothic, but they suffice to proclaim it an architecture barbaric in quality, though suitable to the barbarous people for whom it was invented.

How supremely this opinion has changed! Everywhere in the United States, for instance, Gothic churches are being built at the present day. All denominations are erecting them. The most modernistic preachers round out their periods beneath Gothic arches. Successful millionaire business men are engaged in helping modern universities to house their students in dormitories of severely academic Gothic. Even the great commercial buildings, when graced by a touch of artistry, are constructed along Gothic lines.

As a matter of fact the pointed arch, and the opportunity which it provided for designing lofty churches with large windows in the walls, was admirably suited for the dark northern countries where so many days are foggy and cloudy. Admitting great floods of light, it was an eminently appropriate development for the churches of that period. The classical architecture with its limited window space was more suitable for the cloudless skies of Italy and Greece. But in the Gothic there was a combination of both use and beauty which, in Horatian phrase, carried off every point.

The Gothic cathedrals themselves were marvelously impressive. As John Ruskin said, you cannot enter a Gothic cathedral without lifting your head and your heart toward heaven. These soaring naves and spires represent architectural engineering carried to a climax of power. The use of buttresses, and especially of flying buttresses, which besides being extremely useful were at the same time eminently ornate, added strikingly to the exterior beauty of the churches. It served to show how well these medieval people could solve the most difficult problems. The greatest number of these churches have now been in existence over seven hundred years. They have withstood the neglect of men, the vicissitudes of time, the wear and tear of weather conditions, the changeable climate of northern France and England, and at times as well the deliberate vandalism of iconoclasts, less ruthless only than the Communist haters of God. What better evidence could be had to demonstrate that the medieval builders knew how to build not only for time but almost for eternity! How they were able to do it, with the very limited mechanical aids at their command, is indeed difficult to understand. Having practically no other aid, aside from human muscles, than a draft animal and an inclined plane, they successfully carried out their work of lifting up the beautifully carved stone for hundreds of feet into the air, and so setting it in place that it has stayed there ever since.

In *An Inland Voyage* Robert Louis Stevenson has a paragraph on the old cathedrals which sums up very well the feeling of a great many people concerning these medieval churches, even when they themselves have very little of the faith that inspired the building of them. Robert Louis Stevenson has emphasized above all the magnificent sermon in stone which a great cathedral is, and how much more impressive than any preaching it proves to be for those who visit it:

"I find I never weary of great churches; it is my favorite kind of mountain scenery. Mankind was never so happily inspired as when it made a cathedral, a thing as single and specious as a statue to the first glance and yet on examination as lively and interesting as a forest in detail. The height of spires cannot be taken by trigonometry; they measure absurdly short, but how tall they are to the admiring eye! And where we have so many elegant proportions growing one out of the other, and altogether into one, it seems as if proportion transcended itself and became somewhat different and more imposing. I could never fathom how a man dares to lift up his voice to preach in a cathedral. What has he to say that will not be an anticlimax, for though I have heard considerable variety of sermons, I never yet heard one that was so impressive as a cathedral."

Kropotkin, in his volume *Mutual Aid*,[1] does not hesitate to proclaim the cathedrals the greatest triumphs of human genius in building design and construction. He points out that they illumine the social conditions of the time in which they were built:

"If the medieval cities had bequeathed to us no written documents to testify of their splendor, and left nothing but the monuments of the building art which we see now all over Europe, from Scotland to Italy, and from Gerona in Spain to Breslau in Slavonian territory, we might conclude that the times of independent city life were times of the greatest development of human intellect during the Christian era down to the end of the eighteenth century. . . . Not only Italy, that mother of art, but all Europe is full of such monuments."

Only a marvelously developed social life could have left us such monuments. They were not built by slave labor, but they represent the successful efforts of men to make something worthy of the great Creator in whom they believed and whom they worshiped and who had gifted them with a taste for beauty and a power of artistic expression that was to be a joy forever for those brought in contact with their work.

---

[1] London, 1914.

So, too, Kropotkin cannot help but compare modern structures as we have them in Paris, London, New York, with the structures erected by the medieval guilds and especially the towers which formulate in stone their expectation of a heavenly home in another world. He says: "The lofty bell tower rose upon a structure grand in itself in which the life of the city was throbbing — not upon a meaningless scaffold like the Paris iron tower (Eiffel), not as a sham structure in stone intended to conceal the ugliness of an iron frame as has been done in the Tower bridge (London),"[2] not, he might have added, as a shell of brick or thin marble slab to cover the steel frame of a skyscraper in New York. Their structural work had a meaning that has given it a place forever in the history of human development.

The architectural construction alone of the cathedrals, with its solution of so many of the most difficult problems of architectural engineering, would have afforded a magnificent tribute to the genius of the medieval people, but the interior decorations and ornamentation, and above all the equipment for church services, show clearly the fine artistic ability of the workers and the thoroughgoing critical appreciation of the great majority of the medieval people. All the paraphernalia of the cathedrals and monastic churches of the time was as beautiful as could well be dreamt of. It was designed and executed by those who lovingly strove to create as charming objects for use in the worship of the Creator as the mind of man could conceive and his hand could fashion. Literally, everything about these Gothic cathedrals was supremely beautiful. The hinges on the doors, the locks and bolts and keys — all of wrought iron — have served their several purposes faithfully for six or seven centuries, so that there can be no doubt at all about their utility. They are so beautiful that they are real works of art in themselves.

I have seen three men from distant quarters of the globe

---

[2] *Op. cit.*, p. 159.

sketching the hinge on the cloister door of the cathedral at York. One was from Australia, a second from Russia, and a third from the United States. They came from lands unheard of, almost undreamt of, in England when that hinge was fashioned, but they knew a beautiful thing when they beheld it. Each, to the best of his power, was copying the arborizations of this piece of hammered iron, shaped by a village blacksmith some seven hundred years before, that they might keep it as a precious reminder.

What is true for this piece of hammered-iron work, humble as was the artist's medium for the expression of genuine art, will be found true for everything else made for the service and the ceremonies of the cathedral. Bench ends made by village carpenters, choir stalls completed by some lay brother for the monastery church — these and similar things, when no longer needed in the service of the church in England, find a place in South Kensington Museum as works of artistry, models for a distant generation of what can be accomplished even in seemingly crude material when devotion dictates.

Stone carving took on the character of artistic sculpture finely executed. This was often not only beautiful but educational. Men have come to realize in recent years that the flowers and leaves, and sometimes the fruits of plants which were carved on the old cathedral walls, really represent a sort of textbook of botany with illustrations true to nature. These old medieval people expressed their love of nature and of the natural beauties around them in the decoration of the cathedrals. They felt that they were bringing in the works of the Lord from the fields and the forests to worship Him at His altar. To the people engaged in their devotions they thus became a constant reminder of the many wonderful things the Lord has made for mankind, suggesting in a humble way the riches of His superabounding love for His creatures.

Sometimes the floral pieces in stone were executed most charmingly in dark corners where, with the deficient illumination, they could be seen only imperfectly and with difficulty. The wonder to us may be why men were willing to give so much time and trouble to make something that could afford opportunity for so little admiration. I remember asking the verger in an English cathedral how it came that a particularly charming bit of stone carving had been executed in a corner where it could scarcely be seen at all. The modern electric torch revealed its beauty in detail, but without that it could be seen to any advantage for only an hour or two on the few brightest days of the year. The verger's reply was that he supposed that the artisan had done his work unto God. As God sees everywhere, He was sure not to overlook this humble labor of love. That was quite sufficient for the sculptor who had wrought for the sake of the Almighty.

At times these medieval workmen created exquisite combinations of stone and iron, as for instance the angel choir at Lincoln, fashioned just at the beginning of the thirteenth century. It is so delightful that it has been suggested it must have been made by angels rather than by men. The reason for calling it the angel choir is that the figures of the angels are so exquisitely done in stone that even great sculptors have not hesitated to say that probably nothing finer ever came from the hand of man. As a contrast they have in the midst of them the famous Lincoln imp, sometimes explained to be the devil himself, caught looking on with a grin of jealousy at the beautiful angel figures that men were creating. The choir stalls in wood are charmingly carved, and the whole is surrounded by hammered-iron grille work, strong enough for a bank window in modern times, and yet of such slender construction that at a little distance down the nave it looks like lace.

In countless places marvelous sculptures may be found. In most cases we have no idea of the names of the men who did them. There are some 2,200 sculptured figures on the outside walls and roof of the cathedral at Milan. The sculptures at Rheims, before so many of them were devastated during the war, were looked upon as among the most perfect of all times. So, again, the statue of Christ over the main door of the cathedral of Amiens has been declared by many sculptors to be the most dignified representation of the human form divine that ever was made. The Amiennois call it not *le bon Dieu,* but *le beau Dieu* — not "the good God," but "the beautiful God," and anyone who has ever seen it will be quite in agreement with them. Some of the figures of the apostles in La Sainte Chapelle, St. Louis' architectural gem created as a reliquary for the Crown of Thorns, are amazingly exquisite. Then there is the entrance porch of the cathedral of Chartres with all its wonderful figures, which enable us to realize what a supreme sense of beauty these medieval people had.

Down in Italy they decorated many of their medieval churches in terra cotta. In that medium the work of the Della Robbias was done, whose figures have been ranked among the most delightful ever made. There are pulpits in Italy so artistic that great museums throughout the world insist on having copies, in spite of the precious room they take up in the limited museum space.

Everything else about these cathedrals is just as attractive as men could make it. Time and labor and cost meant nothing to them. They were intent upon expressing in terms of external beauty the profound feelings of their worship of the Creator. They made the altar vessels of the precious metals, gold or silver, and put so much of art in them that the value of the gold and silver was as nothing compared to the workmanship which had created the objects.

We have already referred to the chalice of Ardagh and the cross of Cong in Ireland, made in the very early Middle Ages. These articles as well as the shrines intended for the bells with which the early missionaries used to gather their flocks together, are so fine in execution that they are among the most exquisite of all jewelry. They are not merely settings for precious stones, but the gold and silver are worked up so charmingly that veritable art objects are created. These precious articles were wrought in metal some twelve hundred years ago, and they are just as pleasing to the eye today as they were when they were created. They are now the cherished treasures of the people who have learned through the preservation of these rare things how much of culture and civilization there was in the minds of their ancestors more than a millennium ago.

The vestments of the medieval cathedrals were as remarkable in every way as the precious vessels used in administering the sacraments or in processions. Had we not, in spite of the vicissitudes of time, some of these medieval vestments left, it would seem almost impossible that the supposedly rude people who lived over seven hundred years ago could accomplish such marvelous work.

Some years ago the world was startled by the story of the cope of Ascoli. Copes are garments worn over the shoulders of the priest at Benediction and in processions. The cope of Ascoli was made by the Sisters in the convent of Ascoli, a town of north-central Italy. It was offered for sale, and an American millionaire, assured by his experts that it was the most beautiful piece of needlework known today, paid $60,000 for it and brought it to America. The jewels which originally adorned it had been removed before the article was bought, so that the price was paid for the needlework alone.

The cope of Ascoli was made about the year that Dante was born (1265). About a century later another famous cope was produced, this time not in Italy but in England, a thousand miles away. This is the well-known cope of Syon, which now has a place of honor in the South Kensington Museum. It was the handiwork of the Brigittine nuns, founded by St. Bridget of Sweden, who were invited to establish a foundation in England in the fourteenth century. Embroidery of various kinds, under the name of *opus Anglicum*, was done in England and was looked upon as some of the most exquisite of its kind.

The fact that these two copes were wrought a thousand

miles apart, and within a hundred years of each other, makes it clear that throughout the west of Europe many other such artistically admirable vestments were being created. From their very perishable nature, however, it is easy to understand that only a very few could have survived.

Objects in metal for the service of the Church, even when not made in the precious metals, often shared in this surprising expression of artistry so universal at that time. Some years ago an old thurible, a utensil in which lighted charcoal is placed and incense sprinkled on this in Catholic Church services, was sold at a price that startled even blasé New York. This censer was wrought in bronze with angels holding the chains by which it was swung. It had been designed in the generation immediately after the Middle Ages, following the earlier art traditions. The audience was surprised to hear the auctioneer announce an "upset" price on it of $55,000, below which it was not to be sold. Although here was merely a bronze object, less than a foot high, the first offer was $55,000. The bidding continued until it was "knocked down" at $81,000. Money was no object in comparison with the artistry of the humble thurible that had been in actual service for several centuries in a church in Italy.

Shortly after that, the *Tykyll Psalter* was sold in the Lothian sale at New York for $61,000. This psalter is a book formerly used in one of the medieval churches during the singing of the office by the monks. It was regarded as unrivaled in its time. Bidding began at $20,000, and rapidly advanced to three times that amount. It was bought for the New York Public Library, which now has a precious series of illuminated missals or Mass books and psalters that were used in these old cathedrals.

These marvels of artistry may well have served to turn not a few persons from inherited prejudice to a more tolerant attitude of mind regarding the Middle Ages. Thus Quaritch, the great London bookseller, in his *Contributions to a Dictionary of Book Collectors*,[3] tells of the change that

---

[3] No. 7, London, 1896.

came over Mr. James Lenox, founder of the Lenox Library now united with the Tilden and Astor foundations in the New York Public Library:

"Lenox spent some years in the great libraries of Europe learning, in spite of the rigid Presbyterianism in which his father, a Scotchman, had brought him up, to appreciate the works of art and science which had been produced by the papistical heathens of the late Middle Ages. It proves, we presume, the truth of an idea which has undoubtedly entered many minds, that the people whom living we would have burned are very worthy persons when dead."

It is amusing to have Quaritch, a Jew, thus comment on one of his most valued customers, but the change which came over the mind of Mr. Lenox and of many others, when brought into actual contact with the beautiful products of medieval faith, could not but impress deeply the mind of the very acute bookseller.

Everything, indeed, about those medieval books that were to be used in the service of the Church, was made as perfect as possible. Bookbinding became an art, not a trade. As might be expected, the men who made such wonderful books could scarcely be expected to neglect their external appearance. As a result the art of bookbinding owes much to the Middle Ages and there is a great chapter of education in the reverence for books which should demand for them a fitting enveloping medium. France was particularly enthusiastic in its pursuit of the art of bookbinding, and binders there received a charter from King Charles VI as early as 1401. During the fifteenth and the beginning of the sixteenth century, while the spirit of the Middle Ages in its quest for beauty dominated the scene, some of the finest bindings ever created were made. These must be seen to be properly appreciated, but they are treasures of art, artistic achievements. Rightly they command high prices in the auction room, whenever, because of some cataclysm in social or political life, they find their way out of the hands of holders unwilling to part with them, into commercial avenues once more.

Every art and craft of the Middle Ages came to be practiced, especially when in the service of the Church, with a perfection that has made the products of those times the admiration and envy and not seldom the despair of our modern age. Tapestries, for instance, came to be marvelous examples of art, as exemplified under the difficult conditions of weaving.

Raphael, just after the Middle Ages were over, had so much admiration for tapestry that he was willing to make the cartoons for the tapestries of the Sistine Chapel, though he knew that they would be cut up into narrow strips for the convenience of the weavers, and he must have felt quite satisfied that their only mode of public exhibition should be in the difficult form of woven material. His cartoons were discovered stored away in a Flemish garret. Pieced together they are now one of the precious treasures of the South Kensington Museum in London. They serve to show very clearly that far from doing conventional or sketchy work, or anything less than the best that he was capable of, the greatest of painters actually designed for this purpose some of the most wonderful compositions that ever came from his hand.

This is the finest tribute to medieval tapestry that we have, for it was the tapestry of the Middle Ages particularly which Raphael studied in preparation for his cartoons, and he appreciated how marvelously this work, like every other art and craft, had been developed during that precious time. As in the printing of beautiful books in the first generation of printing, with the charming manuscript material of the Middle Ages before them, so now the inspiration that flowed from medieval tapestry called forth from men their highest artistic achievement.

The tapestries at the end of the Middle Ages represent some of the finest works of art in that mode as yet achieved. The famous set of tapestries of the Apocalypse, now preserved in the cathedral of Angers, is probably the most interesting specimen of this particular art. The set consists of seven large pieces, each five meters high and twenty to twenty-four meters wide. The whole is more than one hundred and fifty meters long and covers a surface of seven hundred and twenty square meters. Each piece contains fifteen pictures arranged in two rows. It took nearly a hundred years to complete this work, which was produced just as the Middle Ages were drawing to a close, and in it the whole evolution of the art of tapestry, composition, design, and technique can be followed. The scenes were copied from illuminations made for a manuscript of the Apocalypse which was in the library of Charles V of France. From the miniatures in the manuscript the painter Jean de Bruges made large cartoons. The weaving then was begun by Nicholas Bataille. The pictures of two of these tapestries, the beast and the false prophet driven into the marsh of sulphurous fire, and the angel leading St. John to the heavenly Jerusalem, are illustrations in *The Legacy of the Middle Ages*.[4] They give an excellent idea of the vividness of the scenes and the perfection of the art of these tapestries at the end of the Middle Ages.

These examples of the textile art illustrate very well that combination of the useful with the beautiful which is such a striking attribute of practically all the arts of the Middle Ages. In the churches such tapestries were hung around the choir and especially behind the choir stalls as screens against drafts. On important feast days they were used to decorate the arches between the nave and the aisles of the church. This position brought out their beauty very well. When religious processions took place through the streets, those who possessed tapestries hung them out for decorative purposes. The same thing was done when they wished to honor the state entry of a sovereign or some important nobleman into

---

[4] Oxford University Press, 1928.

the city. Our decorations for such purposes are flags and
banners, interesting enough for their symbolism, but aside
from that it is easy to understand how prosaic we are as
compared with the Middle Ages in this matter of street
decoration. Indoor tapestries made the cold bare halls of
roughly finished stone castles ever so much more homelike.
Kings and the nobility carried these tapestries with them on
their travels, sometimes to the serious injury of precious
pieces of work, but royal tents were less cold and bald with
these multicolored hangings artistically suspended around
them. Besides, they served the utilitarian purpose of shutting
out cold air and were often used to divide large tents into
various compartments.

The stained glass in the old cathedrals has been left for
our consideration until last because it is one of the most
attractive features of the great churches. The huge windows,
which were the favorite feature of the Gothic churches, presented abundant opportunity for the use of stained glass,
and the figures in the windows became as charming as the
illuminations provided for the missals, psalters, the books
of the priests' office, and other volumes required in church
services. The wonder is how men succeeded in making such
richly colored, glowing stained glass, and how they were able
to discover materials which would not fade though the rays
of the sun came pouring through them for century after
century. Some of these windows have been in position for
seven hundred years, and the sunlight instead of fading them
has, if possible, enhanced the charm of their colors, while
their living tints are the despair of modern makers of
stained glass.

The greatest surprise with regard to these windows is that
the local cathedral builders did not have to send long
distances to secure the stained glass they desired. They seem
always to have made it in the little towns, as we would think
them, in which the cathedrals were so often built. How they
all learned what is to our glassmakers an inscrutable secret

remains a mystery, though the wandering of the journeymen from place to place during the years spent in preparation for their admission into membership in the guild probably led to the diffusion of this knowledge.

Blues were particularly used in these windows, partly because that was the Blessed Virgin's color and partly because it was also the color symbolic of purity, so that all virgins were honored by it. This is the color that is the most difficult for the modern maker of stained glass to obtain in such tints as will not fade under the rays of the sun. The medieval guildsmen succeeded in securing a blue of unfading quality, and some of the most beautiful windows that are left to us from the olden times contain this color in quantity. All the other colors, however, were secured in the same enduring way.

The famous "Five Sisters" window at York, consisting of five lancets, is only done in *grisaille* glass, grayish green in color, without any figures in it, and yet it is often hailed as one of the most delightful examples of stained glass in the world. The Jesse window at Chartres, with its jewellike reds and blues, is a supreme triumph of glassmaking. One of the best stained-glass makers in the United States assumed the obligation of restoring one of the little towns of France that had been destroyed in the war. In return for his interest in them the townspeople presented him with a small stained-glass window, which by good chance had not been injured though the rest of the church was practically destroyed. This window was made some seven centuries ago, in a little town, and yet it is so precious a treasure of artistry that this modern stained-glass maker could appreciate it thoroughly and felt almost as if he had been completely repaid for all that he had done for the people.

Among the most marvelous stained-glass windows in the olden times were those still to be seen in their perfection at La Sainte Chapelle at Paris. Considering the vicissitudes of war and revolution through which Paris has gone, it would seem almost as though it must have been by special Providence that these are preserved for us. "Who is there," says Marcel Aubert, director of the Museum of the Louvre, in his article on "The Decorative Industrial Arts,"[5] "who has not felt the sudden thrill which seizes on the visitor to the Saint Chapelle at Paris when he is brought into the presence of the blaze of color which bursts upon him from a thousand medallions in the fifteen great windows?" There is probably no more glorious sight in the world, but visitors experience here much more than merely the satisfaction of their sense of color when it is presented at its purest and clearest. We have the story of the Bible told succinctly through a medium that is so rich in its perfection of color that it is one of the wonders of the world. Well might visitors proclaim that the Creator has never been more worthily honored than by some of these creations of His own slight creature man. They make it easier to understand the meaning of the expression that man was made in the image and likeness of God.

These great Gothic cathedrals were veritable museums in our modern sense of the term, crowded with art objects of the most precious value and stimulating quality. If our civic and national museums were to be stripped completely of all the objects which have come to them out of the old medieval churches, there would be sad lacunae in the collections. They would lose, in fact, the greatest part of their interest.[6]

---

[5] *Legacy of the Middle Ages,* Oxford University Press, 1928.

[6] It may here be remarked that the Middle Ages are often stigmatized as impractical and, above all, as not given to inventions that would facilitate the solution of problems in which men are interested. Yet Whewell, in his well-known work *History of the Inductive Sciences* (Vol. I, p. 52), enumerates a whole series of inventions that were made by the medieval people, and which still continue in our time to be of the greatest service, as they have been to preceding generations:

"Parchment and paper, printing and engraving, improved glass and steel, gunpowder, clocks, telescopes, the mariner's compass, the reformed calendar, the decimal notation; algebra, trigonometry, chemistry, counterpoint (an invention equivalent to a new creation in music), these are all possessions which we inherit from that time which has so disparagingly been termed the Stationary Period."

Those who know and appreciate best the contents of our modern museums of art are the first to proclaim that it is no exaggeration to state that most of their highly valuable treasures have ultimately come to them from the old medieval churches. But in those churches themselves they were originally assembled, not for exhibition to those who visited there, but as tokens of the worship of the Creator in the hearts of the artists who made them. There was very human rivalry between the various churches, each group of people striving to excel the neighboring city, but the one supreme motive was the adoration of the Most High. In the execution of these marvelous decorative pieces of design the medieval artists and artisans exhibited a power of artistry which we must suppose can only come from intensive teaching and from practice under master artisans, who were also artists. The artistic education of the Middle Ages thus developed is the despair of our time.

We have collected these objects of beauty into our museums, but we find it extremely difficult to bring people to visit them. In New York, with its magnificent Metropolitan Museum, one of the most valuable art collections in the world, it is looked upon as a surpassing achievement if statistically a little more than one in ten of the population residing within an hour of the museum visits it once a year. In reality a great number of the visitors come from long distances, and it is doubtful whether even one in twenty of all New Yorkers visits this place more than once a year. It is a treasure house for kings to envy. No monarch ever had so wonderful a collection of art objects gathered from all parts of the world, and yet more than nineteen twentieths of the people in this metropolitan city have not enough interest to visit their Museum.

In the Middle Ages, even as now, Catholics — and they constituted practically the entire population — were required under pain of serious sin to go to Mass on Sundays and holydays of obligation. This, as we have previously implied, meant that on about ninety days every year, they found themselves for at least the better part of an hour, and often for a much longer time, in one of these lovely churches. Although occupied with their devotion, they, nevertheless, could hardly fail to come under the influence of some artistic object in their vicinity. They knelt beneath the stained-glass windows with their wonderful tints; they could not help but admire the beautiful textile materials with which those who took part in the religious processions were clothed; they often saw the richly wrought chalices and ciboriums close to them during the administration of the sacraments; they were deeply impressed by tapestries and pictures, by statuary, carved stone and woodwork, and all this wealth of artistic beauty was poured over them when they were in quiet and susceptible mood, when, therefore, they might be most profoundly affected by it, even though unconsciously. A man with any appreciation of art in his soul could not help but find satisfaction in contemplation of all these objects of artistic delight.

The great majority of those who visit our museums today are prone to rush through them at sightseer's pace. They have just allowed themselves time to glance at everything in an hour or two. But in the old cathedrals people sat or stood or knelt in one place. They were consequently likely to be brought into intimate association at each visit with some one or two very beautiful things in their immediate neighborhood. Since pews were unknown in the medieval churches, the same persons seldom occupied the same place when they attended services, as is so likely to be the case in our day. The idea of having a family pew, with a definite location, came into church life in modern times. The medieval people naturally took positions that would be quite different on successive Sundays, and so they were likely to see all the different parts of the church and to be brought into intimate association with the various art objects profusely distributed throughout the church.

Churchgoing, under these circumstances, was not merely an

opportunity for devotional worship, but it was also an impressive lesson for the development of artistic feeling and a training for the appreciation of things beautiful. The tapestries, pictures, statuary, stained glass, all represented illustrations of scenes from the Scriptures, and especially from the life of our Lord. They also contained the stories of the lives of the saints and memorials of the work that these heroic men and women of an earlier age had accomplished for the benefit of others. For the medieval people, before the organization of the process of canonization, saints, as we have said, were individuals who had been thoughtful of others and forgetful of themselves. Many of the actions of their lives, then, were presented in the churches for emulation.

No wonder that these old cathedrals were well called great stone books, in which those who came to worship might read the story of Christianity down the ages, as well as the history of the Old Testament preparation for it. True and wise direction for right living was thus impressively built into the structures of which they were all so proud. These churches have continued ever since to be objects of reverence as well as of admiration, and visitors from all parts of the world not merely read in them precious lessons in esthetic education, but not seldom bear home with them rich inspiration from the supremely beautiful objects which the spirit of Christianity can develop when it has the opportunity freely to express itself.

Kropotkin, in his chapter on "Mutual Aid in the Medieval City," in his work already alluded to here, has a note on our modern museums that brings out an important feature in medieval-art education of the people, as contrasted with modern methods:

"Medieval art like Greek art did not know those curiosity shops which we call a National Gallery or a Museum. A picture was painted, a statue was carved, a bronze decoration was cast, to stand in its proper place as a monument of communal art. It lived there. It was part of a whole and it contributed to give unity to the impression produced by the whole."

Our museums are likely to be monuments to the munificence of millionaires who accumulated fortunes at the expense of those around them, and sometimes under circumstances that permitted want and poverty to rule while they were gathering in the dollars, but the cathedrals and abbeys and town halls of the Middle Ages were monuments to the people themselves, the artisans and their guilds, all combining with a common devotion to make their communal monuments so beautiful that they are a joy forever. Even small towns and parishes were able to vie with important cities in lifting up a monument to their pride in community life. Like the Acropolis at Athens, the cathedral of a medieval city was intended to glorify the grandeur of the victorious city, symbolize the union of its crafts, and express the pride and joy of each citizen in the city of his own creation. But above all else, it was to render glory to God.

VI

THE MEDIEVAL UNIVERSITIES

THE greatest achievement of the Middle Ages, greater than even their Gothic cathedrals, if possible, was the foundation of the universities. Sir Charles Grant Robertson, Vice-Chancellor of the University of Birmingham (England), says in the opening paragraph of his volume *The British Universities* :[1]

"The modern university may in its subjects and method of study owe much to the classical world of Greece and Rome, but its origin and its organization can accurately be found in the creative genius of medieval minds — one more striking proof of the debt of the modern world to those Middle Ages which the modern world is so ready either to forget or to deride."

There is often rather serious misunderstanding of the intention of the founders of the old universities, which may be traced to misapprehension of the significance of the word *university* itself, as it came to be used to designate an educational institution of the highest rank. Many modern educators would seem to have assumed that the term indicated a place where opportunity was provided for universal scholarship and where, as a consequence, students could learn all about anything and everything. The Latin word *universitas*, however, meant in the later Middle Ages any community or corporation in its collective aspect. When greetings were sent to a university under the formula *Universitati vestrae*, it simply meant in the Irish way, "To the whole of ye," as applied to an organized group of persons united for a specific purpose. In

---

[1] London, 1929.

brief, as Chancellor Robertson says, "The university was a corporate and privileged guild of a particular character."

The other name for the institution which thus arose in the Middle Ages was *Studium Generale,* and this too has led to misapprehension on the part of those who are not familiar with medieval Latin usage. This "General Study" was not at all "a school of all subjects," but a school or center of studies "for all fit persons and not of all things fit for study." The modern popular notion that the university was an organization which included or was intended to include the study of every subject capable of being studied, has no historical foundation in a medieval university, and has had an unfortunately sad effect upon modern university education by cluttering up our universities with every variety of study. All subjects are not equally suitable for university study and the universities were specifically founded for the teaching of "liberal" studies, as distinct from illiberal or technical studies. As Robertson says:

"The medieval creators of the university bequeathed to the modern world the sovereign lesson that the organization of higher education must be delegated as a responsible trust to those who are prepared to devote their lives to learning its secrets, maintaining its standards, and perpetually training their successors in the discharge of their duties."[2]

What these universities accomplished and how deeply they have influenced the world of education ever since will probably be best appreciated from another significant paragraph in Robertson's work:

"Everyone who has witnessed the installation of a Chancellor at Oxford or Cambridge or a debate on statutes, decrees or graces in the Senate or congregation, who has marked the ceremony at the conferring of degrees, pleaded in the Vice Chancellor's court or fallen under the jurisdiction and administrative law of the Proctors, become a Regent, Master or listened to the Bidding Prayer in the University Church — has stepped

---

[2] *Op. cit.*

back from the twentieth century straight into the thirteenth or fourteenth; and when he visits a modern university he finds that the formulae and phrases, the officers and their powers, the degrees, the hoods and the gowns, the machinery and its nomenclature, are medieval and not modern inventions."

Haskins in *The Renaissance of the Twelfth Century*[3] calls particular attention to the fact that all university degrees are in their origin teachers' certificates granting a license to teach. The names *master* and *doctor* as applied to the advanced degrees show this very well. A master of arts was considered qualified to teach any or all of the seven liberal arts, and a doctor of laws or of medicine was a certified teacher of these subjects. We have had to listen to many a bachelor's and master's oration on commencement day because at the medieval universities it was customary for the accredited teacher on whom a degree was conferred to give an example of his teaching. The discourse he gave was, as it were, a specimen college lecture. Our modern word, *commencement,* has reference to the fact that by their addresses they were beginning to teach. It was the commencement of their careers as teachers. The curriculum, examinations, commencement, degrees, are all inherited from the Middle Ages, and in some form they go back to the end of the twelfth or the beginning of the thirteenth century.

Cardinal Newman, discussing education in the mid-nineteenth century, that is, long before he actually became Cardinal, compared the London University of that time (which was merely an examining board) with Oxford of 1750 when English university education was at its lowest ebb and the men merely "ate their terms," that is, took their meals at the university and received their degrees. The great Oxford scholar, probably the greatest modern authority on liberal education, declared that in his opinion the Oxford degree, though taken under such utterly straitened scholastic requirements, was of far more value than the London degree which

---

[3] Cambridge, 1927.

demonstrated the ability to answer questions. Chancellor Robertson has furnished an excellent explanation for this attitude of mind in a paragraph on the influence that association and fellowship in a university have over the minds of young men in their adolescent period:

"If the founders were inspired by one passionate conviction, it was that membership in a university was membership in a society, that a course of university studies is not merely the process of acquiring knowledge but a life, that praying together and playing together are as important as working together, that examinations are tests of character as well as of capacity, and that a degree is a solemn admission to the full brotherhood of your fellow guildsmen. A university, in short, is as different from a polytechnic as an epic differs from an encyclopedia, or a box of bricks from a living and organic hive of bees."

Professor Leacock of the Department of Political Economy, McGill University, Montreal, has a paragraph in his volume *My Discovery of England*,[4] in which he sets forth what he considers the value of the medieval elements still contained in the curriculum at Oxford. It is precisely because of these contributions, as he finds in his chapter "Oxford as I See It," that this university remains so much more efficient as an educational institution than are our modern universities, in the sense mainly that it cultivates thinking rather than the accumulation of information. Professor Leacock wrote:

"The excellence of Oxford, then, as I see it, lies in the peculiar vagueness of the organization of its work. It starts from the assumption that the professor is a really learned man whose sole interest lies in his own sphere: and that a student, or at least the only student with whom the university cares to reckon seriously, is a young man who desires to know. This is an ancient medieval attitude long since buried in more up-to-date places under successive strata of compulsory education, state teaching, the democratization of knowledge and the substitution of the shadow for the substance, and the casket for the gem. No doubt, in newer places the thing has got to be so.

New York, 1922. Quoted here by permission of Dodd, Mead and Company, publishers.

Higher education in America flourishes chiefly as a qualification for entrance into a money-making profession, and not as a thing in itself. But in Oxford one can still see the surviving outline of a nobler type of structure and a higher inspiration."

John of Salisbury, the distinguished English student at the French university, who before his death became bishop of Chartres, tells the story of some ten years of French education just before the middle of the twelfth century, as he himself came into intimate contact with it. He says that he first went to

"Abelard who then presided upon Mount St. Genevieve, an illustrious teacher and admired of all men. There at his feet I acquired the first rudiments of the dialectical art, and snatched according to the scant measure of my wits whatever passed his lips with entire greediness of mind. Then when he had departed only too soon, as it seemed to me, I joined myself to Master Alberic who stood forth among the rest as a greatly esteemed dialectician, and verily was the bitterest opponent of the nominalists."

John knows that he had surpassing opportunities for education, and yet he realizes very clearly that he thought he knew much more than he really did. He had that precious beginning of wisdom:

"I had learned in the lightness of youth to account my knowledge of more worth than it was. I seemed to myself a young scholar because I was quick in that which I heard. Then returning unto myself and measuring my powers I advisedly resorted by the good favor of my preceptors to William, the grammarian of Conches, and heard his teaching over the space of three years, the while teaching much myself, nor shall I ever regret that time."

John spent some dozen of years in various studies, showing how much the young men of his day, of whom he is a good representative, sought education. He taught for a time, compelled to give up his studies by the smallness of his private means, but also in order to give teaching a fair trial since so many of his friends urged that he should undertake the office of a teacher. After three years of this experience he was glad to return to the university classrooms as a student. No seeker after the degree of doctor of philosophy in our own day has ever had any more zeal in the quest for knowledge than this young man of the middle of the twelfth century. He talks as enthusiastically about his professors as ever does any haunter of colleges and universities in our own generation. His education earned him a guerdon of appreciation from distinguished ecclesiastics in his time. Exiled from his native country, he was elected bishop of Chartres, and spent the last six years of his life in dispensing knowledge and friendship among the scholars of his day.

The earliest of the medieval universities was founded at Salerno not far from Naples, probably at the end of the tenth and the beginning of the eleventh centuries. This location of the first modern university will not be surprising once it is recalled that Greek influences were prominent in southern Italy and this region was spoken of as *Magna Graecia*. According to the oldest tradition, the first portion of the university to come into existence was a medical school, around which were gathered other departments considered of university character. The first teachers in the medical school, tradition goes on to say, were an Arab, a Jew, and a Christian, vividly symbolizing the three great sources of intellectual life to which the university owed its origin.

Salerno had been a health resort to which kings and the nobility as well as the wealthy were attracted by reports of cures of long-standing ills. The higher ecclesiastics on their visits to the pope sometimes stopped there for a health cure. The reputation thus acquired brought students who wanted to learn the secrets of medicine, as they were known in this famous place. The largest influence, in the transmutation of the clinic into a medical school with formal premedical education, was exercised by the Benedictines whose great abbey of Monte Cassino was not far away. The Benedictines had a school of philosophy at Salerno, which afforded a foundation for medical studies, for even thus early students sought the dual degrees of philosophy or logic and medicine.

The teacher of greatest prestige in the medical school of the University of Salerno was Constantine, known as Africanus or the African because of his birthplace, Carthage. He studied Arabian medicine down at Kairouan, a rather large town of the earlier Middle Ages, situated a hundred miles south of Carthage, and containing some hundred thousand inhabitants. In his wanderings through northern Africa and Asia, Constantine gathered a precious collection of manuscript materials relating to medicine. He made a series of translations of these which were destined to affect deeply the theory and practice of medicine on the European continent for the next three or four centuries. What he accomplished in this regard has now come to be considered of very great importance in the history of medicine.

In 1930 the Eighth International Congress for the History of Medicine unveiled a tablet at Monte Cassino, the great motherhouse of the Benedictine Order, in honor of all that Constantine has accomplished for medicine and in reverence for the great monastery of the Benedictines at which so much of his work had been done. In his younger years Constantine had been a Mohammedan, but became a convert to the Church probably through the influence of that well-known Benedictine scholar, Desiderius, who was one of the teachers at Salerno while Constantine was there. Desiderius was elected abbot of the monastery of Monte Cassino, and Constantine went with him to become a member of the community. Due to the encouragement of the abbot, every opportunity was afforded Constantine for the continuance of his task of translating medical and scientific works from the Arabic. A few years later, quite against his will the abbot was elected pope, and assumed that office under the name of Victor III. Constantine continued his work at Monte Cassino, so that we have a series of volumes from the pen of this earliest of medieval medical links between Arabic and modern medicine.

During the past ten years very painstaking investigations of Constantine's work and what it meant for European medicine have been made. These have brought us to a much better understanding of what used to be considered the darkest part of the Middle Ages, the tenth and eleventh centuries. Research studies have been made on Constantine by the Germans, French, and Italians, and special articles with regard to him have appeared in many periodicals, particularly in the proceedings of societies of the history of medicine. All this has quite revolutionized the appreciation of Constantine, and has lifted him up to a position of high prestige as a contributor to medical literature.

Of the School of Salerno, Dr. Garrison, our American authority on the history of medicine says:[5]

"The little seaside town of Salerno near Naples was known even to the ancient Romans as an ideal health resort and here for nearly three centuries we find monastic medicine thriving under conditions most favorable to its development, namely, ecclesiastical organization of hospitals for sick nursing, especially at the hands of women. Here too were those beginnings of organized medical education which were to attain such remarkable development in the great universities of the thirteenth century."

The next university to be founded was probably Bologna in the second half of the twelfth century. This was a development from a law school. Irnerius, an expert in legal lore, and especially Roman law, acquired wide prestige as a teacher of law and a large number of students consequently flocked to Bologna to secure the benefit of his knowledge. One of the most interesting features of the school was that his daughter, Irneria, became interested in the study of law and devoted herself to it with such success that she became a teacher in the school which gradually came into existence around her father in Bologna. There are traditions of women students

---

[5] *History of Medicine*, Philadelphia, 1906.

and even women professors of a still earlier period at the
University of Salerno in connection with the medical school.
De Renzi has given many details of this rather surprising
situation so that the development of feminine education and
the encouragement even of feminine teachers (for they soon
came to occupy positions outside of the legal department) at
the University of Bologna is not so surprising as it would
otherwise be. All during the Middle Ages after this period
women professors of various subjects, including even medical
branches were to be found in the Italian universities, and a
number of women must have been in attendance at them.
Just how many there were it is impossible to determine, since
the Italians had a habit, which has not disappeared in modern
times, of giving masculine or feminine names — sometimes
both — rather indiscriminately to their children. Maria is
often the first name of a boy, and girls are often named after
male saints. In Venice for some time all children born in the
republic were named Maria Giovanni, after the two patron
saints of the city, and then the parents might add any other
name or names they wished. It is easy to understand that the
university records, so far as we have them, under these circumstances do not reveal the numbers of the two sexes that
may have been at the institution.

The third of the medieval universities, that of Paris, was
founded also in the later twelfth century. The principal attraction at this center of higher learning was Abelard, a lecturer on philosophy. It is interesting to note that the first
medieval university was founded in connection with a medical school (Salerno) the second in connection with a law
school (Bologna), and the third in connection with a school
of philosophy and theology (Paris). It has been suggested
that this succession of events in the history of the early universities of the Middle Ages presents a rather striking symbol
of the comparative intensity of man's personal preoccupations
with himself and his environment. He is interested first in his
body, then in his possessions, and finally in the question of

the afterworld and his relations to God and to his neighbor. Many medieval universities came into existence through the withdrawal of students from universities where they considered that they were not being dealt with fairly, or sometimes when they wanted to follow a favorite teacher who had transferred to another institution. Oxford and Cambridge came into existence during the early thirteenth century — Oxford was a daughter of Paris, Cambridge was an offset from Oxford. There are claims connecting Oxford with the name of King Alfred or even with Brutus and the Roman times, but there are no serious foundations for them.

At Paris the unfortunate Héloïse and Abelard incident in the twelfth century created a prejudice against the presence of women students. This led to the elimination of the liberal custom as regards feminine education which had grown up in the Italian universities. Paris proved to be the mother of most of the universities in the west of Europe, or at least exercised a paramount influence on their foundation, and so the result was that none of these schools encouraged in any way education for women. In spite of this fact the Italians had taken it up so heartily there was probably not a century from the eleventh down to our own time when there were not distinguished women professors at the Italian universities. As the result of that Italian tradition, at about the end of the Middle Ages, some women from Spain went to Italy and came back to teach in the Spanish peninsula. Prescott has spoken of their "rare scholarship, peculiarly rare in the female sex." The Renaissance witnessed a definite development of feminine education, but this was not new in any sense and the movement had been in preparation during the concluding centuries of the Middle Ages.

It is at Paris that the connection between the episcopal or cathedral school and the university can be traced most readily. When in the year 1200 the king of France recognized officially the rights and privileges of university teachers and scholars studying at Paris, this first charter of a European university constituted only the institutional ratification and the administrative stabilization of a school that had been in existence for several centuries. Paris soon became the center of scholarship in Europe. The men of prestige either as teachers or as students drifted to that place. They were looking for the chance to teach or to study there. After Abelard there were Adam du Petit-Pont, Thierry de Chartres, Gilbert de la Porrée, Robert Pulleyn, Robert of Melum, Simon de Poissy, Peter Lombard (of the Sentences), Maurice de Sully.

It is interesting to note the cosmopolitan character of the university. Some of the men we have just mentioned, as Adam du Petit-Pont, Robert Pulleyn, and Robert of Melun, are English; others, like Pietro Lombardo, are Italians; Thierry de Chartres and Gilbert, caught by the attraction of Paris, had left Chartres which was at that time a very flourishing school. The students came not only from all parts of France but also from Germany, Spain, and Italy. Hugh of St. Victor came from Saxony, John of Salisbury from England. Ruling princes of Germany, Roman senators and consuls, distinguished men from many parts of Europe, wrote to the king of France, Louis VII (1137–1180), in order to recommend to his patronage young people who were undertaking the long journey to Paris to make their studies under the most favorable conditions in that great mother of studies, the University of Paris.

No wonder that Paris was called the Florence of the twelfth century. The university gained a very high place in the educational world at that time. The familiar bull of Gregory IX which so happily begins with the words, *Parens scientiarum*, "Parent of the sciences," was at once the prototype of the many expressions of praise used at various times by the popes and by high ecclesiastics and also the official sanction of their commendation. Paris was thoroughly appreciated by the men of that generation. The situation is best characterized by that famous old apothegm, "The Italians have the papacy, the Germans the empire, the French have education."

Very probably the most interesting feature of the medieval universities, from a social standpoint, lay in the fact that these institutions were not state supported, but were founded and endowed by the gifts of private individuals. A great many of the teachers, and indeed most of the scholars, were in holy orders and were quite ready to devote themselves to the task of university teaching for a salary that would now be considered little better than a miserable pittance. The universities were all during the Middle Ages celibate institutions, and some of them continued to be so until well on in modern times. Indeed, it is only in our generation that the fellows of certain of the colleges in England have been permitted to marry. Living in common and wearing their academic robes for special occasions, most of the men of the university were able to get along on very modest salaries and found their satisfaction, not in the amassing or the spending of money, but in the doing of work that they cared to do, and in the influence for good which they felt they were exerting upon their students.

The chief function of the university was to train men "fit to serve God in Church and State." The principal idea of the faculty was to make better ecclesiastics and better citizens. This ideal continued to be expressed very emphatically as the supreme purpose of the higher institutions of learning until well on into the nineteenth century. All the colleges that were founded here in America during the colonial period, Harvard, William and Mary, Yale, Princeton, the University of Pennsylvania, Columbia, Dartmouth, and Brown, had for their purpose the proper education of men for the ministry of the Church and the magistracy of the State. All these institutions were emphatic in their declarations that to educate men without making them better citizens was to do harm rather than good.

The great purpose of the universities of the present day is to fit students for doing such things as will help them to make money. Success in life, and by that is meant success in money-making, is the great aim of education. An English educator declared that there were three degrees of comparison in our striving after education in the United States. They were, "get on, get honor, and get honest." In explanation he commented in substance: "Get on, that is, make money, you will surely get honor for it, and then get honest and prevent others from making money the way you did." In the older time the idea was that education, meaning a liberal education, would be helpful in making men generous-minded, less pre-occupied with their personal advancement and more thought-ful of others, readier to be helpful to their neighbors, so that in both Church and State men should be happier and might be rendered more capable of accomplishing all that was best in life. This was an ideal not always attained, but the purpose was very definitely striven for and the effect here in America can be seen in the Constitution of the United States and the constitutions of the several states, which we owe to men who had the advantage of this kind of education.

The medieval universities desired above all to have stand-ards which they should live up to and restrictions which they should adhere to closely. The early universities simply grew into their places and took a long while in growing. It was several centuries before they came to be universities in our modern sense of the word, with an undergraduate department and the graduate departments of law, medicine, and divinity or theology.

When the question of the foundation of newer universities arose it was felt to be important that they should maintain similar standards. Accordingly both State and Church legis-lated for this purpose. Most of the universities had a charter from the pope and a number of them also had imperial charters. The charter from the pope usually required that a new university should have at the beginning professors who had been trained and given the faculties or license to teach at one of the older universities, and also that their courses, and above all examinations, should be held in the same way and should be of the same character as those instituted at the older universities. When Pope John XXII by the bull *Erectio Cathedrarum* granted a charter to the university of his native town, Perugia, it was on condition that the first professors should be graduate *doctores* of the University of Bologna, or of Paris, and that there should be oath-bound examinations in which professors were sworn to the maintenance of standards and bound to refrain from too readily granting academic privileges, that is degrees, to students.

These medieval universities were liberal enough to allow students the freedom of enjoying a diversion in their teaching through attendance at several universities during their course. They had the feeling that it would be mentally broadening for the student to spend at least some of his university semesters at different colleges. They believed that exchange of professors between universities was a good thing not only for the students but also for the professors. We have come back to these ideas only in quite recent years. Before that there was very little interchange of students and still less among the professors of the universities, except that occasionally a very successful professor in a smaller university was invited to a post in a larger institution. Sometimes, in modern days, younger universities with an abundant budget enabling them to offer professors' salaries higher than had been customary, have been known to "grab up" professors quite regardless of the injury that might be inflicted on the institutions from which the professors were drafted. There was a different spirit in the Middle Ages. The underlying idea was the good of the greater number and not such competition as would make for the benefit of one institution of learning to the detriment of another.

The number of students in attendance at the universities is not easy to determine and undoubtedly there have been gross exaggerations as to the numbers. There does not seem to be any doubt, however, that in the midst of the enthusiasm for education which developed throughout Europe in the latter part of the thirteenth century there were larger universities in existence, in the sense of more students in attendance at them, than there ever were before or since until just after the war in our own twentieth century. ⌐

When we recall how scanty was the population of the countries of Europe at that time, compared to ours, it is easy to understand what an ardent enthusiasm for education had developed. England in Elizabeth's time, some three hundred years later, when because of the impending attack of the Spanish Armada the first formal census was made, had only some four millions of population, scarcely more than one tenth of what it has at the present time. In the thirteenth century England had little more than two millions of people, whereas the universities at Oxford and Cambridge had many thousands of students in attendance. It seems clear, then, that in proportion to the population there were more students at the medieval universities than there have been at any time before or since; more than at Athens in its palmiest days, more than at Alexandria even when all the influence of the Ptolemies was exerted in favor of that famous institutiton of learning.

The educators of that time realized very definitely and appreciated thoroughly the magnitude of the number of students in attendance at the universities. Even as early as the beginning of the thirteenth century, about 1210, Guillaume le Breton said: "Never before in any time nor in any part of the world whether in Athens or Egypt has there been such a multitude of students gathered." It was declared that "clerks of all nations came to study and in winter assembled in their legions; they are given lessons and they listen sedulously to instruction, and then in summer they may go back to their homes."

There was a great desire for education abroad in those days and it carried vast numbers of the people away with it. There was a very definite sense of self-sacrifice on the part of parents which made them ready to do anything in their power to secure an education for their boys, especially if they had shown any signs of talent. The religious orders provided the means by which education was obtained for a great many and their teaching at the universities made the fees much more modest than would otherwise have been the case, thus rendering education available even to the poorest if they truly wanted it and showed they had the talents to use it to good advantage.

That university students have not changed their characters to any appreciable degree since the Middle Ages is very well illustrated by their letters home, a number of which have fortunately been preserved for us. Delisle in the *Annual Bulletin of the Society of the History of France*,[6] gives a typical example of these. Two French boys, brothers, were studying in Orleans. In their letters home they described to their parents the environment in which they lived, with special emphasis on the goodness of it. At the end they suggest a number of things they need, and above all the money that will be necessary for them to get on. The letter reads:

"To their very dear and respected parents their sons send greetings of filial obedience. This is to inform you that by divine mercy we are dwelling in good health in the city of Orleans, devoting ourselves wholly to study, mindful of the words of Cato, 'to know anything is praiseworthy,' etc. We occupy a good and comfortable dwelling next door but one to the schools and market place, so that we can go to school every day without wetting our feet. [How this must have appealed to mother's heart, though ordinarily it is presumed that this solicitude with regard to wet feet is a comparatively modern notion.] We have also good companions in the house with us, well advanced in their studies and of excellent habits — an advantage which we well appreciate, for as the Psalmist says, 'With an upright man thou wilt show thyself upright.' [Their father would undoubtedly be glad to know that they were in good company, for that means more than anything else for academic accomplishment.] Wherefore, lest production cease from lack of material, we beg your paternity to send us by the bearer money for buying parch-

---

[6] *Annuaire-Bulletin de la Société de l'Histoire de France,* 1869, p. 149.

ment, ink, a desk, and the other things which we need in sufficient amount that we may suffer no want on that account, but finish our studies and return home with honor. The bearer will also take charge of the shoes and stockings which you have to send us and any news as well."

The very hint of wet feet was presumed to be enough for mother to send them the shoes and stockings.

Another student's letter quoted by Haskins in *The Renaissance of the Twelfth Century*,[7] shows that this first one was not a chance selection but one of a group. It ran:

"This is to inform you that I am studying at Oxford with the greatest diligence, but the matter of money stands greatly in the way of my promotion, as it is now two months since I spent the last of what you sent me. The city is expensive and makes many demands. I have to rent lodgings, buy necessaries and provide for many other things which I cannot now specify. Wherefore, I respectfully beg your paternity that by the promptings of divine pity you may assist me so that I may be able to complete what I have well begun, for you must know that without Ceres and Bacchus, Apollo grows cold."

In the final sentence the student is airing his erudition in a way that would very probably touch his correspondent's heart though he is only suggesting that without bread and wine the successful study of the arts was hard to maintain.

---

[7] Harvard University Press, 1927. Quoted here by permission of the President and Fellows of Harvard College.

VII

THE COLLEGE CURRICULUM

MEDIEVAL schools, with minor and almost negligible differences, all presented the same curriculums. After a preliminary intensive study of Latin in the preparatory schools, which enabled the students to use Latin as a means of communication in the classes, the universities took up the courses in what were called the seven liberal arts. These were divided into the *trivium* and *quadrivium*. The *trivium* originally embraced logic, grammar, rhetoric; and the *quadrivium*, arithmetic, geometry, astronomy, and music. This curriculum was not an invention of the Middle Ages but was adopted and adapted from the ancient Greeks. Medieval teaching approached Aristotle as closely as possible, and his logic in particular was looked upon as the basic study in philosophy.

Almost needless to say these seven liberal arts represented very definite occupation of the mind with science. Logic is the science of ordered thought, grammar the science of language, and rhetoric the science of persuasive speech. The *quadrivium*, as is clear, was almost entirely given over to science, physical and mental. The later Middle Ages modified the curriculum so that higher mathematics and natural philosophy and physics were introduced as well as metaphysics and ethics. They were all embraced under the three philosophies: mental (metaphysics), natural (physics), and moral (ethics), with mathematics and astronomy.

There was comparatively little medieval study of the classics for the sake of their educational value, though undoubtedly they were studied for the sake of their content and in order to render more flexible and also more exact the

Latin speech of the day, keeping it near its vivid Roman original. Much time was devoted to the study of the classical Latin authors both as a preliminary to college or university work and as a source for illustrations in grammatical studies. Dante is an excellent example of the educated university man at the end of the thirteenth and the beginning of the fourteenth century. He was not familiar with Greek, but it is surprising to find how many of the Latin authors he was acquainted with. In general the university scholars of the Middle Ages were doubtless like Dante in this regard, but it must not be forgotten that even some of the learned nuns, such as Hroswitha and Hildegarde, have references to a number of Latin authors with whom they seem quite familiar.

Professor E. K. Rand of Harvard, in an article on "The Classics in the Thirteenth Century,"[1] insists that the classics not only continued to be part of the curriculum of the universities of the thirteenth century, but constituted a very important element in them. The Middle Ages did not, as is so often asserted, see ancient letters engulfed in the fashion for dialectics, but on the contrary, in various ways the influence of the classics grew steadily broader and deeper. Rand says: "The thirteenth century, boldly proclaimed by some as the greatest of centuries, had a rich and varied culture in which, though old and new engaged in mighty conflict, the new did not banish the old but drew from it as ever part of its own strength for progress." The Latin classics particularly were the happy possession of the scholars of this time.

Attention was not given to Greek authors until the Renaissance, in the latter half of the fifteenth century. Medieval college students were expected to know Latin well enough to be able to use it in classwork and to understand Latin dissertations and disputations and take part in them. Our generation inherited from the Renaissance a very definite lack of appreciation of medieval Latin,

---

[1] *Speculum,* official organ of the Medieval Academy of America, July, 1929.

but that attitude has largely passed out of fashion with better knowledge of things medieval and with our recognition of the fact that these medieval scholars were largely engaged, not in mastering Latin for cultural purposes, but in adapting the old Latin tongue as a living language for special use in education.

Under logic, in the college curriculum, not a little of what afterward came to be known as metaphysics was included from an early time. Universals were discussed as well as transcendentals, the true, the good, and the beautiful. The composition of matter, as consisting of prime matter and form, *materia prima et forma,* as well as the distinction between essence and existence, occupied a goodly share of college attention. These subjects were studied more profoundly in courses taken up for the master's and doctor's degrees, after the baccalaureate had been reached. The holder of the master's degree was granted the right to teach a particular subject to which he had given special attention, while the doctor possessed the privilege of teaching all the subjects of the university curriculum.

It has been the custom to make little of this medieval college curriculum, to deprecate it as narrow or at least anything but liberal, in spite of the descriptive term, *liberal arts,* applied to it. The medieval scholars were intent on finding, and indeed were persuaded that they had found, the group of college subjects which were best calculated to free the human mind from the habit of merely accepting the suggestions made by others and to provide it with a stimulus to think for itself.

When Huxley was elected rector of Aberdeen University he took for the subject of his rectorial address the curriculum of these medieval universities of which Aberdeen was one. There is a tradition that he was quite assured that he would be able to show how narrow was the curriculum of these medieval universities, in spite of the fact that they occupied their students with what they called the liberal arts. After careful investigation, however, Huxley in his discussion of "Universities, Actual and Ideal," proclaimed his cordial admiration for the efforts of these medieval scholars to secure a liberal education for their students. Almost needless to say, the distinguished English biologist is perhaps the last man of recent times who would be suspected for a moment of exaggerating the significance of medieval education, so that his opinion is well worth quoting:

"The scholars of the Medieval Universities seem to have studied grammar, logic and rhetoric; arithmetic and geometry; astronomy, theology and music. Thus their work, however imperfect and faulty, judged by modern lights, it may have been, brought them face to face with all the leading aspects of the many-sided mind of man. For these studies did really contain, at any rate in embryo, sometimes it may be in caricature, what we now call philosophy, mathematical and physical science, and art."

But Huxley wanted to leave no doubt of his admiration for these old university authorities whom it was the custom, in his generation particularly, to designate as narrow and illiberal. His studies led him to think that any such condemnation could proceed only from those who knew nothing about the realities of medieval education. The last sentence of his estimate of the comparative significance of medieval and modern education deserves to be put in italics:

"And I doubt if the curriculum of any modern university shows so clear and generous a comprehension of what is meant by culture as this old trivium and quadrivium does."

As time went on additions were made to the curriculum and the *quadrivium* particularly became much broader than before. Logic, grammar, and rhetoric still continued to be the basic elements of education, but arithmetic and geometry developed into mathematics; astronomy, geography, and physics were combined into natural philosophy; metaphysics or mental philosophy became the third of the four major subjects, and ethics found a culminating place at the end of the curriculum. The *quadrivium* then consisted of mathematics and natural, mental, and moral philosophy. The amount of time devoted to physics was much greater than has been thought and that subject was discussed from many angles, as is evident from the old textbooks written by such typical medieval university men as Roger Bacon, and Albertus Magnus, as well as from the time devoted to Aristotle's physics.

The method of teaching during the Middle Ages was by the lecture system, involving note-taking by the students. Paper was expensive, so memory had to be depended on to a great extent. This was further necessitated by the difficulty of obtaining books. Certain books could be secured in the libraries but they were rare, they were costly to produce, and the most precious among them, that is, those most consulted, like the Bible and the works of Aquinas and other popular teachers, were for excellent reasons chained to the shelves, very much as telephone directories have to be chained now, to prevent some ardent seeker after information from walking off with them. The ultimate result was a cultivation of memory almost incredible in our day, when comparatively so little dependence is placed on that faculty.

The students' comprehension of the subject under discussion by the master was secured and tested by means of disputations, which were held weekly or oftener. These disputations were carried on in definite traditional manner. One of the students was selected to defend a thesis and two of his fellow students to make objections to it. The defender was supposed to set forth the thesis in a preliminary exposition in which he marshaled the proofs of its truth. Then the objectors took exception to his demonstration and urged their arguments in opposition to his thesis. They picked flaws in the arguments which he had advanced, and so far as possible disproved his argumentation. All this was done in strict syllogistic form, in Latin, and the exposition and the defense of the thesis took an hour or more. At the end of the period the president of the disputation, usually the professor of the special subject, or sometimes the rector of the university, according to the importance of the disputation, expressed his commendation or criticism of the academic function as it had been carried on. He also apportioned praise or blame to the defender and the objectors in accordance with the way that they had fulfilled their tasks.

Much has been said in recent years in deprecation of these disputations by people who manifestly know almost nothing about them. The disputants are supposed by many to have argued from all sorts of flimsy principles and to have made hair-splitting distinctions, which meant very little though they wasted an immense amount of time. With such a *priori* judgments against them the disputations were set down as utterly trivial in their character, typical of the lack of progressive thinking on the part of university students. So far are these disputations and the defense of theses and the urging of objections against them from being exclusively medieval and confined to this period, that disputations continued to be held in colleges and universities generally, indeed almost without exception, throughout the university world until well on in the nineteenth century. The theses which were presented at the colonial colleges even here in English-speaking America on commencement day, and which undoubtedly provide the best possible material for the proper appreciation of the curriculum followed by American institutions, had to be defended by the candidates for the degree.[2]

---

[2] Some of the theses at the colonial colleges can be traced far back into the heart of the Middle Ages, to the days of the early schools. For instance, one of the theses at Brown was the old ontological argument for the existence of God, originally set forth by St. Anselm in the eleventh century: *Deus potest esse, ergo est,* "God can be, therefore He is." One of the early theses at Harvard ran: "Death must be submitted to rather than a mortal sin committed." Such theses as, *Liberum est arbitrium,* or, *Voluntas est libera,* "The will is free," are to be found on the theses papers in practically all the colonial colleges. There are such variants as, *Voluntas potest pati sed non cogi,* "The will can suffer but cannot be forced." There are many propositions concerning universals and also concerning matter and form, as well as interesting dialectical distinctions with regard to ideas of various kinds which are usually supposed to have been given up at the end of the Middle Ages, or at most to have been kept up only in the Catholic theological seminaries where Scholastic philosophy was still studied. The colonial colleges, like the English and Scotch universities, continued the Scholastic teaching of philosophy both as to content and mode until the end of the eighteenth and even well on into the nineteenth century.

In all of the American colonial colleges it was considered the special duty of the president (the college statutes were very explicit in this regard[3]) to see that the disputations were carried on in Latin every week during the year, and that the commencement disputation, which constituted the examination for the degree, should also be a serious test of the knowledge acquired during the last two college years.

Most of the theses printed for commencement day in the colonial colleges were medieval in origin and were to be defended in exactly the same way and by the same arguments as were customary in the medieval colleges and universities. The reason for printing them was that they might be distributed, not to the audience generally, most of whom would not have understood the Latin, but to select visitors. These were often themselves graduates of colleges, commonly ministers of the Gospel, who were supposed to take part in the disputations with the candidates for the degree. The latter were thus clearly to demonstrate that they were thoroughly prepared to defend these many propositions, often more than a hundred in number, which were presented in their names on the commencement program.

These theses continued to be printed at Harvard until 1820, though during the nineteenth century their character gradually changed. All the other colonial colleges, Yale, Princeton, Columbia, then King's College, the University of Pennsylvania, and Brown had theses of this kind. Columbia has only the receipted bills for their printing, for her library was sadly dispersed during the Revolution; William and Mary has no theses left because of the fire in the library, but the tradition that they were in use at these colleges is well established.

Most of the medieval collegiate traditions remained in vogue here in America long after the Middle Ages were over. For instance, the disputation at the end of the college year was

---

[3] For special references to charters and statutes of the colonial colleges in this matter see Walsh, *Education of the Founding Fathers of the Republic* (Fordham University Press, 1935).

called a Public Act, *Actum Publicum,* the title given to the major disputations in the medieval universities. The degrees — bachelor, master, and doctor — are the same as those of the medieval universities, and other traditions, particularly with regard to college customs, the hazing of freshmen, student privileges, all remain. We have even gone back to the wearing of the academic hoods and gowns of the medieval period which recall the habits of the friars who were so important as students and teachers at the universities.

The American colleges, following in the tradition of Oxford, Cambridge, and Edinburgh, maintained as the basis of their curriculum the *trivium* and *quadrivium.* All of them pursued the liberal arts, logic, rhetoric, and grammar, and then mathematics, including astronomy with the three philosophies. Mental and moral philosophy were considered of such importance that they were usually taught by the president himself and they represented the greatest formative influence in the college careers of the students.

It would ordinarily be assumed that there was not freedom enough of teaching in such a system of education to deserve anything like the term *liberal* studies, but such an objection would come only from someone not familiar with the actual conditions that existed in the universities of the medieval period and continued to exist down to the first half of the nineteenth century. After all, it is of this period that Cardinal Newman, himself a product of the old-fashioned education, said:

"This is the very age of universities; this is the classical period of the Schoolmen; this is the splendid and palmary instance of the wise policy, the large *liberality,* of the Church as regards philosophic inquiry. If ever there was a time when the intellect went wild and had a licentious revel it was at the time I speak of."[4]

The great Oxford scholar was referring to the later Middle Ages and especially the thirteenth century when there was so

---

[4] Newman, *Idea of a University,* p. 469.

much of contention and disputation among the students, and yet so many philosophical principles were firmly laid down while a great wind of the intellectual spirit was abroad so that, as Saintsbury says, if there was one thing that these Scholastic philosophers of the Middle Ages could do it was that they could think. Americans were fortunate indeed that the Fathers of the Republic were educated according to methods that harked back for their origin to the old Scholastic days and ways.

It is often forgotten that these university men were devoting themselves to liberal studies. Instead of feeling hampered in any way they rejoiced in the freedom of mind that came to them as the result of their Catholicity. They felt perfectly free to go on with their investigations, confident that the Church authorities would maintain the theological status, and that the true meaning of their discoveries or conclusions would be pointed out without any danger of their being led astray by the supposed significance of scientific advance. This in fact proved after a time to fall far short of the significance which some were inclined to give it when first promulgated.

VIII

PARISH AND PUBLIC SCHOOLS

FROM the very early days of the Church there were parish schools, that is, schools in connection with the churches. Their origin is not quite certain. There were schools in the bishops' houses in the East as early as the second century, but the origin of the parish schools is usually attributed to the West, and they came into existence in connection with the organization of congregations. Riboulet in his *Histoire de la Pedagogie*[1] mentions the decree of an ecclesiastical council held in Italy about the middle of the fifth century, that is, just at the beginning of the Middle Ages, which imposed on priests the obligation to instruct the youth of their parishes in the priest's house. Riboulet mentions also that in the sixth century the Council of Vaison in the south of Gaul called special attention to this custom which had been established in Italy, and made it incumbent on priests to found schools in which young pupils might learn to read the psalms and pursue the study of Holy Scripture, become familiar with the law of God and be worthy successors in the ministry of the Gospel.

Charity schools were common in the Middle Ages and can be traced back to the third or fourth century, while ecclesiastical authorities assigned deacons and deaconesses to the care of orphans to see that they were brought up in such a way as would enable them to use to good advantage whatever talents they possessed. The obligation of rearing found-

---

[1] Paris, 1925, p. 126.

ling children and orphans was imposed upon certain religious orders by their rules and constitutions. The founders of these institutions recognized the supreme charity that was exercised in this work.

In our day the word *charity* unfortunately carries with it an implication of pauperism, nonexistent in older times. In colonial times we were not afraid of the name Charity School here in America. A striking example of one which bore that name quite frankly was the original Charity School which preceded the College and Academy of Philadelphia, under Benjamin Franklin's sponsorship; a little later in the course of the American Revolution this developed into the University of Pennsylvania. In our own time the Blue Coat School in England, formerly Christ's Hospital, was taken by Thackeray as the background for the character of Colonel Newcome, and the association of the boys and old men proved eminently satisfactory for both.

The palace schools of the Merovingian and Carolingian periods had, as Dr. Hugh Graham writes in his article on "Popular Education in the Middle Ages,"[2] their counterpart in the court schools established by Alfred the Great and other monarchs. J. Bass Mullinger worked out the history of these in *The Schools of Charles the Great,* and C. Plummer gives the details with regard to the schools of Alfred the Great in his *Life and Times of Alfred the Great.*[3] These schools educated the sons of the nobility for their special duties as rulers and defenders of the country. Such education was the type of training necessary for the man of action, the ruler, the soldier, and the courtier. The recent reawakening of interest in the life of Sir Thomas More, saint and scholar, brings out the fact that his early education was secured in the household of Cardinal Morton, where a number of young men of the nobility were gathered in order that they might be trained in mind and body for afterlife. Many of the bishops

---

[2] *Thought,* America Press, Vol. VIII, No. 1, June, 1933.
[3] Oxford, 1902.

had such household groups of students, and the Inns of Court had special schools in which young men were trained by what would probably be called in our time, a pre-law curriculum. Lawyers were very much interested in maintaining the dignity of their profession and in requiring youths who aspired to the status of lawyer to have received proper mental development before being admitted to law study.

J. E. G. de Montmorency, in his *State Intervention in English Education*,[4] said of the Middle Ages in England:

"They have been painted as ignorant, brutal and picturesque. We may have doubts as to the truth of the picture; we may well believe that the eighteenth century in the mass was more brutal, more picturesque and less religious, and we may even believe that it was far more ignorant and far less moral. The Middle Ages left the Reformation educational possibilities [and treasures] that were recklessly squandered."

Indeed the Reformation is responsible for a great many of the defects in education noted at the beginning of modern times and usually attributed to the inhibitory effects on education of medieval ecclesiastics. Speaking of the effect of the Reformation on education in Germany, Professor Paulsen, professor of philosophy at the University of Berlin, in his volume *Higher Education in Germany*,[5] said:

"The first effect of these events [connected with the Reformation] on educational institutions was destructive; the old schools and universities were so bound up with the Church in all respects, socially, legally, economically — that they could not but be involved in its downfall" (i.e., in the countries where the so-called Reformation made its way successfully).

During the Middle Ages the monastic schools were particularly valuable because of the education which they provided for the children of both rich and poor. Practically all the monasteries had inner and outer schools, the inner schools for candidates and members of the order, and the outer schools

---

[4] Cambridge, 1902, p. 60.
[5] *Geschichte des gelehrten Unterrichts*, New York, 1908, p. 64.

for the boys who were being educated for secular positions. The Benedictine monasteries were particularly generous in their provision of education for the youth of all classes. Just before the Reformation there were literally thousands of Benedictine houses throughout the continent, a large proportion of which had schools. Unfortunately these were suppressed and their property confiscated, to be conferred on the noble sycophants of monarchs, thus putting an end to a whole system of education. Modern educational research is bringing out more and more clearly the devotion of the Middle Ages to education.

The decrees of synods and councils of the Church from the sixth century onward show very clearly that there was a definite policy on the part of the Church favoring the expansion of popular education. While the popes and the Church were concerned first of all with making provision for the education in the sacred sciences of those who were to be members of the clerical body, they were also at pains to encourage and promote the education of the laity. Dr. Graham, in the article cited, has given a list of councils and other ecclesiastical bodies which passed decrees not only encouraging but requiring the development of education:

"The Council of Tours (567), Toledo (624), Constantinople (681), Bavarian and Pastoral Instructions (774), Cloveshoe England, (749), the Capitularies of Charlemagne (787–789), the Synods of Aachen (798–817), and the Councils of Chalons (813), Paris (829), Rome (853); the Edict of Emperor Lothair (825), the Canons of King Edgar (960), Lanfranc's Constitutions [this would be the Archbishop of Canterbury] (1075), Synod of Westminster (1133), Lateran Councils (1179–1215)."

Dr. Graham says that this list is not exhaustive but its length is significant of the extent and persistency of the official policy of the Church in diffusing the benefits of education throughout the length and breadth of Christendom. These Church documents represent the most important factors for the positive setting forth of Church interest in education.

In this country unfortunately the translation of Compayré's *History of Pedagogy,* which came to be a textbook in the hands of a great many professors of the history of education, completely ignored medieval education. The author knew nothing about the Middle Ages and very calmly set down the foundation of the Christian Brothers under De La Salle as the beginning of Christian schools. These, in his view, were organized only because it came to be realized that the schools founded by the reformers would have so much influence that they would attract non-Catholics. According to Compayré, Luther in the sixteenth century and Comenius in the seventeenth century are the founders of modern education: "the primary school in its origin is the child of Protestantism and its cradle is the Reformation." Compayré's book was written with the deliberate intention of making little of the religious schools of the Church in order to promote the governmental policy of opposition to religious Orders, just then uppermost in the politics of France. The real authorities on the history of education disagree utterly with this. Luther seriously hurt education rather than benefited it. As for Comenius, whatever importance he was supposed to have had in education has largely disappeared. How little influence in fact he had becomes apparent from a better knowledge of the origin of Jesuit education and from the fact that Scholastic philosophy continued to be used in the schools even here in America until well on in the nineteenth century.

The Middle Ages witnessed the foundation of a number of the well-known English public schools, organized originally for the provision of preparatory training for university education. The oldest of these, Winchester, was founded (1397) by William of Wykeham, Bishop of Winchester, Chancellor of England, and founder also of New College, Oxford. Winchester continued down to our own time to be a training school for intelligence and character, of which English educators have been very proud. Winchester alumni are deeply attached to their alma mater. Something of the well-loved spirit of its great founder has lived on in the school for more than half a millennium and it continues to form the background of sterling English education for the students who attend it.

After Winchester, the most interesting of the public-school foundations which date from the Middle Ages is Eton, founded in 1440 and now nearly 500 years old. It continues to be a favorite school for sons of the nobility in England and especially for those who are expected to take a prominent part in the government of their country. Its situation on the Thames, opposite Windsor, the residence of the English monarchs, gives it a particular prominence and fosters a sentiment of special loyalty to the crown among its students. Its founder was King Henry VI, "Harry of Windsor," as he is known. He was the son of the great English warrior, King Henry V, who won the battle of Agincourt against a French army which outnumbered his own forces more than four to one. His mother was Catherine of France, one of the protagonists in Shakespeare's famous lovemaking scene in *King Henry V*.

Some of these well-known public schools glory in medieval traditions though they were founded after the close of the Middle Ages. Rugby, for instance, though founded in 1574, made its greatest progress under the headmastership of Thomas James (1778–94). James was a graduate of Eton who introduced exhibitions, forms, tutors, preposters, and in general all the traditional methods in vogue at Eton, and made into a national institution what before that had been only a local school.

These English public schools were founded with the idea of training character as well as providing education of mind. It has often been said that Napoleon's army was beaten at Waterloo by men whose characters had been trained on the cricket fields of Eton. Discipline, and above all, the going through hard things without any whimpering of self-pity, have been results of the training afforded by the English public schools. Under the circumstances it is not surprising that caning by the headmaster, corporal punishment for certain offenses, is still maintained as an institution in the enforcement of discipline. Though their alumni have been given the opportunity to vote for its abolition several times in recent generations, they have refused to do so and the practice continues as a precious relic of the medieval customs.

These so-called public schools were for the nobility, but the education of the poor was not overlooked during the Middle Ages. As has been often pointed out in recent years, the chance to rise was afforded to young men of all classes who had special talents. President Woodrow Wilson in his volume, *The New Freedom*,[6] said:

"There was no peasant so humble that he might not become a priest, and no priest so obscure that he might not become pope of Christendom, and every chancellery in Europe was ruled by these learned, trained, and accomplished men — the priests of that great and then dominant church; and so, what kept government alive in the Middle Ages was this constant rise of the sap from the bottom, from the rank and file of the great body of the people through the open channels of the Roman Catholic priesthood."

President Wilson had said that,

"The only reason why government did not suffer dry rot in the Middle Ages under the aristocratic systems which then prevailed was that the men who were efficient instruments of government were drawn from the Church — from that great church, that body which we now distinguish from other church bodies as the Roman Catholic Church. The Roman Catholic Church then, as now, was a great democracy."

That certainly is true in the sense here indicated.

We have seen that Vittorino da Feltre insisted on providing opportunities for poor scholars in his school at Mantua,

---

[6] Published 1913, by Doubleday, Doran and Co., Inc. Quoted here by permission of the publishers.

but this was not a novel idea. Some of the most interesting schools in the Middle Ages in fact are the so-called parish schools, for the duty of teaching *gratis* was laid upon the clergy by a long series of councils and synods as well as by pastoral letters from bishops. These documents ranged over seven centuries from the sixth on. The decretals of Pope Gregory IX, for instance, directed parish priests "to have the clerks sing and read the Epistles, to keep school, and to admonish their parishioners to send their sons to school for the learning of their religion." The chief purpose of these parish schools was to bring instruction to the boys, but provision was also made in them for the girls of the parish. It was to these schools that Roger Bacon referred when he said toward the end of the third quarter of the thirteenth century that, "Everyone who desires it is instructed in those things which are of the Faith."

The history of Florence furnishes an excellent example of the provision of educational opportunities for its people from the elementary schools up to the university. At the end of the first quarter of the fourteenth century, that is, a a culmination of the influence of the great thirteenth century, with some 90,000 of population, Florence, according to Capponi,[7] had 8,000 to 10,000 boys and girls in its primary schools, 1,000 to 1,200 boys in its seven intermediary schools, and from 550 to 600 students in its universities. They displayed enthusiastic devotion not only to education but also for the care of those in need. There were some 30 hospitals belonging to the community containing over 1,000 beds. The more we know of the history of Florence at this time, the clearer does it become that Florentines were anticipating before the end of the Middle Ages most of those social developments of which we are so proud in our time and are so prone to consider as representing recent humanitarian advances.

---

[7] In his *Storia della republica di Firenze*.

When the Franciscans came to England at the end of the first quarter of the thirteenth century they were anxious to set up schools for the poor. This was in accord with the spirit of their founder, and besides they would thus secure recruits for their Order. Once such postulants were received into the Order, all who had the talent were given an opportunity to receive the highest education they could obtain. The friars, Dominicans as well as Franciscans, sent men of special ability to the universities. Gerson, the Chancellor of the University of Paris, to whom the supervision of popular education was committed by the king, inquired whether each parish in Paris had its school and directed the establishment of schools wherever they did not exist.

The best testimony that we have to the determined effort of the churchmen of the Middle Ages to provide education for the poor as well as the rich is to be found in the foundation of the Brethren of the Common Life. Their founder gave up lucrative ecclesiastical preferments to devote himself to the education of the poor. His community spread rapidly throughout the Netherlands in the latter half of the fourteenth century, establishing there and along the Rhine a number of schools in which many sons of poor families secured an education that enabled them to become distinguished scholars later on in life. Hamilton Mabie, the well-known American writer of the turn of the century, in his book of essays, *My Study Fire* (p. 92), paid a sincere compliment to these Brethren of the Common Life that may be taken as a summary of their educational work:

"I confess that I can never read quite unmoved the story of the Brethren of the Common Life, those humble-minded patient thinkers and teachers, whose devotion and fire of soul for a century and a half made the choice treasures of Italian palaces, convents and universities a common possession along the low-lying shores of the Netherlands. The asceticism of this noble brotherhood was no morbid and divisive fanaticism; it was a denial of themselves that they might have the more to give. The visions which touched at times the bare walls of their cells with supernal beauty only made them the more eager to share their heaven of privilege with the sorely burdened world without. Surely Vergil and Horace and the other masters of classic form were never more honored than when these noble-minded lovers of learning made their sounding lines familiar in peasant homes."

These Brethren of the Common Life were founded by Geert de Groote, in Latin, Gerhardus Magnus, called by his contemporaries the Great, because of their admiration for his scholarship. He shares with Albertus Magnus the privilege of having this epithet so attached to his name that most people think of it as his family name. Geert was educated first at Aachen (Aix-la-Chapelle) and then at the Sorbonne in Paris where he studied medicine, theology, and canon law. This seems a very wide program of studies but we are told that he was very successful in them, though when he returned home he was scarcely more than eighteen years of age. He became a teacher at the Chapter School of Deventer, but was manifestly looked upon as no mere dry-as-dust professor — that title had not yet contracted the hint of impracticality that went with it later, particularly in our own time — for when Geert was still under twenty-five his admiring countrymen sent him to Avignon on a special mission to Pope Urban V.

After this he taught philosophy and theology at Cologne and was making a wonderful success in life. He held several ecclesiastical preferments that gave him good salaries and it looked as though he would settle down to be one of the comfortable prelates of his day. About this time he was brought intimately in contact with a fellow student of the Sorbonne, Henry Aeger, of Calcar, who had become prior of the house of Carthusians near Arnheim. Aeger was looked upon as one of the great exponents of the contemplative life and his example touched Geert deeply. A little later he became a close friend of Ruysbroek, the well-known ascetical writer. Under the influence of these two men Geert, or

Gerard, as he is often called, resolved to devote himself to the teaching of the poor, to the giving of himself and not the getting of things. The feelings aroused in him brought him to see the validity of the Scriptural expression which under very similar circumstances Ignatius Loyola used with such telling effect on the brilliant young professor, Francis Xavier, at the University of Paris: "What doth it profit a man to gain the whole world and lose his own soul?"

It was not long before a number of young men gathered around Geert asking to be allowed to share in his labors and his sacrifices for others. In this he had the experience of many other religious founders — Benedict, Bernard, Francis, Dominic, Ignatius. As a result he organized the community of the Brethren of the Common Life whose main purpose was the education of the poor. Geert himself died young, that is, before he was forty-five (1384), carried off by a pestilence while he was nursing those stricken with the disease. His community lived on after him to accomplish an immense amount of good that amply merits for them the tribute of Mabie over five hundred years after his death.

Gerard had the good fortune to have his life written by no less a person than Thomas à Kempis, long known as the author of *The Imitation of Christ*. Recent studies, however, prove that this famous and well-loved book was actually written by Gerard himself, and that for certain reasons his name was withdrawn from it, and the name of the editor, Thomas à Kempis, substituted. À Kempis brings out how much of good Gerard's work accomplished not only among his own people in Holland but also all along the Rhine, where the schools of the Brethren of the Common Life became famous and where they had so many distinguished pupils who left their marks deeply upon the intellectual life of that time. Thomas à Kempis himself and his brother — the sons of a widow — went to school to the Brethren in boyhood years and are striking examples of their education. The Brethren of the Common Life used to take boys from seven to ten years of age, and in the course of five or six years gave them an excellent introduction to Latin and mathematics, as well as whatever scientific knowledge was available at that time. Among their students, besides à Kempis, were such distinguished scholars as Cardinal Nicholas of Cusa, Rudolph Agricola, John of Dalberg, the preceptor of Germany, as well as Erasmus and others who reached distinction at this time. The schools of the Brethren accomplished much for the development of the vernacular languages in Germany and the Netherlands. They constituted an important factor in the early Renaissance as it developed in Europe, and it is surprising how many analogies can be traced between their schools and our own Latin schools here in America just before and after the Revolution.

À Kempis has told of the spread of the community which had been formed by Master Gerard, "a tree which after his death, though but newly set in the ground, ceased not to flourish in the kingdom of the Lord." He adds: "Although this religious Order and these communities of devout persons were first planted in the nearer parts of Holland, Gelders and Brabant, they afterward spread rapidly in the more remote regions of Flanders, Frisia, Westphalia and Saxony." Indeed under Florentius, the disciple of Gerard who carried on his work, houses of the Brethren of the Common Life were founded all along the Rhine and accomplished an immense amount of good by cultivating not only religion but also scholarship. À Kempis has written brief sketches of a dozen of men who were more particularly concerned in organizing this work of the Brethren of the Common Life. There were John Brinckerinck, Berner, Brune, Gerard of Zutphen, Amilius of Buren, James of Viana, John Cacabus, and Arnold of Scoonhoven. All of these men were distinguished scholars and educators and carried on the work that had been so well begun by Gerard de Groote and developed by Florentius. Nearly every one of them risked his life in caring for the ailing poor during the pestilences which occurred so frequently during the fourteenth and early fifteenth centuries. They were educated unto service for others rather than for personal success in life.

That they knew how to study in the Middle Ages is well illustrated by some directions written out for the students of his day by Robert of Sorbonne, the famous founder of the Sorbonne at the University of Paris. In these admonitions he gives advice to the students attending the Sorbonne as to how they should spend their time. Robert had already had many years of experience at the university so that he was thoroughly competent to set down counsels on this subject:

The student who wishes to make progress ought to observe six essential rules.

FIRST: He ought to consecrate a certain hour every day to the study of a determined subject, as St. Bernard counselled his monks in his letter to the Brothers of the Mont Dieu.

SECOND: He ought to concentrate his attention upon what he reads and ought not to let it pass lightly. There is between reading and study, as St. Bernard says, the same difference as between a host and a guest, between a passing salutation exchanged in the street and an embrace prompted by an unalterable affection.

THIRD: He ought to extract from the daily study one thought, some truth or other, and engrave it deeply upon his memory with special care. Seneca said, *Cum multa percurreris in die, unum tibi elige quod illa die excoquas,* "When you have run over many things in a day select one item for yourself which you should digest well on that day."

FOURTH: Write a résumé of what you have learned, for words which are not confided to writing fly as does the dust before the wind.

FIFTH: Talk the matter over with your fellow students, either in the regular recitation or in your familiar conversation. This exercise is even more profitable than study for it has as its result the clarifying of all doubts and the removing of all the obscurity that study may have left. Nothing is perfectly known unless it has been tried by the tooth of disputation.

SIXTH: Pray, for this is indeed one of the best ways of learning. St. Bernard teaches that study ought to touch the heart and that one should profit by it always by elevating the heart to God, *without, however, interrupting the study.*

Robert proceeds in a tone that vividly recalls the modern university professor who has seen generation after generation of students and has learned to realize how many of them waste their time:

"Certain students act like fools: they display great subtility over nonsensical subjects and exhibit themselves devoid of intelligence with regard to their most important studies. So as not to seem to have lost their time they gather together many sheets of parchment, make thick volumes of note books out of them, with many a blank interval, and cover them with elegant binding in red letters. Then they return to the paternal domicile with their little sack filled up with knowledge which can be stolen from them by any thief that comes along, or may be eaten by rats or by worms or destroyed by fire or water.

"In order to acquire instruction the student must abstain from pleasure and not allow himself to be hampered by material cares. There were at Paris not long since two teachers who were great friends. One of them had seen much, had read much and used to remain night and day bent over his books. He scarcely took the time to say an 'Our Father.' Nevertheless he had but four students. His colleague possessed a much less complete library, was less devoted to study and heard Mass every morning before delivering his lecture. In spite of this, his classroom was full. 'How do you do it?' asked his friend. 'It is very simple,' said his friend smiling. 'God studies for me. I go to Mass and when I come back I know by heart all that I have to teach.' "

"Meditation," so Robert continues, "is suitable not only for the master but the good student ought also to go and take his promenade along the banks of the Seine, not to play there, but in order to repeat his lesson and meditate upon it."

In the medieval colleges the students followed the very definite regime which seems to us so laborious and lacking in diversion that we would be prone to wonder how students could maintain their health under its exactions. Certainly if in our time students were kept with their noses to the grindstone of study so much as this we would quite surely explain all the mental breakdowns that might occur as due to it and there would be a clamor for a less severe mode of life. As a matter of fact, they seem to have had fewer breakdowns among young folks than we have in our time, when with our relaxed program of study we are appalled by the ever-increasing number of minds that give way and the fact that the age of the incidence of insanity is constantly becoming younger.

Here is their daily regulation of life as it is to be found in historians of the various universities:

4 a.m. (in summer), 5 a.m. (winter) rising. (The program of the day was changed to accord with the hour of rising, as in our daylight-saving, though they did not fool themselves by turning their clocks back.) During the first hour the students dressed, said their prayers and prepared for the first class.

5 or 6 a.m. One of the minor college teachers, usually called regents, gave the first lesson.

6 to 7 a.m. Breakfast, which consisted of a piece of bread that sometimes needed moistening by water. This medieval custom continued at Harvard until well on in the eighteenth century. After breakfast there was study but no recreation.

8 to 10 a.m. The principal lesson of the morning was given.

10 to 11 a.m. There were disputation and argumentation.

At 11 a.m. dinner. The students were not allowed to talk at meals except on Sundays and feast days, but they listened to the reading of Scripture or the lives of the saints. Various announcements were made after dinner and there were mementoes of benefactors. Punishments and corrections which had been determined on and admonitions were given at this time followed by recreation until noon.

From 12 to 2 there were revision and interrogation regarding the morning lessons.

From 2 to 3, the sleepy period, the serious reading of some poet or orator was listened to, *ne diabolus hominem inveniat otiosum,* or as we should say "lest the devil find work for idle men."

From 3 to 5 the principal lesson of the afternoon was given.

From 5 to 6 discussion and argumentation of the lesson just attended.

At 6 supper.

At 6:30 questionings upon the lessons of the day.

At 7:30 compline and benediction.

At 8 in winter and 9 in summer, bedtime.

With this college schedule before us it is more than a little surprising to learn that with special permission masters and sometimes even pupils might keep their candle burning until eleven o'clock. College authorities were manifestly persuaded that men did not need so much sleep as we think they do at the present time. This special permission was given with reluctance, however. Masters were advised by their directors not to stay up late at night but if they needed extra time for their work to get up earlier in the morning. It is easy to understand that there was no very frequent insistence on permission to take time from sleep when it was proposed that for that purpose you should get up in summer at three instead of four in the morning. It is to the medieval educators that we owe the old formula for the amount of sleep needed for different individuals: "Seven hours for a man, eight hours for a woman, nine hours for a hog."

In many of the medieval colleges Tuesday and Thursday afternoons were free, to the extent at least required for a long walk for exercise. At Fordham, fifty years ago, during the spring and early fall we had the whole of each Thursday for recreation. In winter this was replaced by Tuesday and Thursday afternoons. We rose at 5:30 o'clock and our duties through the day occupied nearly every hour quite as in the medieval colleges, only that we had an hour after dinner in the afternoon and a half hour after supper in the evening for recreation.

They were very practical in their thoughtfulness for others in the Middle Ages. The giving of dowries to maidens about to marry so that the new household might not have to go into debt for its furniture is a striking instance, but not any more so than the provision of libraries and books for poor students. Gerard d'Abbeville, about 1270, bequeathed his library to the students of the Sorbonne, but with the understanding that all clerics and also lettered seculars might have the chance to consult his works on theology.

About this same time Stephen Langton, Archbishop of Canterbury, left his books to the Church of Notre Dame de Paris, with the definite proviso that they be placed at the disposition of poor scholars who needed them in their studies. Robert of Sorbonne himself made it a special practice to collect books for the consultation of students of his college. At his death he bequeathed all his books to the Sorbonne. His library was organized for use. It was divided into two parts. One was called the large library, *libraria magna*, comprising the books which were most frequently made use of. The other part was called *libraria parva* and contained duplicates and works rarely consulted. These would be loaned to applicants upon the deposit of a sum of money or — and this is typically medieval — the deposit of any article of sufficient value to cover the cost of the book. The larger library, where the volumes were in frequent use, had the books chained to the shelves. These are some of the famous books in chains of which we used to hear so much, as if they represented the definite effort of the medieval ecclesiastics to keep knowledge away from ardent students, or at least to limit the opportunities for its acquisition. As a matter of fact our reference books are as summarily bound to the shelves in our day as if they were chained. Before the coming of the telephone directory, when city directories used to be kept in drugstores that they might be consulted for addresses in the neighborhood, they usually were chained in place. Many a druggist knew after costly experience that there was need for such a precaution. The Bible in the old medieval period was oftener chained up than any other book, but that was because there was so much demand for it, and it had to be kept in place so as to be available to as many readers as possible. Manuscript books were very costly and very rare and particular care had to be taken of them, but every effort was made by educational authorities to supply those who could not afford books of their own — as but very few could — with available copies of important books for consultation.

IX

PEDAGOGICS OF THE MIDDLE AGES

O UR generation is firmly persuaded that if there is one phase of education in which we are far in advance of the past, and especially of the Middle Ages, it is in the understanding and education of youth. But more and more in recent years medieval documents of one kind or another treating of education have come to hand and have met with due appreciation. So, by degrees, we have learned that these old-time educators of seven hundred or even a thousand years ago displayed wonderful skill in their knowledge of the human mind and of the methods to be followed to attain its development. It is quite clear that they anticipated most of the ideas in education that are supposed to be very modern or even quite recent discoveries and developments. Probably there is no field in which we have come to appreciate so profoundly how little change there is in mankind as in the department of education. A few examples taken from the works of old educators will serve to make this clear.

We hear much of "flaming youth" in modern times and there is a definite conviction in many minds that adolescents now are quite different from what they used to be even a generation or two ago. It is presumed, therefore, that they must be supremely different from the young folks of centuries ago. Yet, as I have said, only a little study of educational problems, as the medieval teachers faced them over 500 years ago, will serve to show that human nature has not changed in the interval to any appreciable extent. A single medieval book on education, that by Mafeo Vegio of Lodi, a canon of St. Peter's at Rome, demonstrates this very clearly. The canon was a close friend of Cardinal Tommaso Parentucelli, the distinguished Italian humanist scholar, who afterward became Pope Nicholas V. The same pontiff has often been given the title of founder of the Vatican library, because he added greatly to the collection of books already there and was much interested in increasing their numbers. Vegio was also on terms of intimacy with another pope. This was Pius II, who before his elevation to the papacy, at the close of the Middle Ages (1458), was the well-known Renaissance scholar Aeneas Sylvius Piccolomini.

Vegio himself, a noted liturgical scholar, was consulted confidently by high ecclesiastical authorities with regard to church ceremonials and church decoration. But above all he was looked up to as an expert in matters of education. Though he is sometimes spoken of as a product of the Renaissance, his career lies all in the Middle Ages, for he died in the year 1457. He received his impressions as to education and drew his conclusions with regard to it a generation before the first half of the fifteenth century's close, or in other words, before the fall of Constantinople.

His educational work bears the title *De liberorum eruditione,* "The Education of Youth," and outlines the principles to be applied in the education of young folks up to the time of their majority. It contains a series of passages that seem to be the results of much more modern thinking than the early part of the fifteenth century.

Vegio said, for instance: "Certainly youth with its sudden and passing friendships, its violent loves, its zest for gambling and danger, its delights in horses and dogs and birds, needs care. Above all love is strongest at this time."[1]

Vegio understands very thoroughly all the faults of youth

---

[1] These quotations from Mafeo Vegio are from the chapter "Education" in Father Bede Jarrett's book, *Social Theories in the Middle Ages, 1200 to 1500,* Boston, 1926. By permission of Little, Brown and Co., publishers.

but he knows its good qualities as well as its defects and indeed recognizes in quite modern spirit that the two are complementary. Youth has ever the defects of its qualities. Sagely referring to young people of his own day, Vegio writes:

"What fine fellows there are are among them! Freed from the degradation of passion, scorning indecent speech and fellowship, upright, manly, how splendid such a youth can be." But he is no less clear that full recognition was given to the ebullient qualities of youth a thousand years before his time: "How might not St. Augustine, from sixteen years of age upward at the mercy of his passions, regret the irrecoverable fragrance of boyhood. The pages of his *Confessions* are a pathetic warning of the beauties of youth, and the possibilities of their being stained, and the undying sadness if this should be."

Vegio has spoken always of boys throughout his instruction on the education of youth, but he does not hesitate to say that there is hardly anything that he has written that would not equally well apply to girls. He feels that that was the reason why St. Monica understood her son and was able to influence Augustine so deeply. The Italian educator insists that reverence for women should be taught to growing youth, but with that also reverence for himself. He has within him "the secret shrine of the Muses" and he can very easily spoil the beauty of it all: "The young man should be careful of his virtue, particularly when he is alone. Virtue is his one treasure, at once a sea and a shore." As to how he shall accomplish that high purpose of self-preservation, Vegio has only that ever-recurring advice which comes to us down the ages: "The remembrance of God's presence everywhere will support and foster always clean and gentle thoughts."

Undoubtedly the most interesting paragraph in Vegio's treatise on education is his emphatic description of the individuality of children and the absolute necessity there is of constantly keeping that fact in mind when dealing with them.

He takes up first the training of those under the age of seven years. A single passage makes it clear that these educators of the Middle Ages felt that the individual differences of children ought to be properly appreciated in their very early years. We are very likely to think of this specialization in educational development as being reserved for our own time which, because of our peculiar attention to children, we have been pleased to call "the age of the child." Vegio makes it clear that most of what is proclaimed today as recent and novel was anticipated by educators in the later centuries of the Middle Ages:

"It is of gravest necessity that the teacher should prudently and judiciously measure the capacity of each child, so that in correcting their morals we should be able to propose a remedy for their ills, as a doctor would in curing their bodies. . . . Some there are in whom the sweetness of their future virtue is early manifest; timid, sensitive souls, yet often for that very reason with exquisite and elegant taste. Others are bold and full of daring. Some you see talkative, garrulous; others who will hardly answer a word. Many are boastful, more are eager of praise, a few have no ambition at all. Some are inconstant, of unstable humor; others are intrepid and steadfast. Some again know not how to obey. Others are docile even to their inferiors; some there are for whom ease has no attraction and others whose natural bent is to be lazy and do nothing. Some are eager to show you all they know, while others are secretive about things even of no importance; some careless as to eating, others hardly thinking of any other pleasure; some gentle, others quick to anger; some to whom peace is dear, others always in disputes."

Is it any wonder that Vegio, knowing all these different kinds of children as he does, should ask, "How can all these very different children be helped or developed or cared for or cured without an intimate knowledge of each one's character?" He was surely as individualistic as any progressive educator of modern times.

Almost needless to say Vegio is not the only one, and by no means the first, to dwell on this rule of education that in-

dividualizes the subject. Bartholomew the Englishman —
Bartolomeus Anglicus, in the Latin form of his name — in his
well-known encyclopedia, which was the most consulted book
of the later Middle Ages and was constantly referred to by
literary folk in the Elizabethan and Jacobean days, has a
passage in the sixth *capitulum,* Book Sixth, of *The Properties
of Things,* which enables us to judge how slightly, if at all,
children have changed in the seven hundred years that have
elapsed since he wrote (he died before 1250):

"Since all children be tatched [tinctured] with evil manners,
and think only on things that be, and reck not of things that
shall be, they love plays, game, and vanity, and forsake winning
and profit. And things most worthy they repute least worthy,
and least worthy most worthy. They desire things that be to
them contrary and grievous [not good for them], and set more
of the image of a child, than of the image of a man, and make
more sorrow and woe, and weep more for the loss of an apple,
than for the loss of their heritage. And the goodness that is
done for them, they let it pass out of mind. They desire all
things that they see, and pray and ask with voice and with hand.
They love talking and counsel of such children as they be, and
void company of old men. They keep no counsel, but they tell
all that they hear or see. Suddenly they laugh, and suddenly
they weep. Always they cry, jangle, and jape; that unneth
[scarcely] they be still while they sleep. When they be washed
of filth, anon they defile themselves again. When their mother
washeth and combeth them, they kick and sprawl, and put with
feet and with hands, and withstand with all their might. They
desire to drink always; unneth are they out of bed, when they
cry for meat anon."

It is extremely interesting to read these medieval passages
emphasizing the necessity for individualization in education
and the extreme importance of considering the individual
pupil, and to compare them with some recent expressions of
men who are deeply interested in education in our day. Dr.
Ray Lyman Wilbur, for instance, who was Secretary of the
Interior under President Hoover, and in whose department
and under whose supervision the educational interests of the

country were for four years, wrote an article for the *New York Herald-Tribune* magazine section (December 27, 1931). The subject of the article is a report which had just been laid before Congress by the National Advisory Committee on Education. This body had for the preceding two years been studying all the relations of the Federal Government to education. The title of his article is, "End the Intellectual Lockstep," with the subtitle, "Break Away from Hard and Fast Rules; Fit the Course to the Individual Pupil; Provide More Personal Instruction; Look Forward Not Backward in Methods; Substitute Education for Schooling."

This is exactly what five and seven hundred years ago respectively his colleagues in education were emphasizing as regards the education of young folks, before the end of the Middle Ages.

There is scarcely any phase of possible influence over child development that is not discussed in Vegio's work. Today we sometimes hear of women who, during the months before their child is born, try to surround themselves with beautiful things, and above all with beautiful works of art, so that their unborn child shall be affected as deeply as possible by this means. Most people are inclined to think this a very modern notion, consequent on the gradual evolution which is lifting the race up to higher things. It is rather surprising, then, to find Vegio suggesting that beautiful statues be placed in the home, so that these material representations may provoke the imagination of the mother to fixed contemplation of noble forms; for he thinks that this can affect the body of the child while it is in its mother's keeping. The unfavorable influence upon the unborn child of the mother's mental impressions is still believed by many, despite its utter rejection by physicians, but here was a rather striking example of belief in favorable influence.

Vegio was of the very definite persuasion, too, that the relationship between father and mother, especially their affectionate regard for each other during the prenatal life of the child, had much to do with shaping its disposition and molding its intelligence. The mother's mental attitude was an extremely important factor for the formation of the child's character, insofar as that might be affected during its life beneath its mother's heart.

When the child was born the physician was to be consulted as to whether the mother would be capable of nursing her infant. It was recognized that there were some mothers who could not provide properly for the nutrition of their children. In that case a nurse was to be provided, in whose selection great care was to be taken. Curiously enough, Vegio, and those doubtless whom he had consulted in this matter, thought it quite as important that the disposition, character, and intelligence of the nurse be of the right kind as that her physical condition be suitable. The nurse, for instance, must not be half-witted, nor foolish, nor stolid. She must not be of a cranky disposition, nor morose, nor easily stirred to anger. The medieval people had an idea that the nurse's disposition would in some way be carried over with her milk to her nursling. We have learned in recent years how extremely complex may be the composition of human milk. If the mother, for instance, has suffered from certain contagious diseases and acquired immunity to them, this immunization will be transmitted through her milk and protect the nursling so long as maternal nourishing continues. The medieval folk thought that the mental traits would be similarly transferred. They were careful, however, about the physical conditions of the nurse, and especially about cleanliness. Quite contrary to the general impression of the medieval attitude in such matters, they were inclined to think that uncleanliness was a cardinal offense.

Vegio's declarations show that the medieval folk did not think that children should be raised too delicately, and that they objected to fancy clothes for them. Clothes should be simple, and smaller children should go barefooted and without a cloak. So few children any more enjoy the precious privilege of the "barefoot boy" that perhaps only those who shared it will appreciate all that this means. These medievalists were much inclined to think that children caught cold more easily from being overdressed than underdressed. They thought it better to make them accustomed to the cold, for they felt that this made them hardy. We hear today of hardening children by exposure, and anyone who has shivered at seeing the children of Paris on the cold days of late fall or early spring, playing around with their legs bare from well above the knees to the ankles, will realize that this teaching still obtains.

Food and sleep were considered the two most important things for children to have in abundance, but they must not have too much of either. "Too much food," Vegio said, "breeds laziness and ill-shapen bodies and too much sleep fosters stupidity." Medieval counselors in education were agreed that wine should not be given to children until after the age of nine. At a time when all adults took wine at meals this prohibition was like the refusal of tea and coffee in our day. Doctors warned that wine stimulated children overmuch and made them quick to anger. They declared that "the body of a child is already by its nature very full of heat. Wine serves only to increase this in them."

Some very surprising statements on the care of children can be found in these directions. For instance, Vegio says: "Children should not be checked in their crying, for this is thought to develop their strength." It is only in our generation that the practice of letting children have a good cry without interference has come in again. Doctors suggest that a hearty cry, whenever it is clear that there is no physical reason for it, strengthens children's lungs and does them good rather than harm. This is so contrary to the custom of mothers, even a generation ago, of taking up their children at once when they began to cry and endeavoring to soothe and pacify them, that it is worth while to notice how the Middle Ages anticipated us in the recognition of the value of lung exercise. After all, older children delight in making noise and it is healthful for them. Vegio insists that children must have exercise, though care must be taken that suitable gentle exercises are permitted them. Manifestly he felt that arrangements should be made to permit children to play, for without such exercise they will grow up incurably lazy.

Perhaps the most surprising thing is still to be noted. Vegio says that those in charge of children should not indulge in silly baby talk, and that no half words or imitations of baby speech should be used in talking to them, nor should they be given nicknames or baby names, for these often cling to them for life and are a source of chagrin in later years.

Vegio is emphatic in insisting that tales of dreadful monsters should not be told to children, nor ghost stories, and they should not be frightened with names of terror nor threatened with bogies nor told that animals will come and get them. Stories like those with which nurses are prone to terrify them must not be permitted. On the other hand there should be stories about the old times, and about the brave deeds men have done. Manifestly Vegio would be an advocate of the bedtime stories of our modern time if these were properly directed. Above all divine things should be taught them, and reverence for the name of God, and they should learn to esteem the virtue of truth.

Some years ago Professor G. Stanley Hall, of Clark University, shocked the sensibilities of some people by his declaration that the Catholic practice of having young folks read the lives of the saints was excellent pedagogy, because it taught adolescents self-control and self-denial and above all the caring more for others than for themselves. Selfishness is a special characteristic of youth and the neutralization of it is one of the most important phases of education.

The Middle Ages evidently had accepted the maxims which impress upon parents the need of influencing their children's lives as deeply as possible during the plastic or formative period. They were quite persuaded that both parents should share in the exercise of this influence and that it should not be left to one of them alone. This was stressed from many sides during the medieval period. Aquinas wrote in his *Summa*:[2] "Now it is evident that the raising of a human child demands not only the mother's care for its nutrition but much more the care of its father as guide and guardian under whom he progresses in good both internal and external." Women were expected, as the devout female sex, to be more attentive to the religious upbringing of a child than were men, but both were expected to share in the common responsibility of the child's education.

Vegio thought that it was quite as important to select the words that children should hear as it was to select the food that they eat, and he actually makes that comparison. He resents the idea that people of good breeding should entrust their children to servants, for they will learn the speech and the ways of servants. Above all, care must be taken that they shall not hear obscene things nor the scandalous chatter of slaves. He emphasizes the fact that children ought to be kept "from public shows and indecent pictures and whatever else might sully the delicacy and tenderness of their childish minds." One would almost think that one was listening to the advice or reading the admonitions of a modern old-fashioned pedagogue or of a priest counseling against the evils of the movies.

Vegio would surely have been very much disturbed at seeing children wandering around a summer hotel listening to the gossip and scandalous stories that fly about. He declares emphatically that children must be protected from the company found in public inns. He adds:

"Just as modesty and truth should be taught them, so good manners should not be forgotten. The proper ways of salutation, the courtesies of human conversation, methods of address, the time to rise or remain seated, the due reverence for age, and

---

[2] II, II^{ae}.

solicitude for the infirm, all these should be impressed upon children. To the old and to the learned let them acquit themselves well in speech and courtesy and politeness."

Vegio would probably be shocked could he see young men sitting down in subway trains while their elders, especially ladies, are standing around them, and above all he would feel that the boys whom he observed doing this sort of thing had not been properly brought up.

Vegio is persuaded that, "it is a mistake for parents to frighten their children with threats or by whippings." Readers of Vegio have been inclined to think that he represents the milder pedagogics of the pre-Renaissance time, which then were finding their way into vogue, but it must not be forgotten that at the end of the sixteenth century there was plentiful whipping of children both at school and at home. The seal of Shakespeare's school at Stratford had a birch figured on one side of it, as a symbol of the most effective instrument of education. Two generations later the first president of Harvard lost his position because he was too prone to whip and whip severely. Cotton Mather called him in Horatian terms, *plagosus Orbilius*, "Orbilius the thrasher."

On the other hand we find definite expressions in use more than two centuries before Vegio's time as to the harm, physical and mental, that may be done by the whipping of children. Walter von der Vogelweide, "Walter-of-the-bird-meadows," the well-known minnesinger, who received his special title because he said he learned his musical versemaking from the birds, has a quatrain on this subject that is very interesting:

> Children with rod ruling,
> 'Tis the worst of schooling,
> Who is honor made to know
> To him a word seems as a blow.

And yet down to our own time there have been good men and women who have been quite sure that whipping in school was a good thing, and even in my own early days both male and female teachers whipped their boys, and not infrequently their girls. What is interesting is to realize that the motives urged against whipping in school are the same now, five hundred years later, as they were in Vegio's time. He says: "Boys should not be lowered to the level of beasts and horses, and be whipped, nor do their bodies benefit by such harsh treatment. They are to be considered as children and not as slaves." And yet it is in the English public schools, where the sons of the oldest and noblest families in Great Britain are in attendance, that the practice of caning still obtains, and most of the men who have been subjected to it are quite willing to have their sons submitted to it as they were themselves.

Vegio is quite sure that an appeal to the better nature of children will do more good than to their lower nature through whipping. He says: "Whatever there is of generosity in them can be touched easily by kindness." Once more he reverts to his comparison with the animals: "A bullock may have to be struck before it will work properly, but a dog, a beast of nobler worth, is better managed by kindness." One is not so sure that a master of the hounds would entirely agree with the old medieval pedagogue. Trainers of animals have found that kindness is of very great help in making animals obedient, but that physical punishment is absolutely necessary to secure their attention and to overcome their objection to doing things.

Vegio concludes this phase of his pedagogics by saying: "Certainly gentleness is to be used toward boys. This must not be taken to mean lack of discipline, for in these modern (!) days children are being spoiled by softness of education. Let example move them and the stories of the great." The medieval custom was to have them read the lives of the saints and have saints' biographies read to them at mealtime while they were in school. These were the stories of people who had learned to control themselves for high ideals.

One feature of Vegio's treatment of children in order to make them obedient is very striking, but it would not fit in at all with the ideas of modern pedagogy. He suggests that sometimes young folks should be witnesses of the reward of evildoing by the punishment of the wicked, that is, in the pillory and the stocks, and he would also go so far as sometimes "to let them witness a public execution." On this principle modern educators have sometimes insisted on having the punishment of a crime appear on the same film with the crime itself, in order that the suggestion toward crime and the punishment that it entails should counteract each other. Many people, however, are inclined to think that the suggestion to crime is stronger than that of the appreciation of punishment, and that therefore the ultimate results of having children witness a punishment that fits the crime is not so preventive of criminal tendencies as might be thought.

Anyone who reads Vegio, especially in conjunction with some of the other medieval authorities on education, Bartholomew and Vincent of Beauvais, is sure to have the conclusion forced on him that there is nothing new under the sun in education, and that all our supposedly novel suggestions were discussed long ago.

X

METHODS OF PHYSICAL EDUCATION

P HYSICAL education, that is, the training of the body —
as well as the mind in order to secure so far as possible
a healthy mind in a healthy body — is usually supposed to
have been utterly neglected in the Middle Ages. In the monastic schools, as we have seen, manual labor according to
rule supplied all that was needed of physical training. When
the universities developed, certain games and sports were
mentioned, but above all archery was practiced with the idea
that, in anticipation of our student military corps, it might
be useful in time of war.

Near the end of the Middle Ages the attitude of educators
toward physical education was very interesting because it was
so different from what it is presumed to have been. We have
abundant evidence that educators were deeply intent on the
development in their younger pupils of health of body as well
as of mind, and they were manifestly convinced that these
two qualities were well worth the effort it might cost to attain
them.

In this connection attention may be called at once to
Vittorino da Feltre. Educated at the University of Padua,
then considered one of the leading universities of Europe,
he chose teaching as a vocation in life and proceeded to make
it a very popular profession. He taught for a time at Padua,
devoting himself, moreover, to the study of Greek under
Guarino of Verona, the greatest Greek scholar of the day.
In 1423 he was invited by the Marquis of Mantua, Gian

Francesco Gonzaga, to undertake the education of his children. Vittorino accepted the invitation with the stipulation that he be allowed to conduct a school at the court and receive other students. These were to include in particular some of the children of the poor when they exhibited talents of a high order. At his arrival he found in existence what we might call a gymnasium for the Gonzaga family and their friends. A number of sports and games were here carried on. This now became the school building. Under Vittorino's influence it developed into what was called the "pleasant house" or "joyous house," devoted to study, prayer, and play. But play was by no means the least important of the three.

Vittorino himself remained ever young, and while he knew how to make learning joyous he also knew how to take part in the sports and games and exercises of his pupils. One of his biographers says of him that while on entering a classroom he was greeted by the smiles of the students, his arrival on the playing field was the signal for a general rush to tell him of the results of the games and of any incidents that might be of special interest. In the curriculum of his school there were included Latin, Greek, philosophy, mathematics, grammar, logic, music, singing, and dancing, and also physical exercises of various kinds. He taught not only boys but girls, and the girls had to share in the physical exercises. Horseback riding and outdoor sports were insisted upon. His scholars were taught "to live the simple life, to tell the truth, and to remember that true scholarship is inseparable from virtue in the sense of lofty gratitude toward the Creator." Sandys, the well-known English educator, in his Harvard lectures on "The Revival of Learning," has told the story of how successful were some of Vittorino's young women pupils and how gratefully they held in remembrance their distinguished teacher because of the physical as well as the intellectual development they had received at his hands. His most illustrious pupil was Cecilia Gonzaga, who became one of the most cultured women of her time. It is particularly interesting to note that after having had the advantage of all the many-sided education afforded by Vittorino's teaching, and having further attained fame for her ability as a horseback rider and in connection with physical education generally, she ultimately became a nun, attributing the development of her vocation also to the education accorded her by Vittorino. Needless to say, he himself was an exemplary and devout Catholic.

One of the most interesting phases of Vittorino da Feltre's method of physical education is that the pupils were individually directed in the form of physical exercise particularly suitable for each of them. For those of delicate health or constitution the exercise chosen was quite different from that allowed the more lusty in the group. But while the latter were allowed to choose during recreation the particular outdoor exercise they preferred, yet they were not supposed to devote themselves to it exclusively. Certain kinds of exercise were obligatory in all kinds of weather. Vittorino himself took part in the field games with his pupils and in this, as in everything else, he set them the example. No wonder that as the result of his efficient character training many of his pupils felt they owed their success in afterlife to his teaching. He himself as a younger man exhibited a strong temper. In learning to control himself he learned also how to control others. His punishments were intended as remedies and were never administered immediately on the discovery of an offense. Five hundred years ago this prince of teachers anticipated what is best in modern pedagogy.

The school founded by Vittorino is by no means a solitary illustration of what the end of the Middle Ages contributed to the development of physical education. We have a monograph on the education of young folks — in reality a letter to Ladislas, the young king of Bohemia and Hungary — written by Aeneas Sylvius Piccolomini, the well-known Italian Renaissance scholar. It attracts our attention here because of the emphasis placed by its author on the necessity for physical training in conjunction with intellectual studies. Aeneas Sylvius, as we have already seen, later became pope under the title of Pius II. Before his elevation to the papacy he had been sent to distant parts of Europe on missions of many different kinds for the pontiffs who had preceded him. He knew, therefore, the customs of many places and was thoroughly familiar with the ideas of educators regarding physical as well as mental training throughout the Western world. Besides, Aeneas Sylvius himself was looked upon as one of the most distinguished scholars of his day. His ideas about physical education are probably representative of his time. The letter in which he dwelt on the importance of this subject was written just as the Middle Ages were closing and it represents the culmination of medieval thinking on the subject. He said:

"As regards a boy's physical training, we must always keep in mind that we aim at implanting habits in youth which will prove beneficial during his lifetime. So let him cultivate a certain hardness in the sense of determined effort which rejects excess of sleep and idleness in all its forms. Habits of indulgence, such as the luxury of soft beds, or the wearing of silk instead of linen next to the skin, tend to enervate both body and mind.

"Too much importance can hardly be attached to right bearing and gesture. Childish habits of playing with the lips and features, grimacing and jerking should be early controlled. A boy should be taught to hold his head erect, to look straight and fearlessly before him, to bear himself with dignity whether walking, standing, or sitting."

Almost needless to say this is excellent advice in our own day. Neurologists are often brought in contact with young men in whom training of this kind was lacking and who as a result have acquired tics and slouchy habits that are extremely difficult to break in later life.

Piccolomini continues:

"In ancient Greece we find that both philosophers and men of affairs — Socrates, for instance, and Chrysippus or Philip of Macedon, not to mention others — deemed this matter worthy of their concern, and therefore it may well be thought deserving of ours. Games and exercises which develop the muscular activities and the general carriage of the person should be encouraged by every teacher. For such physical training not only cultivates grace of attitude, but secures the healthy play of our bodily organs and builds up the constitution.

"Every youth destined to exalted position should further be trained in military exercises. It will be your destiny to defend Christendom against the Turk. It will thus be an essential part of your education that you be early taught the use of the bow, of the sling, and of the spear; that you drive, ride, leap, and swim. There are honorable accomplishments in every one, and therefore are not unworthy of the educator's care. Ponder the picture which Virgil gives of the youth of Italy, skilled in all the warlike exercise of their time. Games, too, should be encouraged for young children — the ball, the hoop — but these must not be rough and coarse, but have in them an element of skill. Such relaxations should form an integral part of each day's occupations, if learning is not to be an object of disgust. Just as nature and the life of man present us with alternations of effort and repose — toil and sleep, winter and summer — so we may hold with Plato, that it is a law of our being that rest from work is a needed condition of further work. To observe this truth is a chief duty of the master.

"In respect of eating and drinking, the rule of moderation consists in rejecting anything which needlessly taxes digestion and so impairs mental activity. At the same time fastidiousness must not be humored. A boy, for instance, whose lot it may be to face life in the camp, or in the forest, should so discipline his appetite that he may eat even beef. The aim of eating is to strengthen the frame; so let vigorous health reject cakes or sweets, elaborate dishes of small birds or eels, which are for the delicate and the weakly. Your own countrymen, like all northern peoples, are, I know, sore offenders in this matter of eating and drinking. But I count upon your own innate self-respect to preserve you from such bad example, and to enable you to despise the sneers and complaints of those around you. What but disease and decay can result from appetite habitually overindulged?"

Mafeo Vegio in his *De liberorum eruditione* shows very clearly his firm belief in the outdoor life as an ideal stimulus for young fellows no matter what the weather might be. He did not believe that they were likely to be harmed by exposure to inclement weather and even felt that if they were outside it would do them good. Many a young American soldier who had not "slept in a dry bed" for three weeks and "had not had dry feet for three months" in Belgium during the war learned this lesson that Mafeo Vegio emphasized. As he was secretary to Pope Eugenius IV and afterward to his successors, Pope Nicholas V and Pope Pius II — those outstanding end-of-the-Middle-Ages scholars and patrons of book collecting and education — it is very interesting to see what conclusions this latest medieval generation had come to regarding the significance of physical development even under severe climatic trials. To the youths with whom he was brought intimately in contact he said:

"If you want to enjoy the country you must pay no attention to weather. If you are unable to get on without sunshine and fine weather, go back to your cities and the arched street ways [many of the Italian cities like Bologna had their sidewalks beneath the arches of the lower stories of the buildings]. There you can walk securely without the danger of getting wet. If the cold irks you and mud and the baking heat, seek the more artificial life of the towns, but if you are above these fears and have learned a sense of beauty and have gathered from your education a determination to see life whole, then by all means make for the country."[1]

Such sentiments usually are presumed to have been entirely lacking in that period, and yet it would be comparatively easy to add many other quotations from the educators of the later Middle Ages demonstrating their thoroughgoing belief in the value of outdoor air and exercise for growing youth. We have accounts of the sports indulged in at the University of Paris

---

[1] Quoted from Father Bede Jarrett's volume on *Social Theories of the Middle Ages*, p. 67.

on "the fields of the clergy" that were permitted to be used for this purpose. We find that in this, as in so many other phases of medieval education, the only reason for depreciation is that those who are not familiar with actual documents on the subject are prone to assume that since they themselves know nothing about it there must have been nothing to know.

XI

RULES OF CONDUCT

MANNERS are supposed to be one of those refinements of human behavior which had not as yet developed during the Middle Ages. While chivalry cultivated the spirit of courtesy in the noble born, the people generally are supposed to have been rude and uncouth, utterly neglectful of manners, and indeed quite unacquainted with the rules of conduct that make life's contacts smooth and pleasant The surprise is then to find that there was a very interesting group of books on manners written during the Middle Ages which manifestly must have been widely read, for they exist in a series of manuscripts in different libraries. They were meant to teach behavior to children, but they contain many expressions which serve to show how interested were the people of that time in matters of health insofar as good manners conduced to health. For instance, in *The Babee's Book,* which bears the secondary title, "A Little Report of How Young People Should Behave," there is a paragraph of advice similar to that which many a parent has given to a son going off to school in our day:

"And, son, sit not up too long at even, or have late suppers, though you be strong and hale, for with such outrage your health shall worsen. And of late walking comes strife, and of sitting and of drinking out of time, therefore beware, and go to bed betimes and wink [sleep]."

The advice of a father to his son in these medieval books on manners is couched in concise, yet comprehensive terms.

are warned are very nearly the same as those on which the boys were given advice.

Here, for instance, as a companion picture to "How the Wise Man Taught His Son" we have, "How the Good Wife Taught Her Daughter." This advice is in verse or rhyme, like most of these old books of manners. It made it ever so much easier for young folks to commit them to memory as they were supposed to do. The mother insists on attendance at church and charity to the poor, avoidance of gossip, care for the daughter's own reputation and that of others, and touches upon morals as well as manners. Both father and mother ventured to give advice with regard to matrimony, advice that is as valuable in our day as it was in theirs. But youth always prefers to secure its experience for itself though experience is a very dear teacher. Mother said:

Daughter, if thou wilt be a wife,
  Look wisely that thou work;
Look lovely and in good life,
  Love God and Holy Kirk.
Go to church whene'er thou may,·
  Look thou spare for no rain.
For best thou farest on that day;
  To commune with God be fain.
    He must needs well thrive,
    That liveth well all his life,
      My dear child.

Gladly give thy tithes and thy offerings both,
To the poor and the bed-rid — look thou be not loth.
Give of thine own goods and be not too hard,
For seldom is the house poor where God is steward.
  Well is he proved
  Who the poor hath loved,
    My dear child.

When thou sittest in the church, o'er thy beads bend;
Make thou no jangling with gossip or with friend.
Laugh thou to scorn neither old body nor young,

But be of fair bearing and of good tongue.
  Through thy fair bearing
  Thy worship hath increasing,
    My dear child.
If any man offer thee courtship and would marry thee,
Look that thou scorn him not, whatsoever he be;
But show it to thy friends and conceal it naught.
Sit not by him nor stand where sin might be wrought,
  For a slander raised of ill
  Is evil for to still,
    My dear child.

The man that shall thee wed before God with a ring,
Love thou him and honour most of earthly thing.
Meekly, thou him answer and not as atterling (shrew),
So may'est thou slake his mood, and be his dear darling.
  A fair word and a meek
  Doth anger slake,
    My dear child.

While these books of behavior were written mainly with
the purpose of teaching manners, there often occur in them
admonitions so worded as to indicate that these medieval folk
were intent on teaching the rules for good health as well as
good manners. *The Babee's Book*, which dates from about
the middle of the fourteenth century, has a definite anticipation of many of our rules of politeness at table, and yet some
valuable hints about health also. Here is a rather striking
example of that:

Thou shalt not laugh nor speak nothing
While thy mouth be full of meat or drink
Nor sup thou not with great sounding
Neither potage nor other thing.
At meat cleanse not thy teeth nor pick
With knife or straw or wand or stick,
While thou holdest meat in mouth beware
To drink; that is an unhonest chare [manner of acting]
And also physic [medicine] forbids it quite.

Manifestly these old teachers of the young had come to

realize that washing down food with drink and failing to chew it properly was an unhealthy procedure and one which should be avoided as a matter of habit from one's earliest years. This form of health admonition is usually supposed to have been broadcast first in much more modern times, but the medieval physicians had succeeded in popularizing their opinions as to such things in these rhymes which children were required to commit to memory and which continued to be guides for them for the rest of their lives.

It would ordinarily be presumed that the writers of such books knew so little about health that their advice would be of very little value. The surprise is, however, to find how much the medieval people knew about health from the standpoint of common sense. There is a little book called the *Regimen Sanitatis Salernitanum, The Rule of Health of Salerno,* drawn up in the thirteenth century, which because of its enduring value has been reprinted in hundreds of editions in modern times. It was in rhymed Latin verse that made its injunctions comparatively easy to remember and it was read widely.

The celebration of the two hundredth anniversary of the birthday of Washington (February 22, 1932) recalled attention to what is known as Washington's Copybook. This is a manuscript in Washington's handwriting bearing the title, "One Hundred and Ten Rules of Civility and Decent Behavior in Company and Conversation." It bears the date 1745, when Washington was but thirteen years of age. For a long while it was thought that this represented Washington's own precocious thoughts on manners and morals, or perhaps rules adapted from those which had been current in his class books. Careful study of the wording of these rules, however, shows that they are adapted with some, though not very important, modification of the originals, from the rules of behavior and the books of manners of the Middle Ages. Such rules as: "Being set at meat, scratch not, neither spit, cough, nor blow your nose except there is necessity for it," or, "Take no salt nor cut bread with your knife greasy," or, "Put not another bit into your mouth till the former be swallowed; let not your morsels be too big for the jowls," are all to be found in the same or very similar words in the medieval books on manners.

Morals were not neglected, though such rules as, "Speak not evil of the absent for it is unjust," find a place beside such canny good advice as, "In visiting the sick do not presently play the physician if you be not knowing therein." Besides such rules as, "Show not yourself glad at the misfortune of another though he were your enemy," there are to be found such others as, "Wear not your clothes foul, unripped, or dusty, but see they be brushed once every day at least, and take heed that you approach not to any uncleanness."

They were more pious in the Middle Ages and they recommend prayer as an important adjunct for making life happier and better. In Washington's rules, however, the three last of the 110 are all of them in the moral order and make it very clear that the spirit of piety in the Middle Ages had carried over to the eighteenth century to be the guide of the Father of his country:

"When you Speak of God or his Attributes, let it be Seriously & with Reverence. Honour & obey your Natural Parents altho they be Poor.

"Let your Recreation be Manfull not Sinfull.

"Labour to keep alive in your Breast that Little Spark of Celestial fire called Conscience."

XII

ADVANCED FEMININE EDUCATION

FOR most people probably the most astonishing feature in the history of medieval education, so copious in surprises for our time, is the story of feminine education during those ages. Our surprises grow as our knowledge accumulates. It is commonly assumed that no question of an education for women ever arose until almost our own day. Allowance, no doubt, is made for certain individual exceptions depending on family circumstances, as for instance in the case of the daughter of a scholarly father. The better class of women, it was thought, were generally accorded an opportunity for learning the three "r's" so as to be able to keep their household accounts and relieve their husbands' minds of annoying details of domestic expenses, but scarcely more than that. However, the great majority of women — so modern writers summed up their idea of the medieval viewpoint — were considered not to have quite enough intelligence to enable them to secure an education, while anything like hard mental effort would surely cause an intellectual breakdown.

Curiously enough those ideas are not at all medieval; on the contrary, they are very modern and were expressed in no unmistakable terms less than a century ago. We need but revert to the time when, shortly before the middle of the nineteenth century, Mary Lyon undertook to found a school at Mount Holyoke, Massachusetts, to provide for women an education somewhat higher than elementary. Though her proposed curriculum presented what we would now consider scarcely more than high-school work, and her institution bore the charming name of Young Ladies' Seminary, a great many women in New England expressed anxious solicitude over the serious harm that must surely come to her students from this well-meant but ill-advised effort. They were convinced that even the very moderate curriculum which she proposed would put too great a strain on the intelligence of young women, with inevitably serious results.

This was the state of public opinion, affecting women much more than men, about the middle of the nineteenth century. The presumption was that the farther back you went in history the more opposition would be encountered to feminine education. As for the earlier Middle Ages, so long known as the dark ages, it was a foregone conclusion that women must then have been sunk in utter ignorance, ready victims of superstition, and overardent devotees of religion since they had nothing else to furnish them with an escape from their narrow round of thought. They must have been quite incapable of pursuing anything but their domestic and maternal duties, it was deemed, and would not feel their lack of opportunity for education because they had scarcely intelligence enough to appreciate what they were missing.

A great many presumably well-educated people were quite ready to believe almost anything derogatory to the Ages of Faith. For instance, the Diocesan Church Council at Macon in France, at the beginning of the Middle Ages, is often seriously cited by well-meaning modern writers as having debated solemnly whether or not women had souls. The decision arrived at denied women the possession of souls, so it is said. This is only an extreme example of the outrageous nonsense that had been commonly accepted by such as were quite sure that women's intelligence must have been considered an entirely negligible factor for all the ages preceding our own progressive time. What the churchmen actually debated at Macon was whether the Latin word *vir* (which means nearly the same as our term *gentleman*) might, like the word *homo* (*man* in the generic sense), be applied to women as well as to men.

As a matter of fact, at various times during the Middle Ages, efforts were made to afford women opportunities for a higher education, and some of these proved eminently successful. The first chapter in feminine education in what was later to become England is particularly interesting. It all developed under St. Hilda (614–680), at a site we now know as Whitby, though in her day it was called Streonshalh, in Northumbria. We have the story of it from Venerable Bede, whose authority as a historian is unquestionable. His material must have been collected by those who had known her personally and in whose memory were still fresh the details of her career as the great English ecclesiastical historian described them for us.

Hilda was of royal lineage, the daughter of the nephew of King Edward of Northumbria. She embraced Christianity in her girlhood and following the example of her sister became a nun. At first she chose a convent at a distance from home in order to be free from the distractions that would come from the nearness of relatives, and above all to make a complete sacrifice of worldly considerations and home ties in taking up the religious life. She was recalled to England by St. Aidan, the Irish missionary. It was he, as we have already said, who deserves much more the title of apostle to England than Augustine does, since the latter's apostolic labors were confined almost exclusively to Kent. Aidan assured Hilda that there was abundant opportunity for her to devote herself to her own people and accomplish much good among them. After some very interesting experiences Hilda became the abbess of Streonshalh (Whitby), and was superior of a double monastery, comprising a small number of monks and a large number of nuns.

The incident which has kept the memory of St. Hilda alive in the minds of those interested in English literature is the one which connects her name with that of Caedmon, the founder of English literature, and the famous author of a series of poems founded on the Bible. In these the material concerning creation, afterward used by Milton, was first put into poetic form in the west of Europe. Caedmon was not a monk but only a workman attached to the monastery — as Bede says, "of secular habit." He was not educated and his life was spent in manual labor. He had often heard his brother workmen sing in the evening after their work was done, accompanying their songs on the harp. Indeed there was a custom of having something like musical evenings after their work was over. The custom reveals rather surprisingly the state of culture among the working classes in Northumbria about the middle of the seventh century. The story of it serves to contradict much of current opinion as to the popular ignorance and lack of anything like esthetic development at that time.

Apparently everyone was expected to take an active part in these musical recreations. Caedmon, unable to sing or play, left the room, ashamed at not being able to contribute his share. After this had happened on several occasions, he took the matter seriously to heart, withdrawing sadly to the stable where, in charge of the horses, he had his sleeping quarters. One evening, after he had thus left the assembly, a dream came to him. As is common with such dreams, the last thing that he had had in mind before falling asleep recurred to him. But now, in his dream, there stood by him one who called him by name and bade him sing.

Caedmon declared he could not sing. His dream visitant would not take that for an answer. But when Caedmon said that he did not know what to sing, he was told to sing the Song of Creation. Caedmon could not but be familiar with the Book of Genesis, because of the frequent public readings of the Scripture in the monastery for the benefit of all. Obeying then the third behest, he began, still in a dream state, to sing verses descriptive of the creation of man, which under inspiration from on High he was now able to compose in praise of God.

On awaking in the morning he recalled not only the incident of the dream but also the words into which he had shaped the Book of Genesis during his dream. Other poets have had dream poems, but no one has ever dreamed quite so successfully or at such length in verse as Caedmon. When on awaking in the morning he repeated some of the verses for his monastic companions, the latter suggested that the abbess should be told the story. After hearing it Hilda summoned some of the scholarly men of the monastery and asked their advice. Hearing the verses they declared that Caedmon must have been inspired. They were not satisfied with the evidence of the dream poem, but suggested some further sacred studies for his muse, and he confirmed their opinion of his poetic inspiration by turning them into "sweet verse."

The Abbess Hilda then suggested that he become a monk. Apparently he was too modest to think himself worthy to be made a religious. She urged that he would thus secure opportunities for his education and for further occupation with poetry. Accordingly he was taught to read and devoted himself to the Biblical story, which he turned into the same delightful verse. Venerable Bede has told us of his long years as writer and of his holy death. It is no wonder, then, that Caedmon came to be honored as a saint no less than as a poet, and he is recognized as such by the Church. Few, perhaps, who have studied the interesting origin of his great poem — undoubtedly the inspiration of Milton, for an edition of it was printed in England not long before Milton began his *Paradise Lost* — are aware of this title of honor and veneration so lovingly accorded Caedmon by the people of his own time and approved by the Church.

This whole story of Caedmon, with its side light on the occupation of the monks and nuns with music and poetry, illustrates the scholarly monastic interests of that time. Only where men and women are much occupied with the spiritual and intellectual life could the incidents that are told with regard to Caedmon have taken place. We have other sources of information concerning the uplifting influence of the women of that community.

From St. Hilda's monastery came two other women to whom the title of saint has been given, Thecla and Lioba. They were the companions of St. Boniface in the apostolic work for the conversion of the German people, which has won for him the title of apostle of Germany. They volunteered for missionary work in association with Boniface, and their service was rendered the more valuable because of the influence exerted by the women of Germany in the family life of their people. The saint recognized the need for feminine auxiliaries to help him in bringing about the conversion to Christianity of those rugged Teutons, who represented the fertile origins of a great people and who were to be in turn magnificent contributors to civilization and culture in times long after.

For most people the greatest surprise in the life of St. Hilda lies in the fact that she was the superior of a monastery in which there were monks as well as nuns. The tradition under which St. Hilda's monastery was founded was that of St. Brigid in Ireland. Among other Irish customs, St. Aidan, the apostle of Northumbria, brought this with him from Ireland. St. Brigid in the sixth century was the superior of a monastery of monks and nuns in which work very like that accomplished by St. Hilda was done in Ireland. This convent or monastery of St. Brigid supplied opportunities to the Irish women to devote themselves to the intellectual and spiritual life, just as their brothers were doing in the many monastic schools scattered throughout Ireland, making it "the island of saints and of scholars."

The young women under Brigid at Kildare seem to have studied Latin, Greek, and Hebrew, as their brothers studied the same languages, for the sake of the light which they shed upon the Scriptures. They provided this education not only for members of the community, but also for others. They seem, further, to have made marvelously illuminated books, and, to have devoted themselves to the embroidery of altar linens and other materials for use in church services.

Gerald the Welshman, whose acquaintance we have previously made, tells us in the account of his journey through Ireland of the very wonderful book which he saw at Kildare. It was a copy of the Gospels, which he believed was quite unequaled. He had been in Rome at least three times and was a great traveler in his day, always curious about books, so that he had an excellent right to an opinion in this matter. Gerald was not one to be overpartial to the Irish and their achievements, and hence there can be no possible doubt that he was fairly overwhelmed with admiration for the *Kildare Gospels*. It has been suggested that Gerald may have seen the *Book of Kells* at Kildare, but there is good reason to think that the *Book of Kells* was elsewhere, and in that case Kildare must have possessed a rival for the famous *Book of Kells,* which is now recognized as probably the most beautiful book ever made.

Her biographers have told how Brigid in her humility, though the superior of the community, would sometimes take on herself the duty of caring for the sheep and doing other farm work of that kind, but this would seem to have been only her interest in the domestic side of the monastery, in order to emphasize the value of such work. That of the intellectual order nevertheless occupied a paramount place in the interests of the groups of monks and nuns.

Wherever there is a new foundation of education during the Middle Ages it is to be noted that the women were interested in it as well as the men. When Charlemagne called Alcuin to become, as it were, his minister of education, to found schools throughout his empire, opportunities for study were provided for the women as well as for the men. There are letters extant which passed between Alcuin and the daughters of Charlemagne showing their interest in the studies that were pursued at the palace school. Indeed there is a tradition that the young women were more deeply and more successfully interested in their studies than were many of the young men of the time.

In the meantime schools at the Benedictine convents had been growing in numbers and had afforded opportunities for the women of the time to secure higher education. St. Scholastica, twin sister of St. Benedict, endeavored to secure by her foundation the same opportunities for the spiritual and intellectual life of the women of her time as the Benedictine monasteries provided for the men. We have abundant evidence for this, though our sources belong to a somewhat later period in the Middle Ages. All these facts provide the demonstration that Benedictine nunneries, all during the Middle Ages, must have been occupied rather intently with the task of developing the minds not only of members of the community, but of the children of the nobility and even of the tenantry of the monastery who were confided to them.

The most interesting evidence for this devotion of the Benedictine nunneries to education is to be found in the career of a nun dramatist in one of the convents along the Rhine, who wrote a series of plays in imitation of the Latin dramatist, Terence. What may astonish us most is the fact that she did this in the tenth century, a century, often said to have been almost abysmally dark in the midst of the dark ages. The plays were probably not written to be acted, but were meant to be read to the community or intended for private reading by the monks and nuns of her own and other monasteries. Her name was Hroswitha. In the preface to her poems she declares that she wrote them to provide edifying reading for members of the community whose religious peace in the convent might be disturbed by the reading of Terence. She adds that the reading of this often scandalous Latin author was unfortunately indulged in sometimes by the monks and nuns, under pretext of cultivating the pure Latinity of his style. Nearly a thousand years ago men and women were making the same sort of excuses for disedifying reading as they do at the present time.

Hroswitha declared that she took Terence as the model for the Latin of her plays, because she felt that if by this means she attracted the attention of the scholarly members of monasteries and convents the reading of her highly moral Christian dramas would do them good instead of the harm they might derive from the pagan poet. To quote her exact words in a translation from the Latin text:

"I do not hesitate to imitate in my writings a man whom so many permit themselves to read, but my purpose is to celebrate, according to the measure of my feeble intellect, the virtues of Christian women, while employing the same form of composition which served the ancients to describe shameful conduct."

Hroswitha was encouraged in her writing by the abbess of her convent, Gerberga, a daughter of Henry of Bavaria, and a niece of the Emperor Otto I (the Great). The Emperor himself was a special patron of the convent and of Hroswitha. She wrote a number of works besides plays. For instance, she composed in verse the chronicles of the reign of the Emperor Otto, as well as the chronicles of his son and grandson. The nun-dramatist-historian tells us that besides the encouragement of the abbess, she owed much to the inspiration received from one of her teachers, also a member of the community. This was Sister Ricard. Evidently a well-cultivated intellectual life existed in the convent. But Hroswitha's writings attracted attention in all the religious houses along the Rhine, and there were many of them. She was known also in other parts of Germany and in France.

Cardinal Gasquet, the noted English Benedictine writer on medieval history, in his introduction to the English translation of the plays of Hroswitha, calls particular attention to the connotation of art and scholarship among the nuns as revealed by the writings of Hroswitha. "We find here," he said, "an author familiar not only with the Scriptures, the works of the Fathers of the Church, of the hagiographers or

writers of the lives of the saints and of the Christian philosophers, but also well acquainted with Plautus, Terence,
Horace, Vergil and Ovid — an author who on her own
confession took the theatre of Terence as her model."

Hroswitha's plays are called comedies because, like Dante's
Divine Comedy, they have a happy ending in heaven. All
of them end in martyrdom, and then the *personae dramatis*
live happily ever afterward in Paradise. They had the cult
of the happy ending at that time as at the present time.
Critics have suggested that the happy endings to our comedies
in the modern time are not guaranteed to be lasting, but
those of Hroswitha were.

At least one of Hroswitha's plays, *Paphnutius,* has been
presented on the stage in recent years by the Pioneer Players
in London, in 1914. The stage performance was welcomed
with lively interest and a great many expressed themselves
as deeply pleased with the old medieval comedy. Christopher
St. John, the translator of the plays into English, says in
his preface that, "The scenes are well knit, the characterization deft and sure, and the dialogue admirably expressive."
With regard to one of the scenes, the translator writes:

"It is indeed amazing that so true and touching a scene
dealing with a subject which later led dramatists into false
sentiment, coarseness or mere preaching, should have been written
nearly a thousand years ago by an obscure nun in a convent
in lower Saxony."

The fact that it was is a demonstration of how little human
nature changes in the course of a millennium.

One of the comedies is really an old-fashioned morality
play in which a mother, Wisdom, and her three daughters,
Faith, Hope, and Charity, come to Rome in the hope to
exercise a good influence on the citizens of the papal metropo-
lis. They suffer martyrdom at the hands of the Romans, but
not before their missionary endeavors had produced an
abundant harvest of conversions to Christianity, for they
deeply influenced all those with whom they were brought
into intimate contact.

These plays of Hroswitha were preserved in a single manuscript. If anything had happened to that, it would have been almost impossible to persuade scholars generally that a nun could have written comedies in the tenth century.

Even more amazing for our time than the existence of a nun dramatist in a Benedictine convent along the Rhine in the tenth century, is the flourishing of a nun scientist in another Benedictine convent not far away in the twelfth century. Her writings, strangely enough, were all concerned with medicine, and the two books by which she is known are *Liber Simplicis Medicinae* and *Liber Compositae Medicinae*, "The Book of Simple Medicine" and "The Book of Compound Medicine." They are reproduced in Migne's *Patrologia,* the great Latin work in many volumes in which the writings of the Fathers and Doctors of the Church, and other distinguished authors who had intimate relations with the Church in any way, are brought together.

This second nun author of distinction was Abbess Hildegarde, on whom, with the subsequent approval of the Church, the title of saint was conferred by her generation. She was the superior of the Benedictine nunnery of Disibodenberg, in what is now Rhenish Bavaria. On terms of intimate friendship, at least by correspondence, with St. Bernard of Clairvaux, she was consulted by many of the distinguished men of her time, who wrote to obtain her advice. Popes, emperors, and other rulers thus sought her opinions. She was manifestly held in high regard as one of the very learned women of her day, while her deeply thoughtful personality made her advice of precious value on many subjects.

Something of the very practical character of Hildegarde's teaching on medical subjects may be gathered from the quotations from her writing to be found in Lynn Thorndike's chapter devoted to her, in the second volume of his *History of Magic and Experimental Science.* It is astonishing to find how correct many of Hildegarde's suggestions are, though she could not have been aware of the reasons why today we agree with her. Water, for instance, as she tells us, is most important for health. Swamp water, she declared, should always be boiled before drinking, while well water, coming up from the depths of the earth, is better to drink than spring water which bubbles up from the surface. Spring water, on the other hand, is better than river water. This last should be boiled and cooled before drinking. These directions would seem to indicate that Hildegarde was as stern a mentor with regard to the danger of surface water as the army medical service in time of war. Thorndike remarks that Hildegarde is not the first to advise the boiling of drinking water, but she lays such great stress on it as to make her warning strike home.

She said further that rain water is inferior to spring water, and that the drinking of snow water is dangerous to health. Her objection to the drinking of melted snow was probably founded on an old tradition, which accounted for the prevalence of goiter among the inhabitants of certain Alpine villages by the fact that they drank the water flowing out beneath the glaciers, intensely cold, and therefore supposedly productive of various deleterious effects.

Hildegarde in the twelfth century furnishes a typical example of the attitude of medieval scholars toward astrology. A series of church documents were issued at various times condemning astrology mainly because belief in it impaired the validity of the principle of the freedom of the will. Individuals were compelled to shape their lives, willy-nilly, as the result of the influence of the stars. Practically all the medieval scholars condemned belief in astrology, but over and over again the casting of horoscopes was renewed mainly because physicians became persuaded that the stars meant very much for their patients, both as regards the times when medicine and other remedial measures should be administered and also as regards the recovery from disease. Hildegarde insisted that there was no truth in the supposed influence of the stars, and undoubtedly her words impressed her generation deeply. In spite of ecclesiastical condemnations of all kinds, there are still many believers in astrology among us at the present time, and they come mainly from the educated and not from the uneducated classes.

It has been said that any generation that fails to provide a career for the women who for one reason or another do not marry is failing in its humanitarianism in one extremely important particular, and is quite sure to suffer severely for that failure. A certain number of women, many of them very intelligent, either do not care to marry or miss the opportunity to marry. There are in city populations nearly ten per cent more women than men. Modern warfare with its many fatalities has made this problem even more acute than it was before. Unless a career that will occupy and satisfy them is provided for unmarried women their anomalous presence in a generation will make itself felt disturbingly. Medieval encouragement of nunneries, the opportunities which these generations provided for the cultivation of the mind and the heart of the members of religious orders, male and female, supplied an excellent solution of that problem.

Many in our time are prone to think that such a solution of the problem may have proved very satisfactory in the Middle Ages when there were fewer interests in life for women than there are at the present time, but that it would not suffice now. Those who think so, however, are not familiar with the many thousands of women who in our day find happiness and satisfaction in the very monastic life that came to be such a marvelously organized institution during the Middle Ages. As the result of the example set at that time, we have in the United States alone well above 100,-000 members of religious orders for women. The more one knows about them, the more the conviction develops that they find happiness and heartfelt satisfaction in their religious vocation. It is only necessary to know them to understand ever so much better than could otherwise be possible the life of the medieval Benedictine convents and how much it must have meant for the women of that time.

Hildegarde has been the subject of no little study in recent years. It is quite remarkable how modern some of her expressions are. She seems to have had some inkling at least of the circulation of the blood. Five centuries before Harvey she wrote: "Just as the blood vibrates in the veins and causes them to vibrate and pulsate, so the stars move in the firmament." For her the brain was the regulator of all the vital quality, the center of life. She connects the nerves and their passage from the brain and the spinal cord through the body with manifestations of life. She was interested in psychology, normal and morbid, and discussed such subjects as frenzy, insanity, despair, dreads, obsessions, anger, idiocy, and their relation to the personality. She definitely understood how physical conditions might produce mental disturbance and she discounted possession by evil spirits as a cause of insanity. She said: "When headache and migraine and vertigo attack a patient simultaneously they render him foolish and upset his reason. This makes many people think that he is possessed by a demon, but that is not true." Manifestly this twelfth-century nun writer on medical matters was not willing to admit possession by demons as the source of symptoms in mind and body which might be explained in other ways. Spirit possession was not a prominent element in the causation of mental alienation in the thought of the Middle Ages, but is a delusion of the seventeenth and eighteenth centuries in witchcraft time.

Mlle. Lapinska, in her *Histoire des Femmes Medecins,* presented as a thesis for the doctorate in medicine at the University of Paris in 1900, does not hesitate to say that St. Hildegarde must be considered the most important medical writer of her time. Ordinarily it would be presumed that the Benedictine spirit would be rather opposed to the devotion of attention to subjects like medicine by Benedictine nuns. Our generation is prone to picture the monks of the Middle Ages as rather firmly persuaded that while women might occupy themselves with literature, yet science, particularly medical science, was quite unsuitable for their study. As a matter of fact, however, the first great medical school in modern history, founded and continued largely under the influence of the Benedictines, that of the University of Salerno, admitted women students and graduated a number of women who practiced medicine in the south of Italy. Some of their names are well known. It would be in harmony with what we know of these wise old Benedictines to find that they had recognized the fact that there was a definite place for women in the practice of medicine and used their influence to provide opportunities for it.

On the other hand, Hildegarde's devotion to science and medicine did not disturb her religious beliefs in any way. When Hildegarde had attained more than the allotted three score and ten years of the Psalmist, when she felt that she had not much longer to live here on earth, though still in possession of the plenitude of her intellectual powers, she expressed her abiding confidence in her faith as a refuge from all the trials and dreads that might come to her:

"And now that I am over seventy years old, my spirit, according to the will of God, soars upward in vision to the highest heaven and to the farthest stretch of the air and spreads itself to regions exceeding far from me here. Thence I can behold the changing clouds and the mutations of all created things; for all these I perceive not with the outward eye or ear, nor do I create them from the cogitations of my heart."

Mary Agnes Cannon, in her dissertation for a doctorate in philosophy at the Catholic University, under the title *The Education of Women During the Renaissance,* has some informing passages concerning the education of women during the earlier Renaissance. These represent not a new birth but a continuance of the educational traditions of the Middle Ages. She says at the beginning:

"In the general interest in classical learning awakened by its rebirth into Italian life and letters, woman took no insignificant part. From the beginning of the Revival we find the record of her literary taste and accomplishments side by side with those of the leading men of the time. The history of Italian literature makes mention of many women proficient in the Latin and Greek languages which they spoke with ease and in which they wrote familiarly both in prose and poetry."

It is very clear, then, that from the end of the fourteenth and during the first half of the fifteenth centuries, which represent the culmination of the Middle Ages, women were being afforded opportunities for education equal to those of the men, and they were availing themselves of these opportunities very successfully. Some of these women were extremely scholarly. Miss Cannon says: "By the middle of the fifteenth century we find many other girls who like Battista Sforza were remarkable for their early knowledge of Greek as well as of Latin." She names a number of these and gives references which should make it easy for anyone interested in the story of feminine education to find numerous recognitions paid by the scholars of that day to the talents and learning of the young women of the time. During the first half of the fifteenth century it had become fashionable for young women to know Greek as well as Latin. Distinguished scholars even declared that a daughter of the nobility who could not read Latin or Greek was looked upon as a "dumbhead."

After all, whenever anything becomes fashionable we can be quite sure that the leaders of society will have it if it can possibly be secured, and these ladies of the terminal Middle Ages were distinguished for their "agreeable learning." Manifestly they were not bluestockings seeking to display their erudition; their learning added to their charms. Warnings, in fact, came from some of the elderly scholars that women must not expect too much of men in the matter of learning and that scholarly women must permit a young fellow occasionally to be guilty of a solecism without calling attention to it. The women had more time for study than the men but were not to take advantage of their learning to correct a young man of their circle too seriously.

Interesting evidence as to the opportunities afforded to women for education at the end of the Middle Ages is to be found in the story of the monastery of Syon. This was situated on the Thames, near Twickenham. Even in the earlier fifteenth century it was a dual monastery under the rule of an abbess, with more than a dozen of priests, four deacons and eight lay brethren attached to the institute. Its founder was King Henry V (1387–1422), the hero of Agincourt. The chief duty of the community was to pray for the souls of the royal founder and his family, and yet there is abundant testimony to the fact that the members of the community devoted themselves to the artistic and intellectual life, for we have an example of their needlework in the beautiful cope of Syon, one of the precious treasures of South Kensington Museum, London. We have also the catalog of their library of printed books which demonstrates the breadth of their intellectual interests.

King Henry V founded this monastery of St. Saviour and St. Bridget at Syon, in his manor of Islesworth, in response to the enthusiastic devotion of his sister to this community. When his beloved sister, Philippa, married King Eric III of Sweden, the religious Order known as the Brigittines in that country became her chosen friends. The new community became favorites of the royal family in England and grew to be a very wealthy foundation, so that the annual income of the monastery at the end of the fifteenth century was nearly the equivalent of $100,000 in our time. So wealthy a foundation soon caught the avaricious eye of Henry VIII and it was decided to confiscate the property of the monastery, but the commissioners, intent on finding reasons for condemnation and confiscation, discovered little, indeed almost nothing, to bring against the community. This did not save the institution. The Islesworth monastery was conferred on the ninth earl of Northumberland, whose descendants still hold it.

Fortunately the catalogue of the printed books of the library of Syon has come down to us. Miss Mary Bateson, lecturer at Newnham College, Cambridge, edited this *Catalogue of the Library of Syon Monastery.*[1] It serves to show how broad and serious were the interests of the nuns at the beginning of the sixteenth century before the Reformation came to disturb them.

Among the books at Syon were 67 volumes of grammar and classics; 55 on medicine and astrology, some of them classics; 46 on philosophy; 128 commentaries on the sentences, that is, on the work of the Master of the Sentences; 75 Bibles and concordances; 232 commentaries on the Old and New Testament; 65 on history. There were no less than 58 dictionaries; 121 lives of the saints; 88 works of the Fathers; 98 devotional tracts; 70 books of sermons; 104 on canon law, and 21 on civil law. Space was left in the catalogue for nearly 1,500 books, and the titles of 1,421 are given. Most of them are incunabula and the latest published was probably in 1526.

It is clear, then, that the Reformation had nothing to do with the gathering of the books nor with their character, because that movement did not begin to make itself felt in England until later than this date. Miss Bateson says:

"The catalogue of Syon Library has a special interest inasmuch as it offers a means of estimating the intellectual and literary resources which were at the disposal of a flourishing religious house shortly before the Reformation."

Most of these books represented gifts which had been made by friends of the monastery or bequests by will, because books were considered very precious and were mentioned particularly in testamentary documents. Undoubtedly many of them were purchased by the ample funds

---

[1] Cambridge University Press, 1898.

of the monastery, for though books were extremely expensive, religious superiors were ready to be liberal in appropriations for reading material. The catalogue offers positive evidence of the deep interest there must have been among religious in the new art of printing. Almost within the incunabula period this community had gathered some 1,500 printed books.

After going over the catalogue there is no doubt left that the monastery kept pace with the New Learning in Latin Renaissance literature. All of the Italian writers whose names are familiar from this period are represented in the library, but none of them by their Italian works. Petrarch appears as a Latin writer on the Penitential Psalms, and Boccaccio as the author of a dictionary of classical antiquities. Dean Colet and Dr. Linacre (afterward a priest) as well as St. Thomas More, are represented in the library, but by their Latin and not their English books. The library was pre-eminently a library of Latin books. At that time Latin was the language of scholars and anyone with any pretense to education was supposed to be able to read Latin at least, and Latin was talked in the schools. The total of works in English consisting chiefly of small theological tracts, was twenty-six; in French four. The comparative absence of books in English is more remarkable as the foundress of the Brigittine Order in Sweden sought to enforce the use of the native language, requiring it to be spoken at such times as conversation was allowed and with a penalty for the use of Latin. At Wadstena, the parent house in Sweden, many Swedish translations were prepared and printed. The religious women of the later Middle Ages were evidently not lacking in interest in books nor in the intellectual power to comprehend and appreciate them. They were educated, scholarly examples of the training of mind afforded them by their generations.

XIII

WOMEN IN THE MIDDLE AGES

THE commonly accepted opinion is that women in the Middle Ages were almost entirely confined in their interests to what the Germans in the modern time termed the three "k's," *Kinder, Küche, Kirche,* "children, cooking, and the Church." The daughters of the medieval nobility married when in our estimation they were scarcely more than children — about fifteen or sixteen — very often having spent the preceding seven years or more away from home under the tutelage of their mother-in-law-to-be, so as to be sure that they would be properly sympathetic toward their "in-laws" in afterlife. They were supposed to begin having children within a year after marriage, and if in good health they were expected to continue this maternal process so that they might often have a dozen or even more in a family. No wonder that under these circumstances, in such striking contrast with our customs, modern women are almost forced to the conclusion that life could not have meant very much to their medieval sisters, and that they represented, as it were, merely so many units to carry on the race.

As a matter of fact, the interests of the women of the Middle Ages were as broad as at any time in history. The responsibilities placed on their shoulders developed their characters and brought out their personalities as well as trained their intelligence in ways that made them quite as capable of solving the problems of life as are the women of our time. Indeed the more we know about medieval women and what was expected of them the clearer it becomes that a great many of the women of the Middle Ages were thoroughly prepared for life; that, after all, is the essence of education. Christine de Pisan (*c.* 1363–1431), herself a rather striking example of the achievements of the medieval woman, contradicting in her own career so many false impressions that have been rife with regard to the opportunities for education accorded the medieval women, has provided us with some definite information as it was derived from her own personal experience and her acute powers of observation, impressions that are very different from those now current in regard to the women of her time.

Christine was married at fifteen, only to be left at twenty-five an inconsolable widow, without means and with three children to support. She proceeded to make a living for them by her writing and is the first example that we have in history of a woman becoming self-supporting by means of her pen. Among other things that she has told us, manifestly with wholehearted sincerity, is the happiness of the years of her married life. Though hers was a marriage of arrangement with which the young folks themselves had very little to do, her life with her husband proved eminently full of happiness and she tells us how much of joy there was in her family life when her children came. She tells further how united she and her husband were in their mutual love and what a profound sadness came over her as the result of his death.

Much has been said in the modern time about the unhappiness that seems to so many of our day almost inevitable when marriage is contracted at so early an age, with no question of love or personal preference as the stimulus for it. Yet here is a thoroughly intellectual woman, quite as advanced mentally as any of her modern sisters, who personally went through the experience of early arranged marriage and found her married life happy beyond almost anything that romance could picture. The fact that so many of the married folks during the Middle Ages were very young when they began their married life was in their favor, because youth is supremely adaptable and at the same time untrained in concealing its feelings. As a consequence the young married couple came to know each other very well, but as they had no strongly marked prejudices their minds were readily molded into harmony. Christine did not hesitate to say that she had been *given* to her husband when she was young. Yet they developed such deep love for each other that after a few years of married life their two hearts beat as one. She declared that their affection, even in their early years of marriage, came to be much greater than that of brothers and sisters, and so they were ready to share the joys and griefs of existence together as the years went on.

Christine, in her best known book, *Livre des Trois Vertus*, "The Book of the Three Virtues," written toward the close of the Middle Ages (about the beginning of the fifteenth century), gives a list of the things which a lady or baroness living on her estates, far from city life, ought to be capable of doing in the fulfillment of her household duties. The principal thing expected of her was that she must be able to replace her husband in every way whenever political or military duties required his absence. As Miss Eileen Power says in her essay, "The Position of Women":[1]

"The lady must therefore be skilled in all the niceties of tenure and feudal law in case her lord's rights should be invaded [while he was absent]; she must know all about the management of an estate so as to supervise the work of the bailiff and she must understand her own métier as housewife and be able to plan her expenditures wisely."

Now that we have heard so much about the household budget it is extremely interesting to meet with Christine's suggestion that the income of a great lady should be divided into five parts, of which the first should be devoted to alms-

---

[1] *The Legacy of the Middle Ages,* Oxford University Press, 1926.

giving (for in the Middle Ages they were supposed to think about others before themselves); the second to household expenses; the third to the payment of officials and women; the fourth to gifts; while the fifth should represent the amount of the budget to be drawn upon for jewels, dresses, materials for personal adornment, and miscellaneous expenses as required. Note that the personal expenditure of the lady of the house occupies the last part of the budget, a long distance after charity.

This arrangement of life and income, often thought of as a very modern development, was no empty pretext in those days, held up for conventional consideration without a serious belief that it could be realized in practical life. On the contrary, it represented what was demanded of medieval women in the actual conditions in which they were living. It is not surprising to learn under the circumstances that their husbands recognized how valuable their services were in the care of the household and appreciated them very thoroughly. They realized that the good management of the family is sometimes worth more to the husband than the income which he receives from his tenants. As in our time it was the feeling in the Middle Ages that the wife should be the treasurer of the household, in the sense that all moneys received should be handed over to her and that she should dispose wisely of what her husband brought into the family exchequer, whether this represented the patrimony of a nobleman or only the wages of a worker.

Women occupied very much the same position in the household in the Middle Ages in this regard as they did in the simpler traditions of our own country a generation or so ago. How many of us can look back on our own home experiences and appreciate this status of our mothers as the economists of the family, the financial directors, as it were, of the household? It must not be thought that the relation of husband and wife in the Middle Ages was confined to their domestic concerns. There was often the fondest affection between them, as may be readily seen from some of the expressions that have come down to us in their letters. Miss Power has quoted some of these.[2] For instance, an obscure Flemish weaver, writing to his wife from England signed himself with a phrase that seems strangely modern, "Your married friend." In our days when introductions at bridge or at the theater are likely to take such form as, "Meet friend wife," or, "friend husband," most people will find it hard to believe that the formula is well over five hundred years old.

Women are usually supposed to have had very few or practically no rights during the Middle Ages, but in this as in so many other things, it was the nineteenth century and not the later centuries of the Middle Ages that was lacking in humanity. Certain very definite rights were claimed for women by their male relatives at the time of their marriage, and these were accorded. For instance, the father of St. Birgitta of Sweden, at the beginning of the fourteenth century, put in this claim at the time of his daughter's marriage:

"I give you my daughter as wife, full of honor and fidelity, on condition she partake of your bed and roof; that she has the control of your keys, the symbol of her authority; and that she enjoys the tithes and offerings as well as the rights which King Erik and the law of Upland accord her."

Birgitta was a very busy woman in her household, the mother of a dozen children, and the mistress of the family directing her domestics in the manufacture of many things for the household. She was famous for her charity and succeeded somehow in finding time to establish on her estate a monastery for men and women of which Catherine, her daughter, became the first abbess soon after her mother's death. Manifestly these women of the Middle Ages had an abundance of energy and the opportunity to exercise it.

Occasionally medieval wills, even through the stiff legal phraseology of the times, reveal something of the tender

---

[2] *Op. cit.*

feelings a husband entertained for his wife. One testator left this injunction for his executors: "I pray you pray Thomas, my son, in my name and for the love of God, that he never enter into strife with his mother if he wishes to have my blessing in the after time, for he shall find her courteous to deal with always."

The women of America gained their freedom in the frontier days when wives and mothers so often had to care for home and children while their husbands were away. They had to defend the house and the family against wild beasts and against still more terrifying Indians. As a journey to the settlement often meant days of absence, and husbands sometimes had to be away for months at a time on business, at war or in defense against the Indians, it is easy to understand how a spirit of independence came to the women and their husbands learned to appreciate them as real helpmates in life.

Something very like that happened to the medieval women. As Eileen Power says:

"While her lord was away on military expeditions, on pilgrimages, at court or on business, it was she who became the natural guardian of the fief or manager of the manor, and Europe was full of competent ladies, not spending all their time in hawking and flirting, spinning and playing chess, but running estates, fighting lawsuits and even withstanding sieges for their absent lords. When the nobility of Europe went forth upon a crusade it was their wives who managed their affairs at home, superintended the farming, interviewed the tenants, and saved up money for the next assault. When the lord was taken prisoner, it was his wife who collected his ransom, squeezing every penny from his estate, bothering bishops for indulgences, selling her jewels and the family plate."[3]

The intellectual development of these poetic ladies of the later Middle Ages was often admirable in breadth and depth. Christine de Pisan knew not only Latin and French, but she

---

[3] *Op. cit.*

had also learned Italian from her father. Marie de France, so well known for her poetry, knew Latin and French, and also English. Yet these two women were not bluestockings in the sense that they thought more of intellectuality for women than they were concerned about woman's power to heal the ills of mankind by her love for those near and dear to her, and to aid by her charity those in need.

Marie wrote a series of legends or fables, one of which is the story of the young knight who scorns love and devotes himself to the chase and to other manly sports, rather despising the young men around him who preoccupied themselves with women. On one of his hunting expeditions the young knight was turned on by his quarry and sadly wounded. He was told by a very wise fairy that he would not recover from his wounds and no one would bring him the balm of healing until he would meet a woman who would be willing to suffer for him, provided at the same time that he himself was ready to suffer even more for her than she suffered for him. This is the lofty unselfish love that was exploited by the poets, particularly at the beginning of the great movement of love poetry. It was not passion but true devotion and readiness to bear pain for others that was the subject of the poetry.

Reverend Bede Jarrett has called attention particularly to "this romance of youthful manhood which shows us the daintiness of women's minds under the influence of the literary movement of the time." It is usually around a girl that the love story turns, not the illegitimate passion of the later fourteenth century's praise, but the "delicate, secret, and subtile love of a maiden." This is well illustrated in the familiar lines from Bernart de Ventadorn, one of the Troubadours to whom Dante refers. Dante seems to have read Bernart with special attention since their poems contain similar errors of mythology. Chaytor, in the introduction to *Troubadours of Dante,* says that toward the beginning of the thirteenth century a gradual change came about in the mind of the Troubadour. "Seeing that love was the inspiring force to good deeds," he gradually dissociated his love from the object which had aroused it. Among them, "as among the minnesingers, love is no longer sexual passion. It is rather the motive to great works, to self-surrender, to the winning an honorable name as courtier and poet." The lines already referred to illustrate this very well:

> for indeed I know
> Of no more subtle feeling under heaven
> Than is the maiden passion for a maid,
> Not only to keep down the base in man,
> But teach high thoughts and amiable words
> And courtliness and the desire of fame,
> And love of truth and all that makes a man.

Surely this represents the best solution ever put forth for certain social problems that have always been with us and always will be. Here is nature's own panacea for ills that may be serious and that other remedies can, at the most, only palliate.

The women whom we know best in the Middle Ages are those who attracted the attention of contemporaries because of the position which they came to occupy in the intellectual and spiritual life of this time. It is perfectly easy to select a group of women, taking one or more from each century of the thousand years of the Middle Ages, whose memory will doubtless continue to be cherished so long at least as Christianity lives. We wonder whether their feministic sisters of the present day who have achieved at least notoriety will live on in the memory of succeeding generations for 500 years or more as these have done.

In the fifth century there were Brigid and Scholastica, both founders of religious orders, long to be remembered by their daughters in religion and looked up to as channels of strength in the conventual movement which absorbed so many of the talented women of the time. Fifteen hundred years after their death their names are still in benediction.

Brigid, as the Mary of the Gaels, is the woman best remembered by her people in all secular history, while more of the daughters of the nation have been called after her than is true of any other woman patron of a people.

Thus, then, in the sixth and seventh centuries there were Hilda, the abbess of Whitby, patroness of our earliest English poet, as well as Thecla and Lioba, who after their training at Whitby went over to Germany to help St. Boniface in his great mission of converting the Teutonic peoples to Christianity. Women's hands and ways, and women's educated minds were needed to introduce Christianity to the woman-respecting Germans. In the ninth century there was the Irish girl, Dymphna, in whose honor a shrine with its organization of care for backward children was founded at Gheel, which still exists as a beneficent work down to our time. In the tenth century we have the nun dramatist, Hroswitha, and in the twelfth, the Abbess Hildegarde, a writer on scientific subjects whose name has won an enduring place in the history of science and whose career has been the subject of devoted research in our day.

It would be easy to mention others. Toward the end of the Middle Ages women whose names were destined for immortality occur in numbers. This is due not so much to any greater distinction than that of the women of previous periods as to the better preservation of the records. Among them were St. Elizabeth of Hungary whom the Germans called *Heilige Frau Elisabeth,* "St. Mrs. Elizabeth," just a good mother who was a saint; St. Clare, founder of the Second Order of Franciscans and preserver of Franciscan traditions, followed by a group of wives and mothers who stamped their imprint deeply not only on their own generation but on the generations that followed; Blanche of Castile, mother of St. Louis of France, herself a great ruler who saved and strengthened his kingdom; Berengaria, her sister, mother of the equally beloved St. Ferdinand III of Castile; Mabel Rich, the London tradesman's wife of the same century, mother of

St. Edmund of Canterbury; while the fourteenth century gave to us St. Catherine of Siena, and the fifteenth saw a galaxy of Italian women whose names will not be readily forgotten.

But particularly interesting, in addition to all this, is a group of women in the thirteenth century, all bearing the name of Gertrude, whose memory continues to be cherished in certain parts of Europe even down to our own day, seven centuries after their deaths.

There was, for instance, Gertrude of Aldenberg, as she is known, the abbess of the Benedictine convent of Aldenberg in the Rhineland. She was the youngest daughter of that dear Duchess of Thuringia, whom we know as St. Elizabeth of Hungary, and who has been held in such high honor by the German people ever since. And yet her all too brief life closed some seven hundred years ago. Gertrude attracted much attention because of what seemed to be an inheritance from her mother, an intense solicitude for the poor, which preoccupied her thoughts more than anything else. At the age of twenty-one she was made the abbess of her convent and continued to occupy that position for some forty-nine years. She made it her principal business as abbess to help those who needed to be helped in any way. The Germans look upon her as in every sense worthy of her mother, the *Heilige Frau Elisabeth.*

Another of the well-remembered Gertrudes was Gertrude of Heckerborn, a relative of the family to which St. Elizabeth belonged and a sister of St. Mechtilde. Royal families in that day were often distinguished by the number of saints whose love for God and neighbor was heroic. Gertrude of Heckerborn devoted herself particularly to the development of the education of her nuns and insisted on procuring for them an opportunity for training in the liberal arts combined with special devotion to Holy Scripture. This is worth noting, particularly because such devotion to Holy Writ is often declared to have been anything but characteristic of that time. Gertrude did not hesitate to say to her nuns that the more they knew and the more developed their intelligence was, the more their worship and prayer would mean in the sight of God. This attitude of mind with regard to the relations between education and worship is so different from the conceptions often entertained of medieval religious superiors that it deserves to be especially noted.

Then there was a third Gertrude who is usually spoken of as Gertrude the Great. In spite of that lofty title she was only a simple nun of lowly birth, living in the convent which was ruled by Abbess Gertrude of Heckerborn. Yet the attention she attracted even in her own time was quite exceptional and even exceeded that given to her mother abbess, although both of their names are likely to be kept on the honor roll of mankind until this stage of existence is at an end. Gertrude the Great wrote on mysticism. A series of her books have been published and republished in our own day. One of these is the *Legatus Divinae Pietatis, The Legate of Divine Piety;* another is the *Liber Specialis Gratiae, The Book of Special Grace.* The scholarly world of the time wrote in Latin. The educated read it fluently and so it was the language that these nuns all used in their writing.

Among the admirers of Gertrude the Great have been many distinguished thinkers and writers, some of them known for high accomplishment in the same fields as Gertrude, such as St. Teresa of Spain; Francisco Suarez, the Jesuit philosopher of Spain, whose influence continues in the philosophic world of today; St. Francis de Sales, the "gentleman saint," as he has been called, the great evangelizing bishop of Geneva, who said in relation to conversions that more flies are caught with a drop of honey than with a barrel of vinegar. These were sixteenth-century admirers of Gertrude, and in the following century M. Olier, the founder of the Sulpicians, whose work has meant so much for the training of zealous priests must be added to their number. In our time we may

mention in this same list Dom Gueranger, the great Benedictine writer on the liturgical year, whose works are so
often read in the refectories of religious orders, and finally
Father Faber, the English Oratorian, the distinguished
convert of the Oxford movement, who influenced England in
his own time almost as deeply as Cardinal Newman. He was
looked upon as a remarkable thinker and writer, especially
on mystical subjects.

The sketch of Gertrude the Great in the *Catholic Encyclopedia* states that "her writings are colored by the glowing
richness of her Teutonic genius which found its most con-
genial expression in symbolism and in allegory." It is interesting to note that the fervent admirers of Gertrude whom
I have mentioned are all from the nations outside Germany,
from Spain, France, Switzerland, and England. When such
tributes come from peoples as strikingly individualistic as
these, one can rest assured that nothing less than genius in
some form is the object of them. Admiration for Gertrude
is not conventional. It is forced from hearts like her own
who recognize that her thoughts had their origin so close
to the heart of human nature that they will always be of
interest to humanity.

But this does not conclude the roll call of the famous
Gertrudes who lived at that period. Scarcely more than a
generation had passed when another Gertrude appeared, this
time in Holland, who attracted such wide attention in her
own age that the memory of her has been cherished ever
since. She was the lady known in her day as Gertrude van
der Oosten, and her death took place in 1358. She occupied
herself with the charitable purpose of bringing aid to the
poor at Delft in Holland and asked to be admitted among
the Beguines, those devoted apostles of the poor who lived
in little groups of houses and did so much, particularly for
the care of poor children. Besides her charity she was deeply
occupied with the contemplative life. As a reward for her

intense devotion she suffered, like St. Francis of Assisi, from the stigmata or wounds of the crucified Saviour. After a time she asked that the external manifestations might cease so that they would attract less attention, but the suffering of the Passion made itself manifest in her every week. She deeply influenced the people of her time and is remembered faithfully by the Hollanders.

Most of us are interested in knowing something not only about the nuns and married women of the Middle Ages, but also about those who remained unmarried in the world and especially those whom we would call old maids. There is a passage in Father Bede Jarrett's *Social Theories of the Middle Ages*,[4] taken from Messer Donato Velluti's autobiographical manuscript of the fourteenth century, which shows clearly that an old maid might be very happy in the Middle Ages "once she gave up struggling." The Florentine gossiper tells the story of two such lives:

"Cilia and Gherardina never married. For a great while they remained maids in the world hoping to have husbands, but when they lost all hope they became sisters of San Spirito (a non-conventual confraternity for works of mercy not unlike our hospital auxiliaries). They earned much money, more indeed than sufficed for their support, by winding wool, and their brothers did never need to keep a servant. They were exceedingly kind of heart and great talkers. They died in that same pestilence of 1348, being both forty years of age or more."

Father Jarrett's comment on this is very interesting: "It is a peaceful, quiet picture, the long wait [not so very long if they died in their forties], the half-conventual life, the kindness, the chatter, the home attended to, the equal end."

The general impression, however, is that women in the Middle Ages were rather frequently the subjects of severe treatment at the hands of their lords and masters and bore it almost as patiently as Boccaccio's patient Griselda, often

---

[4] Boston, 1926. Little, Brown and Company.

considered as a type of the long-suffering women of the time. But the people of the Middle Ages had a strong sense of humor. And when we turn to find what it was they laughed at, we discover that one of the commonest sources of boisterous laughter was the occasional temper of wives and their readiness even to let their lords and masters feel at times the impact of their hands.

One of the very popular mystery plays was that of Noah and his wife. Noah was usually represented as a little old man with a long white beard, which might be expected to command reverence, but he always came off second best in the quarrels with his wife. As the story was usually told, when Noah began to build the ark Mrs. Noah was perfectly sure that there must be something wrong with him, that he was wasting his time and not properly providing for the household. In some of the mystery plays of the Middle Ages she is represented as talking very freely with her gossips about the foolishness of this old husband of hers and the crazy notion that has come into his head. When the ark was finished and the rain had already begun and when all the animals were aboard and the family was ready to embark, Noah invites his wife to come into the ark so as to be ready for the worst. She refuses to accept his invitation, so he turns to the boys, and they proceed to bundle mother in. As she passes her husband on the way into the ark he receives a good box on the ear, after which his wife seems better satisfied. Almost needless to say this bit of what we would call slapstick humor was welcomed with loud guffaws of laughter by the medieval audiences.

Only that such relationship between husband and wife was recognized as one of the realisms in life as it was lived, this would not have been so popular a scene as it was. Manifestly some of the men suffered occasionally at the hands of their wives and the women in the audiences rejoiced thereat. Noah's appeal to his boys to manage their mother makes it clear that he must have had no little experience on other occasions with similar conduct on this particular matron's part. The medieval husbands laughed at the scene because they understood the quandary of the husband. The wives laughed because they were glad that some husbands at least "got what was coming to them."

If there is any one conclusion that would be forced on the reader of medieval documents relating to women it is that the women were very individual, and that the men complained of them for very contradictory qualities. For, as pointed out by Father Bede Jarrett, there are complaints that some women are constantly running in search of idle pleasure, and that they are powdering and painting themselves — surely not for the sake of winning their husbands' affections — and that they are following all the vagaries of fashion, not so much for the men's sake as because they want to be like other women. On the other hand, there are complaints that some women pay too much attention to their homes, and some are too devoted to their children, and they thus do not make home as pleasant as it ought to be for their husbands. We hear the echo in our own time that "the wife must keep her man." Some are blamed for being too occupied with their home affairs and with details of their husbands' business, sometimes even when that business is not conducted according to Christian practice, as for instance usury or certain phases of politics. The result is that they are said to have little time for their religion and for God.

There are passages in medieval sermons which make it very clear that there was just as severe a denunciation of fashions in the older time as in ours. Preachers complained of the foolishness of homely women who tried to make themselves appear beautiful by artificial means, and of the beautiful women who tried to enhance their beauty by like means. Some of their special denunciation was reserved for the hair dyeing, so common at various times during the Middle Ages.

The friars complained of "the vagaries of fashion that changed hair from black to white and from white to gold and from gold to black again." These complaints were so common that "it is hard to find a theologian or a Scriptural commentator or a preacher or even a poet who did not denounce these and similar practices and describe instead the charm of natural beauty and the untouched complexion and the fragrance of the rose."[5]

No wonder that there are frequent denunciations in medieval literature of the evil effects of women upon mankind, and of the insidious snares which they spread abroad for the capture of poor innocent man. Sometimes, to read the sermons that have come down to us, it would seem as though women were mainly occupied with just one thing — wasting their husband's goods. Manifestly women were just about the same in the Middle Ages as they are in our time, and just as different from one another, some of them too domestic and some of them too gadabout, and all of them probably too good for their husbands as a rule.

The more we have come to know about the women of the Middle Ages, the deeper is the realization that feminine human nature has not changed any in the centuries since. Some of the medieval women had no inclination for marriage and they found an occupation for mind and body in a convent or sometimes in the care of their own folks who needed them. Some of them, who were not able to attract or to secure a husband, found that life could be happy enough once they gave up their efforts and they became the beloved aunts of growing nieces and nephews, and held a very interesting place in the affections of their relatives. Some of them as Mother Superiors of religious communities became managing women, thoroughly capable of organizing and developing not only a convent but a whole series of them, with sometimes hundreds of Sisters under their control. More than one of them

---

[5] Jarrett, *op. cit.*

proved wonderful helpmates for their husbands, and in case of his untimely death managed the affairs of his estate for the benefit of his children, or sometimes they acted as regent in a principality or kingdom and achieved quite as great success in such positions as did the men. A great many of them had intellectual tastes and aspirations, and secured opportunities to satisfy them. A few of them even found that they could make a success in law or medicine and prove a help to their generation and especially to their own sex.

XIV

THE MEDIEVAL ENCYCLOPEDISTS

A VERY common impression exists that the men of the Middle Ages were lacking in that special quality of inquisitiveness which is the source of success. They are supposed to have cared little for information for its own sake and are often declared to have shut their eyes to the world around them. In a word, it is thought that they preferred to use their imagination to account for things rather than make investigations which would secure for them definite knowledge. Impressions like these vanish as soon as men acquire even a slight familiarity with the books to which the people of the Middle Ages turned so frequently for knowledge on matters dubious or unknown. As a result of their desire for facts, many manuscript copies of books of information, some of them well deserving the name *encyclopedia*, were made. With the invention of printing numerous copies of these were called for, showing how thoroughly the men of the Middle Ages appreciated them and how ready they were to make sacrifices of all kinds in order to secure the diffusion of information.

ISIDORE OF SEVILLE

Almost at the beginning of the Middle Ages there was such a demand for information on many topics that one of the most important ecclesiastics of the time, Isidore of Seville, compiled an encyclopedia which for nearly a thousand years proved a popular source of knowledge for clerics, that is, for all persons who could read and write. It circulated very freely during the Middle Ages in manuscript and was among the very early books to be printed, although by the time of the invention of this art some 900 years had elapsed since its original composition. Isidore's work was reprinted a number of times. A superb edition of it, edited by a distinguished German scholar, was issued in our generation.

Isidore came of one of those families who are proud to have the privilege of giving a number of their members to the service of the Church. No less than three of them became important members of the hierarchy in Spain. Isidore's elder brother, Leander, was his immediate predecessor in the archbishopric of Seville, while his younger brother, St. Fulgensis, was the bishop of Astigi. The distaff side of the house was represented, also, for Isidore's sister, Florentina, was the Mother General of over a thousand religious women distributed in some forty convents throughout the Spanish peninsula. We have such religious families in our own day who give proudly and freely of their members to the Church. This makes it easy for us to understand the situation and to realize what little change there is in a matter of this kind even after the lapse of nearly 1,500 years.

Isidore received his elementary education in the cathedral school of Seville where besides following the *trivium* and *quadrivium,* the so-called seven liberal arts, he devoted himself also to Latin, Greek, and Hebrew. This meant that besides a good working knowledge of the three languages most helpful in the understanding of Scripture, he had a training in logic, grammar, and rhetoric, and a scientific mental development, since the *quadrivium* embraced not only arithmetic and geometry, but astronomy and geography, as well as music, from the standpoint of the Pythagorean rhythms.

It is not quite certain that in his early life Isidore was a monk, but as soon as he became a bishop he announced himself as a patron of the monks and did everything possible to make their work effective. He felt that they were the right hand of the Church. His own broad scholarship enabled him to realize how devoted monks were to the preservation and diffusion of learning, and he wanted to do as much as possible to encourage this spirit. The spread of education was his particular aim and he set himself to doing everything he could to further this cause among the people of Spain.

Without question, Isidore was the most learned man of his age. One of his colleagues among the Spanish bishops, Braulio, bishop of Saragossa, proclaimed him a man raised up by God to save the Spanish people from the tidal wave of barbarism which threatened to submerge their ancient civilization. This was then due to the invasion of the Visigoths.

Isidore has the distinction of being the last of the ancient Christian philosophers as well as the last of the great Latin Fathers of the Church. As a writer he was prolific and versatile to an extent that is extremely surprising for the period in which he lived. The best known of his writings and the most important is the *Etymologia* or *Origines* (the titles being translated into English as *The Etymology* or *Origins*). It is really an encyclopedia containing a vast storehouse of information. In it is gathered, systematized, and condensed all the learning possessed at this time. It was the most used book in the schools during the entire Middle Ages and was the favorite authority on all dubious questions, consulted freely on all manner of occasions.

The first printed edition of this book appeared in 1470 and it was reprinted nearly a dozen times during the next sixty years. There was manifestly a great demand for it. The work truly deserved the prestige accorded it, for it is a precious treasury of ancient lore. In all, Isidore quotes from 154 authors, Christian and pagan, most of whom he had evidently read in the original. When the originals of many of these authors ceased to be available, owing to conditions induced by barbaric invasions in the early Middle Ages, men supplied for them in a measure by the numerous citations made from them by Isidore.

We owe Isidore's *Etymologia* to the urging of Bishop Braulio. The bishop was so grateful for the immense amount of information he had himself personally secured from Isidore, that he pleaded with him to commit that information to writing for the benefit of others who could not know him personally and for the men of subsequent generations. Manifestly, conditions leading to authorship were not unlike those of the present time. Under the circumstances it is only proper that the work was dedicated to Bishop Braulio. He had a good deal to do with arranging it and it was he who divided it into twenty books.

Isidore wrote much besides the *Etymologia*. He published for instance a dictionary of synonyms under the title, *De differentiis verborum, The Differences of Words,* and another volume, *De differentiis rerum, The Differences of Things.* Then there is a volume, *De natura rerum, The Nature of Things,* which is really a manual of physics so far as natural philosophy was known at that time. It treats of astronomy and geography, as well as certain phases of physics. Isidore touched also upon history and biography. The first of these, the *Chronicon,* is a universal chronicle. This was followed by a volume, *De viris illustribus,* a work of Christian biography.

Some idea of the value attributed to Isidore's work as a source book of history may be gathered from the fact that Theodor Mommsen, the distinguished German historian, was willing to take up the task of editing the historical writings of St. Isidore for the *Monumenta Germaniae Historica.*[1] There is also a German translation, made about the same time, of Isidore's history of the kings of the Goths, the Vandals, and the Suevi. Some 350 years ago a complete edition of Isidore in folio was printed in Paris (1580). About the beginning of the nineteenth century a complete edition of all of Isidore's authentic works, very well edited, appeared in seven volumes.[2]

---

[1] Berlin, 1894.
[2] Rome, 1797–1803.

DURANDUS

Another writer who deserves to be counted among the medieval encyclopedists is Durandus, author of the volume, *Rationale divinorum officiorum, Significance of the Divine Offices.* He was the bishop of Mende in France about the middle of the thirteenth century, and died in Rome. His tomb, with its inscription in the handsome church of *Santa Maria Sopra Minerva* in Rome, shares with the incorrupt body of St. Catherine of Siena the distinction of a place in the only Gothic church in the city and attracts many visitors. His book has been translated into English under the title, *The Symbolism of Churches and Church Monuments.* This work has been very widely read and is highly appreciated by all students of the Middle Ages.

It is a huge volume but in spite of that is a favorite work of scholars. The best possible idea of the appreciation that came to it even two centuries after it was written can be gathered from the fact that the *Rationale* was among the first works from the pen of an uninspired writer to be accorded the privilege of print. The *editio princeps,* a real first edition of supreme value, appeared from the press of John Fust in 1459. That first "Durandus" remains one of the triumphs of printing and the charm of the typography has seldom been exceeded.

For some five centuries this work continued in such high esteem that ecclesiastical scholars considered it a disgrace not to be familiar with it. The style of Durandus has been praised highly by critics of many centuries for its straightforwardness, simplicity, and brevity. These qualities Durandus evidently owes to the hours spent in the reading of Holy Scriptures, so that he is fairly permeated by the spirit and mode of expression of the Gospels. Durandus fashions his style, consciously or unconsciously, so much on the Sacred Writings that most of his book possesses something of the impressive character and even the unction of the Bible. The impression derived from reading it is that of being brought into contact with a book on a religious subject, written in eminently appropriate tone and spirit. Durandus not only forms his style on the Scriptures but actually incorporated Scriptural extracts in his writings to such an extent as to make his work almost Scriptural. This style is eminently suitable to the subject and the method of his treatment. A quotation from the "Preome" (as it is written in the quaint spelling of the English translation) will give the best possible demonstration of this:

"All things, as pertain to offices and matters ecclesiastical, be full of divine significations and mysterious, and overflow with celestial sweetness; if so be that a man be diligent in his study of them, and know how to draw *HONEY FROM THE ROCK, AND OIL FROM THE HARDEST STONE.* But who *KNOWETH THE ORDINANCES OF HEAVEN, OR CAN FIX THE REASONS THEREOF UPON THE EARTH?* For he that prieth into their majesty, is overwhelmed by the glory of them. Of a truth *THE WELL IS DEEP, AND I HAVE NOTHING TO DRAW WITH:* unless he giveth it unto me *WHO GIVETH TO ALL MEN LIBERALLY, AND UPBRAIDETH NOT:* so that *WHILE I JOURNEY THROUGH THE MOUNTAINS* I may *DRAW WATER WITH JOY OUT OF THE WELLS OF SALVATION.* Wherefore albeit of the things handed down from our forefathers, capable we are not to explain all, yet if among them there be any thing which is done without reason it should be forthwith put away. Wherefore, I, *WILLIAM,* by the alone tender mercy of God, Bishop of the Holy Church which is in Mende, will knock diligently at the door, if so be that *THE KEY OF DAVID* will open unto me: that the King may *BRING ME INTO HIS TREASURE* and shew unto me the heavenly pattern which was shewed unto Moses in the mount: so that I may learn those things which pertain to Rites Ecclesiastical whereof they teach and what they signify: and that I may be able plainly to reveal and make manifest the reasons of them, by His help, *WHO HATH ORDAINED STRENGTH OUT OF THE MOUTH OF BABES AND SUCKLINGS: WHOSE SPIRIT BLOWETH WHERE IT LISTETH: DIVIDING TO EACH SEVERALLY AS IT WILL* to the praise and glory of the Trinity."

What becomes very clear from even a few passages like this

from Durandus is that the old calumny against the Catholic Church which declared that the reading of Scriptures was discouraged in any way, is entirely without foundation. Here is a scholar who, three centuries before Luther's time, was so saturated with Scriptural lore and Scriptural style that his writing is a marvelous echo of Holy Writ for the benefit not only of ecclesiastics but also of the laity. Anyone reading Durandus would quite surely be tempted to go back to passages in Scripture to which directly or indirectly he referred.

For those not able to secure a copy of Durandus in the original, or some of the many translations that have been made, an excellent idea of Durandus' style and his method of presentation can be obtained from the often quoted chapter of the *Rationale* on bells and their use in churches, the first paragraphs of which we quote. They are as full of interesting information as any modern writer could have possibly brought together, while they have the dignity and simplicity of the best modern prose:

"Bells are brazen vessels, and were first invented in Nola, a city of Campania. Wherefore the larger bells are called Campanae, from Campania the district, and the smaller Nolae, from Nola the town.

"You must know that bells, by the sound of which the people assembleth together to the church to hear, and the Clergy to preach, *IN THE MORNING THE MERCY OF GOD AND HIS POWER BY NIGHT* do signify the silver trumpets, by which under the Old Law the people was called together unto sacrifice. (Of these trumpets we shall speak in our Sixth Book.) For just as the watchmen in a camp rouse one another by trumpets, so do the Ministers of the Church excite each other by the sound of bells to watch the livelong night against the plots of the Devil. Wherefore our brazen bells are more sonorous than the trumpets of the Old Law, because then *GOD* was known in Judea only, but now in the whole earth. They be also more durable: for they signify that the teaching of the New Testament will be more lasting than the trumpets and sacrifices of the Old Law, namely, even unto the end of the world.

"Again bells do signify preachers, who ought after the likeness of a bell to exhort the faithful unto faith: the which was
typified in that the *LORD* commanded Moses to make a vest-
ment for the High Priest who entered into the Holy of Holies.
Also the cavity of the bell denoteth the mouth of the preacher."

VINCENT OF BEAUVAIS

The greatest of the encyclopedists of the Middle Ages, using
that term in the sense of the man who wrote by far the greatest
collection of information upon a great variety of subjects,
is the Dominican writer, Vincent of Beauvais. Unfortunately
we know comparatively little of him personally. He was apparently so preoccupied with his works that he took no pains
to leave behind him details of his life. We know that he was
subprior of the Dominican monastery in the city of Beauvais
just before the middle of the thirteenth century. We possess
no information enabling us to determine even approximately
the year of his birth or of his death. We know that he was
regarded by his contemporaries as one of the most learned
friars of his time when so many of the members of the recently
founded Franciscan and Dominican orders were deservedly
looked up to as thorough scholars. The fortunate circum-
stance of his life was his attachment to the court of King
Louis IX. St. Louis came to esteem him highly and Vincent
occupied the triple position of royal librarian, royal chaplain,
and tutor to the children of the king.

Vincent's work bears the title *The Great Triple Mirror*. It
consists of the Mirror of History,[3] the Mirror of Nature, and

---

[3] Vincent begins the first part of his great encyclopedia, the *Speculum
Historiale* or *Historical Mirror,* with the reason why he has taken up
this task. It is extremely interesting now that books have multiplied to
such an extent in our time to have Vincent insist on the impossibility for
anyone to hope to exhaust the knowledge contained in all the books that
had been written down to that time, and make it available in any way.
He said: "Since the multitude of books and the brevity of time and the
slipperiness (*labilitas*) of memory do not permit that all that has been
written can be kept in the mind," therefore he who had had the opportunity to read many books is glad to facilitate knowledge for others by
gathering together what has seemed the most important to him in the
midst of his reading.

the Mirror of Christian Doctrine. History is recounted from the standpoint of the place of Christ in the world, with many references to Augustine's *City of God*. The *Speculum Doctrinale* is a great summary of theology and of Church teaching which reveals Vincent's thoroughgoing orthodoxy and at the same time shows how simply the doctrine and mysteries of religion can be presented for the sake of such as may not have had philosophical and theological training. The Mirror of Nature holds up the mirror of the human mind to all the details of natural history. It tells besides the story of the world so far as it was known at that time. A fourth volume in this series, with the title, *Speculum Morale,* once attributed to Vincent, is now generally considered not to be from his hand.

In spite of the size of the work, which would occupy some sixty octavo volumes if printed in modern fashion, a great many manuscript copies were made. They exist to the present day in a number of great European libraries. Some of them have been purchased in recent years by Americans at very startling prices, for collectors have learned to appreciate these old books. Vincent's encyclopedia was not a popular work like that of his Franciscan rival in encyclopedic authorship, Bartholomew, but it was frequently referred to by scholars and had a place in important libraries, while universities kept copies of it for consultation by students.

Vincent's work was one of the earliest accorded the distinction of being printed. The printing was done with the loving care that makes the *editio princeps* (1459) one of the most precious bibliographic treasures in existence. The type faces are excellent, the spacing makes reading easy, paper and ink are almost untouched by time, and the margins are nicely measured to bring out the printed pages. The beautiful example of this edition in the reserve collection of books at the New York Public Library was the copy which belonged to William Morris. When the English poet artist was designing houses for his compatriots that would make worthy homes for people of taste, he found that the books being printed in the last quarter of the nineteenth century were so ugly that he did not want to give them a place in his houses. He went back then to the first generation of printing for models and on his own Kelmscott Press imitated some of the early printed books with such excellent results that now the Kelmscott volumes themselves command high prices.

Vincent's main purpose was to collect information on all possible subjects from the writings of older authors whose books would not be available for the great mass of readers. Authors of every description, from the pagan philosophers of Greece to the literary and historical classics of Rome, down to the various Arabian writers, were put under contribution by Vincent, so as to secure information from original sources. Aristotle, Augustine, Albertus Magnus, particularly Pliny and Isidore, were quoted frequently. The famous Arabs: Rhazes, Avicenna, Averroës, and Albumaser, are repeatedly referred to.

Vincent had the good fortune to enjoy intimate relations with Louis IX and was able to employ a group of his Dominican brothers in the collection of this information, though he probably had himself the duty of arranging and editing it. The result was the huge encyclopedia deserving that name even in our broadest sense of the word, since it compares in size with our encyclopedias of modern times. The many copies of it that were made by hand show how deeply interested were the scholars of earlier days in having near them a source of information on which they could depend.

Vincent's discussion of dreams and their meaning gives an excellent idea of his method of imparting information. He quotes half a dozen of the older authors who had written on this subject as well as his own contemporaries. He was very concrete in his explanation of the origin of these natural phenomena, stating that they were due to a full or an empty stomach, and were also caused by the train of thought of the dreamer, so that people dreamt of what they were thinking about before going to sleep. He suggested, however, that dreams might be due to demons acting upon the sleeper and might be revelations from on High made through angels.

Lynn Thorndike in his *History of Magic and Experimental Science,* boiling down some of Vincent's work with regard to dreams, quotes him as saying substantially: "Dreams are powerfully affected by the disposition of the sleeper, so that peculiarities of his make themselves felt in dreams which are not observed in waking hours." In a word, the interpretation of a man's dreams would help us to understand his character better than by any other way. Professor Thorndike finds in this a striking medieval anticipation of the Freudian theory of dreams. It certainly serves to show how notions, supposedly so modern, were bobbing up in men's minds in those olden times.

The smaller works of Vincent of Beauvais throw strong light on his personal character and especially on his genuine piety. Four of his opuscula were printed in a single volume at Basle (1481). They are, *The Book of Grace, The Book of the Praises of the Glorious Virgin Mother of God, The Book of St. John the Evangelist,* and *The Book for the Teaching of Royal Children.* This latter has such interesting chapter headings as: "The Selection of a Teacher," "The Method of Teaching," "The Impediments to Learning," and others of like tenor. There were few ideas in relation to education, its method and content, that Vincent did not describe. He has a series of chapters also dealing with the education of girls, which make it very clear that women were not to be left in ignorance. He emphasizes particularly the place of modesty in a young woman's life and dwells on superfluous ornaments as a serious fault. He thinks that women even more than men have a need of moral instruction. Vincent has much sane advice on education which makes it clear that the development of pedagogy, so far at least as serious thought of its problems is concerned, was not left for modern times. From his writings it is perfectly manifest that men of experience and teaching were deeply devoted at this time to applying very definite principles to the task which they considered so important.

GERALD THE WELSHMAN

A typical medieval scholar, the details of whose career and the consultation of whose works make one realize better than in any other way the breadth of the interests of many of the scholars of the Middle Ages, is *Giraldus Cambrensis*, Gerald the Welshman. He lived at the end of the twelfth and the beginning of the thirteenth century. There were few things that Gerald was not interested in. He had what we speak of now as an encyclopedic mind. Yet his manifold intellectual interests did not swamp him. The distinguished English historian, who knew so much about this period, Professor Freeman, in the preface to his edition of the last volume of Gerald's works in the Rolls series, refers to him as "one of the most learned men of a learned age." He thinks that he eminently deserves the title of "the universal scholar," nor does he hesitate to call him "the father of comparative philology." Evidently, then, he was not a mere accumulator of information but a thoroughgoing scholar who could synthesize his knowledge and analyze it in such a way as to enable him to make additions to the information of his time.

Professor Brewer, Gerald's earliest editor in the Rolls series, is even more laudatory, if possible, than Freeman. Brewer was himself a man of wide interests and therefore could appreciate Gerald very well. He did not hesitate to say of the Welsh scholar: "Geography, history, ethics, divinity, canon law, biography, natural history, epistolary correspondence and poetry employed his pen by turn and in all these departments of literature he has left lasting memorials of his ability."

Gerald is particularly noteworthy for his command of languages, not only the classical tongues but also the modern languages, and he used them all with surprising facility. Gerald quotes Welsh, Irish, English, German, and French as readily as Hebrew, Latin, and Greek. He was particularly interested in the languages of the Scriptures with which every scholar was familiar in that day. With half a dozen of these languages Gerald had an intimate scholarly acquaintance.

With all this linguistic knowledge and his deep learning in the classics, he had, as Professor Freeman says, "mastered more languages than most men of his time," but what was particularly interesting was that "he had looked at them with an approach to a scientific view which still fewer of the men of his time shared with him." English historians particularly have been enthusiastic in their acknowledgment of Gerald's learning. John Richard Green, historian of the English people, does not hesitate to go so far as to call Gerald, "the father of popular literature."

In the introduction to Gerald's *Itinerary through Wales* in the Everyman series, Llewelyn Williams says that, "Gerald is the most 'modern' as well as the most voluminous of all the medieval writers." He quotes Miss Kate Norgate who, he believes, in her *England Under the Angevin Kings,*[4] has perhaps most justly estimated the real place of Gerald in English letters:

"Gerald's wide range of subjects is only less remarkable than the ease and freedom with which he treats them. Whatever he touches — history, archaeology, geography, natural science, politics, the social life and thought of the day, the physical peculiarities of Ireland and the manners and customs of its people, the picturesque scenery and traditions of his own native land, and the scandals of the court and the cloister, the petty struggle for the primacy of Wales and the great tragedy of the fall of the Angevin empire — are all alike dealt with in the bold, dashing, offhand style of a modern newspaper or magazine article. His first important work *The Topography of Ireland* is, with due allowance for difference between the taste of the twelfth century and that of the nineteenth, just such a series of sketches as a special correspondent in our own day might send from some newly colonized island in the Pacific to satisfy or whet the curiosity of his readers at home."

---

[4] Vol. II, p. 457.

XV

THOMAS AQUINAS, GREATEST OF SCHOOLMEN

MORE than twenty-five years ago, when writing the opening sentences of the chapter on "Aquinas the Scholar" in *The Thirteenth Greatest of Centuries,* I ventured to say:

"No one of all the sons of the thirteenth century, not even Dante himself, so typifies the greatness of the mentality of this wonderful time as does Thomas, called from his birthplace, Aquinas, or of Aquin. On him his own and immediately succeeding generations, because of what they considered his almost more than human intellectual acumen, bestowed the title of Angelical Doctor, while the Church for the supremely unselfish character of his life formally conferred on him the title of Saint."

Since these sentences were written added prestige has come to Aquinas all over the world. Many universities that knew him not or knew almost nothing about him at the beginning of the twentieth century have now come to offer courses in Scholastic philosophy, in which he more than anyone else is the representative teacher and the supremely great authority on whom all students depend.

The life of Aquinas is of special interest because it serves to correct many false impressions that are only too prevalent with regard to the intellectual life of the period in which he lived. Though Aquinas came of a noble family closely related to many of the royal houses of Europe, the son of the Count of Aquino, then one of the most important nonreigning noble houses of Italy, his education was begun in his early years and was continued in the midst of opportunities such as even the modern student might envy. It is often said that the nobility at this time paid very little attention to development of the intellect and rather prided themselves on ignorance of even such ordinary attainments as reading and writing. The falsity of such assertions, however, becomes very clear with actual knowledge of conditions as they were. Doubtless many of the nobility of the time neglected education, but many more did not, and those who had the talent took advantage of educational opportunities quite as in our own day.

Aquinas' early education was received at the famous monastery of Monte Cassino, in southern Italy. Here for some seven centuries, since the very beginning of the Middle Ages, the Benedictines had been providing magnificent opportunities for the studious youth of Italy. Serious-minded students from all over Europe had the chance to secure here their higher education. When scarcely more than a boy, Thomas proceeded to the University of Naples, which at that time was under the patronage of the Emperor Frederick II and was being encouraged by him not only to take the place so long held by Salerno as the leader in the educational world of Europe but also to rival the rising universities of Paris and Bologna.

At the age of seventeen, still in the midst of his university studies, Aquinas felt a call to the Dominicans. Founded only a short time before by St. Dominic, they had already begun to make their influence deeply felt throughout the religious and educational world of the time. This determination on the part of her son, as is easy to understand, met with decided opposition on the part of his ambitious Countess mother. The Dominicans, at that time in their first generation, did not have the traditional prestige of the Benedictines. Besides, they were "mendicant friars," that is, they lived by begging alms or receiving voluntary support from their hearers, for they were the Order of Preachers. People generally had not grown accustomed as yet to the idea of mendicancy. Moreover, the family influence could be exerted to only a very slight degree among the Dominicans. As the Countess further pointed out, if her son wanted to be a clergyman he might, because of his noble connection, rise high in the hierarchy and come to occupy a very prominent place in the Church.

Every possible effort was made by the family to break Aquinas' resolution, but without avail. He was immovably steadfast, and the Dominicans prevented further efforts to nullify his vocation by sending the young scion of nobility up to Cologne where he would be far from family interference.

Providentially, as it would seem, at Cologne Thomas came under the influence of the greatest teacher of the Dominican Order, Albertus Magnus. Aquinas was far from being the most brilliant among the young men who were receiving the benefit of Albert von Bollstadt's teaching, and in his quest of thoroughness he seems even to have appeared slow witted, so that he was the butt of some of his more successful fellow students. They are said even to have dubbed him the "dumb ox," partly because of his slowness of speech and partly because of his bulkiness even as a youth. But his distinguished teacher was not deceived in his estimation of the capacity of the young Italian student, and according to tradition is said to have declared that "the bellowings of this dumb ox will be heard throughout all Christendom."

In his early twenties Thomas, after some years spent at Cologne, accompanied Albert who had been called to a teaching position at the University of Paris. There Thomas received his bachelor's degree and also took out his license to teach — the doctor's degree of our time. After this some further years were spent in the quiet and intense study of philosophy and theology at Cologne. Then at last it was that the greatness of the man began to dawn on his generation. He was called back to Paris and became one of the most popular professors at this university which had now attained the height of its fame. Perhaps no greater group of scholars and teachers has ever been gathered together than shared with Aquinas the honors of the professors' chairs at that institution. In his life

of Thomas Aquinas the Reverend Dr. Vaughan has told the
story of the group of supremely great men who were teaching
at Paris at that time:

"Albert the Great, Roger Bacon, St. Bonaventure, and St.
Thomas Aquinas, form among themselves, so to speak, a complete representation of all the intellectual powers; they are the
four doctors who uphold the chair of philosophy in the temple
of the Middle Ages. Their mission was truly the re-establishment
of the sciences, but not their final consummation. They were not
exempt from the ignorances and erroneous opinions of their day,
yet they did much to overcome them and succeeded better than
is usually acknowledged in introducing the era of modern
thought. Often, the majesty, I may even say the grace of their
conceptions, disappears under the veil of the expressions in which
they are clothed; but these imperfections are amply atoned for
by superabundant merits. Those Christian philosophers did not
admit within themselves the divorce, since their day become so
frequent, between the intellect and the will; their lives were
uniformly a laborious application of their doctrines. They realized in its plenitude the practical wisdom so often dreamed of
by the ancients — the abstinence of the disciples of Pythagoras,
the constancy of the stoics, together with humility and charity,
virtues unknown to the antique world. Albert the Great and St.
Thomas left the castles of their noble ancestors to seek obscurity
in the cloisters of St. Dominic; the former abdicated, and the
latter declined, the honors of the Church. It was with the cord
of St. Francis that Roger Bacon and St. Bonaventure girded
their loins. When the last named was sought out that the
Roman purple might be placed upon his shoulders, he begged
the envoys to wait until he finished washing the dishes of the
convent. Thus these men did not withdraw themselves within the
exclusive mysteries of an esoteric teaching; they opened the doors
of their schools to the sons of shepherds and artisans, and, like
their Master, Christ, they said: 'Come all!' After having broken
the bread of the word, they were seen distributing the bread of
alms. The poor knew them and blessed their names. Even yet,
after the lapse of six hundred years, the poor in Paris kneel
round the altar of the Angel of the Schools, and the workmen
of Lyons deem it an honor once a year to bear upon their
brawny shoulders the triumphant remains of the 'Seraphic
Doctor.'"

These four men represent the intellectual supremacy of the culminating period of the later Middle Ages. They were the fruit of the educational system of their day. Never has genius developed more richly than when these four flourished and influenced so deeply their generation. They are the flower of university life, such as it is, while the best possible index of the results achieved by university training is to be found in what they accomplished. The most interesting feature of their work is that all four of them are extremely different from one another. This individuality was emphasized and by no means merely modified in the direction of assimilation, as might have been expected from what modern critics have been wont to refer to as an illiberal and hidebound education. Medieval education was not of this kind. After seven centuries these four men are recognized as among the great lights of human genius. Their prestige is likely to endure as long as this stage of our civilization lasts.

The most interesting feature of the life of Aquinas is his almost unlimited capacity for intellectual work. He was born in 1225, or perhaps 1227, and died in 1274, so that he was not yet fifty years of age at his death. To have Albertus Magnus, who lived to be over eighty, leave many huge tomes on profound philosophical subjects is astonishing enough, but without those thirty additional years of life to have accomplished as much as Aquinas did is indeed astounding. The books he wrote fill nearly a score of folio volumes. Each one of these folio volumes contains from half a million to a million of words, so that altogether we have many millions of words on the most intricate and esoteric subjects from the pen of St. Thomas. The French have defined genius as an infinite capacity for taking pains. Aquinas had an infinite capacity for taking thought about the deepest subjects that occupy men's minds when in serious mood.

How much he was esteemed two hundred years after his death is well demonstrated by the attention accorded him by the early printers. Altogether some 300 editions of various of his works were issued in the incunabula period, that is, before 1501. Every printer of the day seemed to think it necessary to publish some work by Aquinas for the sake of the prestige which it brought to his press, but also for the very practical reason that no author that he could print commanded a better sale. This intense attention to him two centuries after his death is indeed a tribute that reveals how deeply the philosophy and theology of St. Thomas satisfied the minds of men

The greatest surprise for most people in connection with the life of Aquinas is to learn that besides being a supremely profound philosopher he was also one of the world's greatest poets. Thomas' favorite devotion, as also that of Cardinal Newman in our time, was to the Sacrament of the Holy Eucharist. This was well known, and because of it Thomas was asked by the pope to compose the Office for the then recently established Feast of Corpus Christi. Certain hymns are always incorporated in the offices of the special feast days. Ordinarily it would be presumed that a scholar like Aquinas would write or select the prose portions of the office, leaving the hymns for some other hand, or making suitable selections from the great collection of sacred poetry already in the service of the Church. Some of the hymns of St. Bernard would, it might seem, have been supremely suitable for this purpose. Aquinas, however, selected the lessons and psalms, but wrote both the prose and the hymns. Surprising though it may be, the hymns are some of the most beautiful religious poetry ever composed. They have continued to be the admiration of posterity ever since.

It is to be recalled that Thomas lived during a period when Latin hymn writing was at its highest achievement. The *Dies Irae* and the *Stabat Mater* were both written during the thirteenth century, and most of the precious Latin hymns that have been used in the Church ever since were composed in the century and a half from 1150 to 1300. The wonder is that Aquinas' hymns challenged comparison with the finest of these. While he had the advantage of an eminently devotional subject in the Blessed Sacrament, it must not be forgotten that on the other hand he had to give lyrical expression in brief formulas of words to a supremely difficult set of theological problems, providing appropriate devotional words in rhymed Latin for the worship of the Blessed Sacrament. In spite of the difficulties, Thomas succeeded not only in writing good theology but supremely great poetry. A portion of one of these hymns, the *Tantum Ergo,* consisting of the last two stanzas of the *Pange Lingua Gloriosi,* is more used in church services than any other, with the possible exception of the *Dies Irae.*

Neale, the English hymnologist, usually considered the best authority on the subject, says of this great hymn of Aquinas, the *Pange Lingua:*

"This hymn contests the second place among those of the Western Church with the *Vexilla Regis,* the *Stabat Mater,* the *Jesu Dulcis Memoria,* the *Ad Regias Agni Dapes,* the *Ad Supernam,* and one or two others, leaving the *Dies Irae* in its unapproachable glory."

Aquinas' other hymns are scarcely less beautiful than the *Pange Lingua* and have proved more stimulating in promoting devotion to the mystery of the Blessed Sacrament than any other sacred hymns we have.

Doubtless one of the greatest tributes to Aquinas is the devotion which so lofty a mind as that of Dante, so penetrating in its power of understanding human nature, had for him. It has been said that Dante's sublime poem, so supremely interesting to this modern generation of ours that some twenty-five hundred books have been written about it in the twentieth century, is the *Summa Theologica* of St. Thomas Poetized. It is not that the great Florentine poet has in any sense put Aquinas into verse, but that he has surrounded with an aureole of the sublimest poetry the profound thinking with regard to man's relations to the Deity, to his neighbors, to himself, and to the universe, which are to be found in Aquinas' writings. In a certain broad sense the two men might be called contemporaries. Dante was not yet ten years old when Aquinas was called from his great teaching work, but they represent between them the culmination of the intellectual genius of that supremely great century, the thirteenth, in its effort to solve the mystery of human life and state its meaning in terms comprehensible and satisfying to mankind. It would seem from the attention still given to the works of both these men that they have come as close to the heart of that mystery as any in the history of the race. With Aristotle, at whose feet they both sat with reverence, they constitute a trinity of intellectual geniuses that will ever command the respect and reverence of all thinking men.

Perhaps the best way to give those who have not had time or opportunity to delve into philosophic subjects, some appreciation of what the Angelic Doctor accomplished for theology and its handmaiden, philosophy, is to quote his passage on the proofs concerning our knowledge of God. His argument on the subject and its mode of presentation is not only extremely interesting but is typical of his style and manner:

"If a truth of this nature were left to the sole inquiry of reason, three disadvantages would follow. One is that the knowledge of God would be confined to few. The discovery of truth is the fruit of studious inquiry. From this very many are hindered. Some are hindered by constitutional unfitness, their natures being ill-disposed to the acquisition of knowledge. They could never arrive by study at the highest grade of human knowledge, which consists in the knowledge of God. Others are hindered by the claims of business and the ties of the management of property. There must be in human society some men devoted to temporal affairs. These could not possibly spend time enough in the learned lessons of speculative inquiry to arrive at the highest point of human inquiry, the knowledge of God. Some again are hindered by sloth. The knowledge of the truths that reason can investigate concerning God presupposes much previous knowledge; indeed almost the entire study of philosophy is directed to the knowledge of God. Hence, of all parts of philosophy that part stands over to be learned last, which consists of metaphysics dealing with divine things. Thus only with great labour of study is it possible to arrive at the searching out of the aforesaid truth; and this labour few are willing to undergo for sheer love of knowledge.

"Another disadvantage is that such as did arrive at the knowledge or discovery of the aforesaid truth would take a long time over it on account of the profundity of such truth, and the many prerequisites to the study, and also because in youth and early manhood the soul, tossed to and fro on the waves of passion, is not fit for the study of such high truth; only in settled age does the soul become prudent and scientific, as the philosopher says. Thus if the only way open to the knowledge of God were the way of reason, the human race would [remain] in thick darkness of ignorance, as the knowledge of God, the best instrument for making men perfect and good, would accrue only to a few after a considerable lapse of time.

"A third disadvantage is that, owing to the infirmity of our judgment and the perturbing force of imagination, there is some admixture of error in most of the investigations of human reason. This would be a reason to many for continuing to doubt even the most accurate demonstrations, not perceiving the force of the demonstration, and seeing the divers judgments, of divers persons who have the name of being wise men. Besides, in the midst of much demonstrated truth there is sometimes an element of error, not demonstrated but asserted on the strength of some plausible and sophistic reasoning that is taken for a demonstration. And therefore it was necessary for the real truth concerning divine things to be presented to men with fixed certainty by way of faith. Wholesome, therefore, is the arrangement of divine clemency, whereby things even that reason can investigate are commanded to be held on faith, so that all might be easily partakers of the knowledge of God, and that without doubt and error."[1]

A still more striking example of Aquinas' eminently sympathetic expression of a most difficult problem occurs in his treatment of the question of the resurrection of the body. The doctrine of the creed that men will rise again on the last day with the same bodies which they had while on earth has been a stumbling block for a great many persons from the beginning of Christianity. In recent times the indestructibility of matter and the ever-growing identification of matter and

---

[1] Book I, cix.

force have put an entirely new aspect on this problem, but have left Aquinas' argument untouched and still convincing. While the material of which man's body is composed is never destroyed, it is broken up largely into its original elements and is used over and over again in many natural processes, entering into the composition of plants and animals but also other men's bodies during the years as they flow. Here is a problem upon which it would ordinarily be presumed at once that a philosophic writer of the thirteenth century could throw no possible light for modern scientific-minded people. We venture to say, however, that in spite of all the modification of scientific thought in the twentieth century, as to the composition of matter, St. Thomas' paragraph on the resurrection of the body remains the most satisfying presentation of the subject:

"What does not bar numerical unity in a man while he lives on uninterruptedly, clearly can be no bar to the identity of the arisen man with the man that was. In a man's body, while he lives, there are not always the same parts in respect of matter but only in respect of species. In respect of matter there is a flux and reflux of parts. Still that fact does not bar the man's numerical unity from the beginning to the end of his life. The form and species of the several parts continue throughout life, but the matter of the parts is dissolved by the natural heat, and new matter accrues through nourishment. Yet the man is not numerically different by the difference of his component parts at different ages, although it is true that the material composition of the man at one stage of his life is not his material composition at another. Addition is made from without to the stature of a boy without prejudice to his identity, for the boy and the adult are numerically the same man."

In a word, Aquinas says that we recognize that the body of the undeveloped boy and of the grown man were the same, though composed of quite different material. With this in mind the problem of the resurrection takes on quite a new aspect from what it held before. What we would call attention to, however, is not so much the matter of the argument as the mode of it. It is essentially modern in every respect. Not only does Thomas know that the body changes completely during the course of years, but he knows that the agént by which the matter of the parts is dissolved is "the natural heat," while "new matter accrues through nourishment." The passage contains a marvelous anticipation of present-day physiology as well as a distinct contribution to Christian apologetics. This co-ordination of science and theology, though usually thought to be lacking among Scholastic philosophers, is constantly typical of their mode of thought and discussion, and this example, far from being exceptional, is genuinely representative of them, as all serious students of Scholasticism know.

Perhaps almost the last thing for which the ordinary student of philosophy would expect a modern teacher to recommend the reading, or rather the deep study of St. Thomas, would be to find in his writings the proper doctrine with regard to liberty, and the remedies for our modern social evils. Those who will recall, however, how well the generations of the Middle Ages faced social problems even more complex and more serious than ours — for the common people had no rights at all at the beginning of the thirteenth century, yet secured them in the course of several generations so satisfactorily as to lay the foundation of the modern history of liberty — will realize that the intellectual men of the time must have had a much better grasp of the principles underlying such problems than would otherwise be imagined.

As a matter of fact, St. Thomas' treatment of society, its rights and duties and the mutual relationship between it and the individual, is one of the triumphs of his wonderful work in ethics. It is no marvel, then, that the great pope at the end of the nineteenth century, Leo XIII, whose encyclicals showed that he had been occupied profoundly with these social problems which demand the attention of our time, recognized their tendency, appreciated their dangers, and

recommended as a remedy for them the reading of St. Thomas.
The pope in his great encyclical said:

"Domestic and civil society even, which as all see, is exposed
to great danger from the plague of perverse opinion, would
certainly enjoy a far more peaceful and a securer existence if
more wholesome doctrine were taught in the academies and
schools — one more in conformity with the teaching of the
Church, such as is contained in the work of Thomas Aquinas.

"For the teachings of Thomas on the true meaning of liberty
— which at this time is running into license — on the divine
origin of all authority, on laws and their force, on the paternal
and just rule of princes, on obedience to higher powers, on
mutual charity one toward another — on all of these and
kindred subjects, have very great and invincible force to over-
turn those principles of the new order which are well known to
be dangerous to the peaceful order of things and to public
safety."

Some people are inclined to think that the papal encyclical
recommending St. Thomas as the guide and master in the
schools will inevitably hamper the progress of thought. The
pope himself answers this question. The Scholastic philosophers were never opposed to investigation, and indeed "they
well understood that nothing is of greater use to the philosopher than diligently to search into the mysteries of nature and
to be earnest and constant in the study of physical science."
As Dr. Kennedy, in his article on Aquinas in the *Catholic
Encyclopedia,* notes: "This principle was reduced to practice
at the height of the devotion to Scholasticism when men like
Albertus Magnus and Roger Bacon as well as St. Thomas
himself and many others at that time gave large attention to
the study of natural science."

The pope also dwelt on the fact that philosophy and physical science are inseparable, for investigation alone is not sufficient for physical science: "When facts have been established
it is necessary to rise and apply ourselves to the study of the
nature of corporeal things, to inquire into the laws which

govern them, and the principles whence their order and varied unity and mutual attraction and diversity arise."

Above all the pope recommends that Catholic universities and seminaries throughout the world adopt the methods and principles of St. Thomas, and not merely the material gathered by him and the system of thought he elaborated. Pope Leo warned of the abuses that might readily creep in should we content ourselves with only a slavish adherence to medieval philosophy instead of following the methods of these philosophers themselves. They were ever intent on increasing their knowledge by observation of the facts on which they were to reason. The great pope of the end of the nineteenth century was not tying modern thought to old-fashioned ideas, but rather suggested how modern thinking might be enlarged and co-ordinated by Scholastic methods. He said: "If anything is taken up with too great subtlety by the Scholastic doctors or is too carelessly stated; if there be anything that ill agrees with the discoveries of a later age or in a word is improbable in any way, it does not enter into our minds to propose that for imitation to our age."

Aquinas' English biographer, the Very Reverend Roger Bede Vaughan, a worthy scion of that distinguished Vaughan family which gave so many zealous ecclesiastics to the Catholic Church in England and so many scholars to support the cause of Christianity, manifestly felt that he could scarcely characterize appropriately St. Thomas' great work, the *Summa,* or accord it its proper place in the realm of theology. When it is recalled that Father Vaughan was not a member of the Dominican Order, to which St. Thomas belonged, but was a Benedictine, we can understand that it was not because of any *esprit de corps* but out of the depths of his great admiration for the saint that his words of praise were written:

"It has been shown abundantly that no writer before the Angelical's day could have created a synthesis of all knowledge. The greatest of the classical Fathers have been treated of, and the reasons of their inability are evident. As for the Scholastics who more immediately preceded the Angelical, their minds were not ripe for so great and complete a work; the fullness of time had not yet come. Very possibly had not Albert the Great and Alexander (of Hales) preceded him, St. Thomas would not have been prepared to write his master-work; just as, most probably, Newton would never have discovered the law of gravitation had it not been for the previous labors of Galileo and of Kepler. But just as the English astronomer stands solitary in his greatness, though surrounded and succeeded by men of extraordinary eminence, so also the Angelical stands by himself alone, although Albertus Magnus was a genius, Alexander was a theological king, and Bonaventure a seraphic doctor. Just as the *Principia* is a work unique, unreachable, so, too, is the *Summa Theologica* of the great Angelical. Just as Dante stands alone among the poets, so stands St. Thomas in the schools."

XVI

DANTE, THE MEDIEVAL UNIVERSITY MAN

DANTE is the typical university man of the Middle Ages. During his youth he had the benefit of a well-developed education in his birthplace, Florence. During his exile he spent some time at the University of Bologna but seems to have been also at the universities of Naples and Paris, and perhaps at Oxford. During his banishment abundance of time for study accrued to him and he used it to the best advantage in securing a deep and broad mental development, as well as an immense amount of information. His *Divine Comedy* reveals that he had absorbed practically all the learning of his time: philosophic, literary, theological, and also scientific.

This last is but another of the instances already cited to show how ill-founded was the conviction of those who believed that science was despised by scholars and banned by ecclesiastics in the Middle Ages. There is no doubt as to Dante's scientific attainments. Many modern scientists are agreed in recognizing Dante's observations of nature and his knowledge of many phases of science. There was nothing in the intellectual order that Dante was not interested in. His educational career, then, is of supreme interest.

Dante Alighieri was born in Florence in 1265 and died in 1321, at the age of 56. Shakespeare was born almost exactly three hundred years later, in 1564, and lived to be only 52. In their short lives and comparatively brief careers these two men accomplished work that has preoccupied the attention of the educated men of the twentieth century more than any other. Altogether, the librarian of Cornell University Library tells me, more than 2,500 books have been issued about Dante in the twentieth century. Cornell has the second largest Dante library in the world, the Laurentian Library in Florence being first. More than 12,000 books about Dante have been gathered at Cornell in a collection made some six hundred years after his death and more than 5,000 miles away from his place of birth. It is probable that altogether some 15,000 books have been written about Dante and these mainly by men who were themselves of far more than average mental power. Their high appraisal of Dante was due precisely to the fact that they were so capable of appreciating the realities of human interest in life. The authors who have written on Dante constitute an unusual intellectual elite, and this is even truer now in the twentieth century than it was a century ago.

As for articles about Dante in periodicals, no bibliography lists of them exist, but their number is legion. In America alone during the twentieth century literally thousands of articles on Dante must have appeared in newspapers and magazines. Especially was this true at about the time of the six-hundredth anniversary of the poet's death, in 1921. In spite of the disturbing conditions which had developed after the war a flood of Dante articles issued from the press, many of them from the hands of men and women who were looked upon as intellectual leaders in their countries.

Dante has been the subject of profound and productive study not only in Italy but in France and Spain, and also, during the twentieth century particularly, in England and in distant America. All of the American countries, including particularly Latin America, have made important contributions to Dante literature. Without exaggeration Dante may be said to be the man who has attracted most attention from the educated class of the world. He has probably been for them the subject of more study and a stimulus to more writing than any other man who has ever lived, with the single exception of Shakespeare.

This Dante who has so riveted the attention and caught the admiration of the literary world, of the poets, critics, scholars, historians, and university professors, is by universal consent the incarnate spirit of the Middle Ages. If you would understand the Middle Ages, study Dante. That is the proclamation of many who best know the great poet and his age.

There are a great many who insist that they do not like Dante, and above all that they cannot find in him all that his admirers point out. Indeed many readers are almost inclined to think that something of a conspiracy exists to exaggerate the significance of this medieval poet. They are quite frank to declare that there cannot be so much in Dante since they fail to find it in his work. The only appropriate response to that state of mind is the answer which Turner, the great English painter, made to a supercilious member of the English nobility who was looking at one of his paintings and remarked, a little petulantly perhaps, "Do you know, Mr. Turner, I don't see all that in nature." To which Turner, with a sad lack of gallantry, replied, "Aren't you sorry, Madame, that you don't?"

There is such a universal accord of praise for Dante on the part of all who have the best right to an opinion with regard to great poetry that those who cannot bring themselves to join with it must just feel sorry that they are lacking in some quality of mind which makes admiration of Dante a significant mental trait in nearly all the distinguished men since his time — if only they have once been drawn into close touch with him.

To be even a little familiar with the literature that has gathered around Dante is to be inevitably brought to the conclusion that if ever a man deserves to be characterized as a poet, which in its Greek etymology means a creator, surely it must be Dante. Competent critics of all nations are united in proclaiming his power. Our own James Russell Lowell said of him: "In all literary history there is no such figure as Dante, no such homogeneousness of life and work, such

loyalty to ideas, such sublime irrecognition of the unessential."
It has been suggested that art is the elimination of the obvious
and the superfluous, and our American poet critic felt that
Dante was the very incarnation of the poetic art.

Lowell's comparison of Dante and Milton brings out clearly
how far above his English brother poet, great as he is recognized to be, was the Italian. The two poets dealt with the
spiritual world; God and the angels and men's relations to
them were the theme of their epics. Lowell said: "Milton's
angels are not to be compared with Dante's, at once real and
supernatural; and the Deity of Milton is a Calvinistic Zeus,
while nothing in all poetry approaches the imaginative grandeur of Dante's vision of God at the conclusion of the
Paradise."

In that same generation, when Dante's work was already
some six hundred years old, another distinguished critic and
literary man of the English-speaking countries, John Ruskin,
said of Dante: "I think that the central man of all the world,
as representing in perfect balance the imaginative, moral, and
intellectual faculties all at their highest, is Dante." Ruskin is
not now accepted as the significant leader that he was in the
Victorian period, nor does he sway such critical influence as
was accorded him at that time, but after a period of comparative neglect he is coming to be thought more of in our day
than at the beginning of the twentieth century. If there is one
thing in the world that is true it is that Ruskin could think.
He possessed a critical faculty far above the average, so
that he could express his thoughts in an English style which
has been equaled only by Cardinal Newman and never excelled by anyone. His opinion carries weight.

Dante, it may be said, has all the elements that would seem
to make him an almost inevitable object of neglect in our
day, for the very heart of Dante's thinking is a profound
belief in a spiritual world so lacking with us. And yet, so far
from being neglected, he has been studied deeply and read
by distinguished intellectuals not once but over and over

again. As we shall see, the tributes of James Russell Lowell and of Ruskin have been multiplied many times over from the pens of those who have the most right to an opinion with regard to him. Dante, true medieval as he is in every way, breathing the very spirit of the Middle Ages, must be considered to be probably the greatest secular poet who ever lived.

Dante's greatness was recognized in his own Italy just as soon as his writings began to be disseminated among his people Giovanni Villani, who died in 1348 and had been Dante's neighbor in Florence, besides being with him at the jubilee in Rome in 1300, has given us a brief sketch of his life, mentioning his studies at Bologna as well as at Paris and his travels in many parts of the world. He gives a list of all his principal works and deems him worthy of perpetual honor. Within scarcely more than twenty-five years after his death Dante had already become one of the great names of Florence and he was hailed as one whose works were destined not to perish.

Shortly after the middle of the fourteenth century both Boccaccio and Petrarch recognized Dante's genius. In 1373 Boccaccio at the request of the civic authorities of Florence gave public lectures on the *Commedia* every Sunday in the cathedral! In view of all that has been said of ecclesiastical opposition to Dante it is of particular interest to note the place where these lectures were delivered.

To Boccaccio we owe the details of the personal appearance of the poet. There was nothing very striking about this except his deep seriousness, but Boccaccio spoke of him as *il divino poeta*. It is to him that we owe the tradition that Petrarch deliberately refrained from reading the *Commedia* through fear of impairing his own originality if he came under the spell of so great a master.

According to tradition Boccaccio wrote out the whole poem as a gift for Petrarch and thus tempted him to read it. Petrarch at once recognized Dante as the prince of Italian poets who had written in their mother tongue and he proclaimed that "the subtle and profound conception of the *Commedia* could not have been set in writing without the special gift of the Holy Spirit." The cult of Dante proved contagious and professorships for lectures on the *Commedia* were founded in other cities in Italy not long after that of Florence. At Bologna Benvenuto Ramboldi da Imola was the lecturer. His lecture notes were afterward written out by him in the form of a Latin commentary, thus bringing them better to the attention of the scholarly world. Other cities were not laggard in following the example of devotion to Dante.

In another way Dante was springing into fame. The painters of Italy, just then at the beginning of a great renaissance of art, found a wide choice of subjects in the *Commedia.* Already at that time the application of Cornelius' law was making itself felt. Cornelius formulated the law that whenever Italian art has been under the influence of Dante it has been strong and vigorous, whereas it became weak and sensuous in proportion as Dante's influence over it waned. In the second half of the fifteenth century came Botticelli's illustrations for Dante, which represent an important landmark in Dante appreciation. Dean Plumptre, distinguished English Dante student and commentator, said in his *Dante: Studies and Estimates*:

"In Sandro Botticelli we have one whose mind fed on Dante until it was interpenetrated with his mind and emotions, so that he was of all artists perhaps the one in most entire sympathy with him; and he aimed at nothing less than complete illustration of the whole poem."

Orcagna in the fourteenth century, Luca Signorelli in the fifteenth, as well as Michelino, all reveal Dante's deep influence over Italian art which always made itself felt with the happiest effect.

What they thought of Dante in Italy in the fifteenth century will be best appreciated from the editions of his *Divine Comedy* issued as incunabula during the first generation of printing down to 1501. What is now considered the *editio princeps*, the first published edition of Dante, was printed at Foligno in 1472. That same year, however, two other editions were issued, one at Iesi, the other at Mantua. These command very high prices now, especially the Foligno edition because there are so many Dante lovers or book collectors — there is a distinction, almost needless to say — who would like to have them. All three of these editions are in the Morgan library in New York, where modern New Yorkers and others interested in Dante may see them. The next edition was that of Naples in 1476. Then came the much-prized edition of Dante published in Venice (1477), with Boccaccio's life of the poet as an introduction.

In 1481 was issued the Landino edition with a copper-plate illustration, almost the first copper-plate illustration for any work. The value of this is greatly enhanced by the fact that the plates for it were made by no less a person than Botticelli, the great Florentine painter who was a profound lover of Dante and who has made some very sympathetic presentations of Dante's ideas in his painting. As might have been expected, however, Botticelli's illustrations have a certain naïveté that add supremely to their interest. It has been said that no one was ever so interested in Dante as this brother Florentine. Finally, in 1487, came the Brescia edition, not by any means the last of the Dantes of the incunabula period, but having the special distinction of being illustrated by charming woodcuts, no less than 68 in number. It is not surprising that when a perfect copy comes into an auction room it commands a high price. There was more than one edition of Dante for every year after the *editio princeps*, down to the end of the incunabula period. Dante was coming into his own and his place as the supreme poet of all time was coming to be recognized.

The greatest Dante lover of Italy was Michelangelo, also a

fellow Florentine, who died just two months before Shakespeare was born. As he lived to be ninety he bridges one of the two centuries between the two greatest of modern poets. Michelangelo was himself the greatest of sculptors since the time of the Greeks — witness his David and Moses. He was the greatest decorative artist that ever lived — witness the Sistine Chapel. He was further the greatest of architects — witness, again, St. Peter's at Rome. But he was also a poet, whose sonnets equaled those of Dante and Shakespeare and in fact have never been exceled by anyone. His opinion, then, with regard to his Italian brother poet is of the highest value.

Two sonnets to Dante written by Michelangelo exist. In one of these he declares of the poet of the *Divina Commedia*:

"Nor did the world his equal ever know,"

while in the other he practically avows that he would give up all he had ever achieved to have shared Dante's exile:

"Would I were such to bear like evil fate,
To taste his exile, share his lofty mood!
For this I'd gladly give all earth calls great."

Probably the greatest loss the world of Dante appreciation — and of art — ever suffered was the loss at sea of the designs which Michelangelo sketched to illustrate the *Commedia*. They perished in the Gulf of Genoa with the sinking of the ship that carried them. The *Last Judgment* in the Sistine Chapel, with its many reminders of Dante, enables us to realize that no one could have illustrated Dante like Michelangelo.

Raphael manifestly cherished an admiration for Dante at least equal to that of Michelangelo and fortunately has left us definite evidence of that admiration. Great critics have declared that Raphael's greatest work is to be found in his frescoes in the *Camera della Segnatura* in the Vatican. Here Raphael has pictured for us the greatest men of all the world. There is a group of philosophers, a second of theologians, and a third of poets. Raphael's genius as a creative artist is attested to by the fact that he has depicted the countenances of the supreme thinkers of all time in such a way as to make the beholder appreciate their intellectual supremacy while their individuality is equally emphasized. Men who have studied these frescoes profoundly have declared that you can see the evidence of their genius in the faces Raphael created for them. In two of these galaxies of supreme genius, Raphael puts Dante — the only man to be repeated. He is among the poets, but also in the graver company of the Doctors of the Church. "In both pictures," says Plumptre, "Dante stands out and his figure most attracts the spectator's eye and lingers longest in the memory."

The Italians of the nineteenth century, just as soon as the modern Renaissance began, the *Rinascimento,* manifested their love and reverence for their divine poet. Over a hundred editions of Dante were issued between 1800 and 1865 when the whole world joined in the celebration of the sexcentenary of Dante's birth. Alfieri was particularly attracted to Dante and it is said that he even thought of himself as a second Dante — which was the highest compliment he could pay his brother Italian poet of six centuries before. During the first half of the nineteenth century a series of important lives, more than a score in number, of Dante made their appearance in Italy. Mazzini, the Italian revolutionist, looked upon Dante as the prophet of unity for Italy. The medieval poet, Plumptre held, was "the first of the great witnesses that Italy had, as a nation, the right to live not broken up into a host of petty principalities but strong and mighty, taking its place among the great powers of Europe."

The greatest of the Dante scholars of the nineteenth century in Italy was Rosmini. He was the founder of a religious order, himself given to metaphysics rather than poetry, and often considered the reviver of the study of Thomas Aquinas in the nineteenth century. Rosmini found, as did Pope Leo XIII in the generation after him, evidence abundantly satis-

fying that Dante was a faithful son of the Catholic Church,
above all a devout believer in her tenets, and a practicer of
her precepts as well as a devoted patriot. It is said that Pope
Leo XIII could take any line of Dante and go on with the
passage attached to it, for he was so faithful a Dante lover
that he knew all of the *Divine Comedy* by heart. Rosmini
and Leo represent the beginning and the end of the nineteenth
century so far as Italian reverence for Dante goes.

Toward the end of his life Rosmini passed on the torch of
honor for Dante to Manzoni, who did for Italy what Scott
did for the English-speaking people in the revival of roman-
ticism and the understanding of the Middle Ages. When
Rosmini died, Manzoni, who had been frequently with him
during his last illness, wanted to have some appropriate
memorial of his friend. He found a copy of the *Paradiso* in
which Rosmini had been reading often during the months
before the end of his life. Rosmini had found it a source of
the greatest consolation and now Manzoni was to cherish
it as a precious relic of the friend who had brought him to
the love of Dante.

One of the great Dante lovers of the first half of the nineteenth century was Silvio Pellico, who, because of his connection with the revolutionary movement in Italy, was arrested
by the Austrian government which then ruled over most of
the northern part of Italy. The story of his imprisonment
My Prisons (*Le mie prigioni*) is one of the little books that
all literature lovers confess to having read more than once.
During his imprisonment he had but two books, the Bible
and the *Commedia*, and he learned that for one as for the
other there was no end to the meaning that might be evoked
as the result of repeated reading. All his life afterward he
continued to be a devoted student of Dante, one of those who
led his fellow countrymen of the nineteenth century to appreciate the fact that they had the good fortune to be the brothers
in language of the greatest poet of all time.

The celebration of the sexcentenary of the birth of Dante,

in 1865, was the signal for a great outburst of literature of all kinds with regard to the divine poet and led to the publication of all manner of editions of his work. In 1921 came the six hundredth anniversary of his death and it was celebrated quite literally all over the world. Most of the American universities, situated five thousand and more miles away from Dante's Italy, celebrated the death of the great poet almost as if he were a fellow countryman. Meantime Dante had be. come recognized as one of the three or four universal geniuses of mankind who had expressed in words the deepest thoughts it has ever been given man to utter.

In France, just as soon as there came to be modern interest in literature, a translation of Dante was published (1596), it being the first translation of the *Commedia* into any modern European language. Then came a period of devotion to the classics and for two centuries there was almost no French interest in Dante. It was not until almost the last quarter of the eighteenth century before there was a French critical estimate of Dante, and that came from Voltaire. Nothing that I know shows so clearly the character of the mentality of Voltaire as his passage on Dante:

"You wish to know Dante? The Italians call him divine, but his is a hidden divinity. Few understand his origins. He has commentators. That is one reason more why he is not well understood. His reputation will doubtless go on increasing because no one reads him anymore. There are a score of traits of his that everyone knows by heart. That is enough to spare us the trouble of examining the rest of his work.

"This divine Dante was, they tell us, a man who was unhappy enough. Do not think for a moment that he was divine in his own time, or that he was a prophet among his own people."

That is the sort of apothegmatic writing that has made Voltaire the favorite reading of so many who like to have someone else do their thinking for them. It may be recalled that Voltaire declared once that some of the ballad singers in the streets of Paris were as great as Homer. He also suggested that Herodotus was called the "father of history" but should be called the "father of lies." Voltaire also found it very difficult to take the Almighty seriously. His mind had a very definite tendency to satirize whatever was above it. It is no wonder that he did not understand Dante and that his conclusions with regard to him served to show that he knew but very little about Dante and that little was superficial. For that reason he disposes of him all the more completely and confidently.

With the revival of Catholicism in France after the restoration of the Bourbons, and especially after the revolution of 1830, a group of illustrious men devoted themselves to bringing out the treasure inherited from the old Church, and Dante came into his own. Montalembert, Ozanam, Chateaubriand, Ampère, Lacordaire, de Lamartine, and de Lamennais, all of them representative Catholic authors and thinkers, did their share to bring the fame of Dante into the hearts and minds of their countrymen and to enable them to understand something of the environment which produced him so as to make him better appreciated.

Ozanam, above all, was the apostle of Dante not only for modern France but for the world. He visited Assisi, studied the Franciscan poets, wrote about them sympathetically yet critically, and in his monograph *Dante and Catholic Philosophy* may be said literally to have given new life to the old poet. It was as the result of his Dante studies that Ozanam was invited by Fauriel to share his work of professor of foreign literature in the Sorbonne.

Dean Plumptre has not hesitated to set this Dante monograph of Ozanam beside Dean Church's essay on Dante, James Russell Lowell's disquisition, and Hettinger's monograph written on Dante in Germany. He regards these as the four critical appraisements that must be read by anyone who hopes to have a proper understanding of Dante. Ozanam's study of Dante, the English Dante scholar holds, is "well nigh indispensable to anyone who wishes to enter into the deep

things of the *Commedia* and to understand Dante's attitude
to the mysteries of the faith. It embodies the results of a
vast range of study. It is besides lighted up here and there
by pregnant thoughts embodied in epigrammatic language."

Since Ozanam's time Dante has remained a constant subject of study for French scholars. Many books on the great
Florentine poet have been written by Frenchmen. The greatness of Dante has grown and not diminished in the course of
time. Very probably the supreme tribute to Dante from a
French poet is that attributed to Victor Hugo: "He knocks
bravely at the door of the infinite and says, 'Open, I am
Dante.' " This is one of these cryptic expressions like Carlyle's
"Dante is a promontory jutting out into the infinite," which
may mean much or little according to the temper of the reader.

Germany waited until almost the end of the eighteenth
century for any proper appreciation of the great Italian poet.
Goethe like Voltaire has pilloried himself for all time, thinking that he pilloried Dante. He thus summed up his judgment
of the *Commedia:* "The *Inferno* is abominable; the *Purgatorio*
doubtful; the *Paradiso* tiresome." Plumptre has suggested that
"the closing scene of Goethe's *Faust* seems almost a deliberate
travesty of Dante's *Paradiso,* just as the opening scene is of
the prologue to the Book of Job, Gretchen taking the place
of Beatrice." Probably nothing has so diminished the estimation of Goethe, and especially eclipsed regard for his critical
acumen, as his utter failure to appreciate or sympathize in
any way with Dante. With the nineteenth century the
Schlegels, Friedrich and August, come on the scene in Germany, and there is a new revelation in criticism. August
Schlegel names Aeschylus, Homer, Dante, and Shakespeare as
the poets who stand above all the others. He hails Dante as
the father of modern poetry and says that "acknowledging
Virgil for his master he has produced a work which of all
others most differs from the *Aenead* and in our opinion far
excels his pretended model in power, truth, compass, and
profundity."

Friedrich Schlegel, who had become a convert to the Catholic Church in that first half of the nineteenth century when the Oxford movement in England and the neo-Catholic movement in France and the yearning after something broader and deeper in religion than the popular Lutheranism of Germany, led to so many conversions, was particularly devoted to Dante. His enthusiasm carried him into a climax of estimation: "This work [the *Divine Comedy*] will ever remain an extraordinary, wonderful and characteristic monument wherein the peculiar spirit of this first Scholastico-Romantic epoch of European art and science is displayed in the most remarkable manner."

About the same time Alexander von Humboldt, the great German scientist and explorer of the beginning of the nineteenth century, was paying in his *Cosmos* a high tribute of a very different kind to Dante. What surprises him is the marvelous power of observation for the natural world around him that is to be found in Dante. The medieval people are usually said not to have been observant, indeed to have neglected observation of nature to a very great extent. Humboldt who more than anyone else in his generation might speak with authority here, was very explicit in his proclamation of Dante's power of observation. He said: "We find in the great and inspired founder of a new era, Dante Alighieri, occasional manifestations of the deepest sensibilities to the charms of a terrestrial life of nature." He further notes the inimitable grace of some of his pictures of storms, of dawn, and of appearances of the sea which make it very clear that the Italian poet was seeing things for himself and with marvelous insight into nature.

The latter half of the nineteenth century witnessed intense preoccupation with Dante on the part of Germans. Karl Witte for more than sixty years consecrated his life to scholarly Dante studies which have proved a precious treasure for succeeding generations. His editorial work in the collation of texts of manuscripts has of itself been of immense value, but besides he unearthed sonnets that had not hitherto been attributed to Dante. He translated not merely these and the other minor poems, but also the *Commedia*. He further annotated all of these translations in a way that makes his work extremely precious for Dante students of all times. Probably no foreigner has done so much for Dante as Witte.

After Witte came a group of men making translations, writing articles, presenting contributions to the German *Dante Gesellschaft*. Plumptre considers it no exaggeration to say that the Germans have taught Italians to understand and appreciate their own poet just as they have at least helped Englishmen to understand Shakespeare.

Of all the European countries the most astonishing in its relation to Dante is England. Foggy England is so different from blue-skied Italy that it would not be surprising if the poetry that appealed poignantly to one of these peoples would have little appeal to the other. Though they are separated by a thousand miles of physical distance, and are farther far from each other in mental temper, practically all the distinguished English writers who knew Dante well were deeply enthusiastic devotees of the great Italian poet. English interest began almost in Dante's lifetime, making it clear that there was much more intimate touch between distant parts of the Christian world at that time than has been thought. Chaucer's acquaintance with Dante, though Dante's death and Chaucer's birth occurred in the same third decade of the fourteenth century, began when he was a young man and continued all his life. Many of the Canterbury tales carry references to Dante, and Chaucer seems to have taken special delight in translating Dante's hymn to the Blessed Virgin, which occurs in the first part of the thirty-third canto of the *Paradiso*. Even in those manuscript days, when the multiplication of copies was so difficult, Chaucer seems to have had the opportunity to study Dante's great poem in its entirety.

Gower, Chaucer's friend, mentions Dante the poet, and Lydgate in his *Fall of Princes* speaks of Dante as, "of Flor-

ence the laureate poet, demure of loke, all filled with patience,"
so that, as Plumptre suggests, he would almost seem to have
seen the Bargello portrait. Lydgate mentions the three parts
of the *Commedia*. Many other English writers, before the
Reformation and after it, were well acquainted with Dante.
One of these English students thoroughly appreciative of
Dante was Sir Philip Sidney. While the structure and style
of the *Faërie Queene* are modeled upon Tasso rather than
Dante, it has been pointed out that there are many parallel-
isms with Dante in the poetic writings of Spenser. Similarly
it is hinted that certain passages in Shakespeare's Sonnets indicate that the greatest of English poets was in intimate
touch and deepest sympathy with the greatest of Italian poets.
It has even been suggested by a writer in *Blackwood's* that
the *Vita Nuova* of Dante holds the key to the yet unsolved
mystery of Shakespeare's Sonnets.

England of the nineteenth century is the special jewel in
the crown of Dante. Translations of him began at the end of
the eighteenth century and Dante attracted the attention not
only of literary folk but also of painters. Sir Joshua Reynolds'
picture of Ugolino was the first of English illustrations of
Dante and this was followed, just as the nineteenth century
began, by Blake's illustrations. These have attracted attention for their weird, titanic conception. Blake declared that
he had received visits not only from the spirit of Dante but
also from those of Shakespeare and Milton. Within the first
decade of the nineteenth century Flaxman was commissioned
by Mr. Hope to make a series of illustrations for Dante. He
had already made illustrations for the Greek poets and so had
the inspiration that would fit a supremely great poet of the
modern time. He made no less than one hundred engravings
of scenes from Dante. Distinguished Dante scholars have
declared that Flaxman was finely in tune with Dante's genius
and that his illustrations are the most satisfying, not except-
ing even those of Botticelli. The Englishman's illustrations
for the *Paradiso* are particularly sympathetic.

The translation by Cary in blank verse became the popular edition of the poet in English and practically all quotations are made from it. Cary undoubtedly was very largely responsible for the great revival of interest in Dante which now took place in England. His greatest auxiliary was Samuel Taylor Coleridge whose lectures contain some very illuminating passages with regard to the great Italian. One of Coleridge's statements is: "You cannot read Dante without feeling a gush of manliness of thought within you." In another passage he says: "Dante is the living link between religion and philosophy. He philosophised the religion and Christianised the philosophy of his day." The profundity of Scholasticism and of Aquinas' great works itself were almost entirely unknown in the England of Coleridge's time and so the English philosopher was quite unaware that Dante represents to a large extent Scholastic philosophy adapted to poetry, while his great source of philosophic truth was Aquinas.

Practically all the writers who reached distinction in England in the first half of the nineteenth century paid their tribute to Dante. Lord Brougham declared in his inaugural address as Lord Rector of Glasgow University that there can be "no better training for pulpit or forensic eloquence than the verse that embodied the suffering of Ugolino and the scorn of Farinata."

Lord Macaulay's essay on Milton contains some rather unexpected passages in the comparison drawn by him between Dante and Milton, in which he decidedly favors Dante, in spite of the fact that he was never prone to put foreigners above Englishmen. Hallam in his *Literature of Europe,* deals similarly with Dante. All this was likely to make English readers suspect something of Dante's commanding genius, since their own most ardent lovers of English literature placed Dante above Milton. Other factors, too, contributed to this end. It was told of Sidney Smith, for instance, that he found solace in his old age in the study of Dante.

Wordsworth, Shelley, Southey, Byron — all show their acquaintance with Dante. Indeed Byron in his *The Prophecy of Dante* manifests that he had penetrated the meaning of Dante better than any Englishman of his day. Friedrich Schlegel noted in his *History of Literature* that Dante's chief defect is a lack of gentle feelings. Byron's comment was:

"Lack of gentle feelings? With Francesca da Rimini and the father's feelings in Ugolino and Beatrice and La Pia! Why there is a gentleness in Dante above all gentleness. . . . Who but Dante could have introduced any gentleness at all into hell? Is there any in Milton's? No; and Dante's heaven is all love and glory and majesty."

Unfortunately Robert Browning's cordial tribute to Dante is contained in *Sordello*. This represents a striking effort of the modern poet at an expression of appreciation for his brother seer of six centuries before, but it is so obscure, especially in the introductory passages, that all but the most enthusiastic Browning lovers have been deterred from it. His wife, Elizabeth Barrett Browning, was more fortunate in her tribute, and with her all the poets who attracted any attention in England at this time proclaim their admiration for Dante. When in 1865 Florence celebrated the six hundredth anniversary of the birth of Dante, it invited among others Tennyson, the English poet laureate, to send his tribute. In it Tennyson graciously expresses a sense of his own inferiority to the world's great bard and acknowledges the supreme genius of Dante:

> King, that hast reigned six hundred years, and grown
> In power, and ever growest! Since thine own
> Fair Florence, honouring thy nativity —
> Thy Florence now the crown of Italy —
> Hath sought the tribute of a verse from me,
> I, wearing but the garland of a day,
> Cast at thy feet one flower that fades away.

Perhaps almost the last man one might think of as feeling that he was deeply indebted to Dante would be Gladstone, the great practical-minded politician whose thirst for information would seem to preclude the possibility of his having that refinement of critical judgment that would enable him to appreciate Dante. His Homeric studies, nonetheless, might well warn us as to the superficiality of such a judgment. The fact is that Gladstone hailed Dante not only as a supreme poet and a solemn master but proclaimed his poem a "vigorous discipline for the heart, the intellect, the whole man." When far advanced in years Gladstone said in a letter to an Italian friend: "In the school of Dante I have learned a great part of that mental provision which has served me to make the journey of life up to the term of nearly seventy-three years."

But the greatest surprise is to find John Ruskin and Thomas Carlyle in agreement in their lofty estimation of Dante. While Ruskin thought of him as the central man of all the world, with the imaginative, moral, and intellectual faculties all at their highest, Thomas Carlyle wrote:

"For the intense, Dante is intense in all things; he has got into the essence of all. . . . For rigor, earnestness and depth he is not to be paralleled in the modern world. To seek his parallel we must go into the Hebrew bible and live with the antique prophets there."

Add to these two judgments that of a third writer with individual peculiarities so striking that it is astonishing to find three such men at one in their enthusiastic estimate of Dante. That third personality is Cardinal Manning, who believed that Dante was just below the inspiration of Holy Writ. A passage from a letter of his written to Father Bowden, in commendation of the Oratorian's translation of Hettinger's work on Dante's *Divine Comedy*, runs:

"There are three works which always seem to me to form a triad of Dogma, of Poetry and of Devotion, — the *Summa* of St. Thomas (Aquinas), the *Divina Commedia* and the *Paradisus Animae*. [This last, the *Paradise of the Soul*, is a little volume of mysticism from the Middle Ages that many people have found extremely beautiful.] All three contain the same outline of the faith. St. Thomas traces it on the intellect, Dante upon the imagination, the *Paradisus Animae* upon the heart. The poem unites the book of Dogma and the book of Devotion, clothed in conceptions of intensity and of beauty which have never been surpassed nor even equalled. No uninspired hand has ever written thoughts so high and words so resplendent as the last stanza of the *Divina Commedia*. It was said of St. Thomas, *post summam Thomae nihil restat nisi lumen gloriae* (after the *Summa* of St. Thomas nothing remains except the light of glory). It may be said of Dante, *post Dantis Paradisum nihil restat nisi visio Dei* (after the *Paradise* of Dante nothing is left for us except the vision of God Himself)."

There was scarcely a great scholar in England who did not lay his tribute at the feet of Dante. Dean Milman, the dean of St. Paul's, the well-known translator of Aeschylus and Horace, and the historian of Latin Christianity, did not hesitate to say: "Christendom owes to Dante the creation of Italian poetry, through Italian, of Christian poetry." He can only compare him with Tacitus whom, almost needless to say, Dean Milman considered one of the greatest of historians.

Probably the best summary of the place that Dante holds in the modern world not only for his fellow countrymen but for all the cultured nations, comes to us from Professor Edmund G. Gardner, who has published a series of books with regard to Italian subjects and who is the professor of Italian literature at University College, London. In his little volume, *Italian Literature*,[1] he speaks of Dante as "the supreme poet of the Italian nation — perhaps the greatest figure in the literature of the world." He adds that Dante is "to some extent the father of the Italian language and Italian literature; the incarnation of Italy's genius, the interpreter of her past and the prophet of her future." And then there is a paragraph that helps to the understanding of Dante better than any other such brief passage anywhere:

"Dante is not only the supreme poet but the national hero of Italy. A man of action no less than of thought, he strove

---

[1] London, 1927.

in the turbulent politics of his time to translate his dreams in the sphere of ideas to the sphere of facts: first his dream of a city-state for which he strove so manfully within the walls of Florence, 'Florence the most beautiful and most famous daughter of Rome'; and then, when he went forth into exile (1302) under sentence of death and his eyes opened to a wider political horizon, his dream of a restored unity of civilization in a renovated Roman empire, a dream of peace and freedom for mankind in which Italy should have a leading part to play. Thus it has been said that Dante died for Florence and rose a citizen of Italy — to become the greatest citizen of the world."

One is tempted to quote still further from Gardner because his profound knowledge of Dante cannot but help others who have not had his opportunities for study to an understanding of the majestic figure that Dante is in the literature of all time:

"Dante is the supreme interpreter of an epoch of abiding significance in the history of man. He interprets it not only by rendering intelligible the intellectual, political and religious heritage of the later Middle Ages but also by his unique revelation of the passions and motives of his contemporaries; the men and women with whose souls he meets and speaks in his visionary journey through the three spirit realms, stand out from his cantos with an actuality, a dramatic power of delineation that Shakespeare himself was hardly to surpass. . . . Dante is the poet of what Francis Thompson called 'love's possible divinities and celestial prophecies'; and he is the poet of Eternity when he ends by realizing this soul's whole capacity of love and knowledge, sees 'bound by love into one volume what is dispersed in leaves throughout the universe,' and finds desire and will brought into perfect harmony with 'the love that moves the sun and the other stars.'"

Probably the most surprising feature of the immense Dante literature that has accumulated during the past hundred years is the contributions that have been made to it by Americans. The subject of Dante's great poem, the other world, has been losing its interest for the men of these later generations because their religious faith has been sapped. Dante was medievally minded to the core of his being, and it would seem as though anything that he wrote could have very little appeal to the practical-minded men of our American republic of the late nineteenth and the early twentieth centuries. In spite of these considerations, which would seem to preclude the possibility of Dante's being more than a subject for study by a very few dry-as-dust devotees, his modern American admirers have been many in number, enthusiastic in character, and have cordially devoted themselves to the study of him and spent much time and effort writing about him, so that their fellow countrymen might be able to appreciate him adequately.

The American Dante movement began with the group of literary men of whom we think the most in this country, Longfellow, Lowell, Oliver Wendell Holmes and, as so many thought him, his even cleverer brother John, Charles Eliot Norton, and a group of other men only less widely known in the history of literature. They founded the Dante Club at Cambridge which held its meetings every week during the scholastic year and formed a kind of committee of consultation for the discussion of the difficulties of the text and the elucidation of the meaning of difficult passages during the progress of Longfellow's translation of the *Divine Comedy*. This Dante Club later expanded into the Dante Society which continued to exist for many years at Cambridge and continued to publish its transactions until the beginning of the twentieth century.

The supreme American tribute to Dante was Longfellow's devotion of his leisure hours for many years to the translation of the great Florentine poet, with such notes and commentaries, as well as literary parallels, as would enable brother Americans to comprehend all the more readily and thoroughly the meaning of this supreme poet. Longfellow had the feeling that if he could lift up American scholarship and criticism to a better understanding of the genius of this great Florentine poet he would accomplish much more for the culture of our people than anything he might be able to do by means of his own poems. At this time Longfellow was looked up to as probably our greatest American poet, and therefore his worship at the feet of his Italian colleague of six centuries before meant all the more for his readers.

The next greatest American tribute is the essay on Dante by the poet, James Russell Lowell, which may be found in the first volume of his collected essays, *Among My Books*. Of this tribute Plumptre remarks: "Take it all in all it seems no exaggeration to say that it is simply the most complete presentation of what Dante wrote, of what the man himself was, that exists in any literature." Dean Plumptre himself spent many years in translating Dante's supreme poem into *terza rima,* and adding annotations which have rendered his edition invaluable for serious students of Dante.

While James Russell Lowell's essay on Dante is an acknowledged masterpiece of critical appreciation, his essay on Shakespeare is probably one of the finest contributions to the proper appreciation of the greatest of English poets that has been written. It is important therefore to note the comparison he institutes between these two supreme poets. He says:

"Almost all the other poets have their seasons but Dante penetrates to the moral core of those who once fairly come within his sphere and possesses them wholly. His readers turn students, his students zealots, until what was a taste becomes a religion. If Shakespeare be the most comprehensive intellect, so Dante is the highest spiritual nature that has expressed itself in rhythmical form."

A very interesting feature of the literature that has gathered round the name of Dante lies in the fact that the great Italian poet, who was thoroughly steeped in Catholic philosophy and theology and whose sublime masterpiece has been declared to be Catholicity itself in poetry, has won and retained the enthusiastic devotion of countless non-Catholic scholars of many countries, most of whom had little sympathy with the Church itself. In an article on "Philip Wicksteed, Dante Scholar"[2]

---

[2] *The Moraga Quarterly*, San Francisco, Winter, 1931, p. 30.

Brother Leo in fact states: "In England, where for more than a century Dante studies have found favor, nearly all the eminent commentators on the *Commedia* have been non-Catholics." This same thing is true of the men in the United States who have been most ardently enthusiastic in Dante studies and who have devoted themselves to long years of writing about Dante in order to make the great medieval poet better understood and appreciated. Monsignor Slattery in his volume, *My Favorite Passage from Dante,* in which people all over the world have set down the Dante quotation which recurs oftenest to their minds, makes it very clear that in many countries throughout the world, indeed in practically all the civilized countries, a very considerable number of Dante enthusiasts are not sharers in Dante's religious convictions. Dante has drawn all hearts to himself in spite of even that almost insurmountable obstacle, religious prejudice.

Dante is the typical representative of the Middle Ages. He has the faith and the knowledge which during that thirteenth century built the wonderful cathedrals, founded the vast universities, and created great literature in every language of Europe as well as in Latin. All his thoughts are deeply influenced by Scholastic philosophy. To know Dante is to know the Middle Ages better than in any other way. He is above all the representative of the education of that time. Professor Caesare Foligno, Serena Professor of Italian Studies in the University of Oxford, in his monograph on Dante,[3] points out that early in his exile Dante went to Bologna and he is convinced that Dante studied there. The evidence offered for this is that in his later works Dante showed much more than average familiarity with Roman and ecclesiastical law. As a result, lawyers have confidently asserted that he must have spent some time at Bologna which was the great center for the study of law at that time. But Dante spent some time also at Padua. Indeed there is a well-established tradition that

[3] London, 1929.

Dante was on a visit in Padua at the time his friend Giotto frescoed the walls in the chapel of the Arena, which spot has ever since been a favorite place of pilgrimage for Dante and Giotto lovers. The corroboration of this is declared to be the "Dantean character" of Giotto's allegorical figures in that chapel.

The tradition as to Dante's stay in Paris and his attendance at the university there is not so well assured as his stay at Bologna and Padua. Dante lovers and students have always been prone to believe that Dante must have heard some of Siger's lectures in the straw market or he would not refer to them so concretely. The question of his having been at Oxford is more dubious, but there are good reasons to think that he visited the English university sometime toward the end of the first decade of the fourteenth century.

Dante was thus in intimate personal relationship with the most important universities of that time. He is a type of the university man of that period. Poets in the modern time gather at our universities the information that will enable them to express their thoughts most poignantly for their generation. They pick up the science and the philosophy of their time, as well as the literature, and then use the information to bring home the significance of their thoughts to their contemporaries. This is just what Dante did and he manifestly gathered up all the current information of his time and used it to help him express his thoughts in terms of his day, and yet in the very few words that he knew so well how to use for that purpose. Dante, as the university man of his time, is a very striking figure in the history of education.

Dante's exile, so hard to bear, that made his life seem such an utter failure judged by human standards, was really a most fortunate event. The tearing at his heartstrings for his beloved country and for his wife and children stirred the spirit of poetry deep in him, while his wanderings brought him in contact with many different men of many different moods and gave him a knowledge of human nature that otherwise would never have been acquired. As a successful politician in Florence he would be remembered, if at all, for some minor poems. Beyond that, he would have been looked up to as a more or less distinguished citizen of Florence. As it is, he became one of the greatest citizens of the world and during his wanderings had the opportunity to be brought in intimate contact with the great teachers at the universities of that greatest of centuries, the thirteenth, when the nascent institutions of learning were doing so much to rouse the energies of the human mind and illuminate the spirit. He learned how bitter it was to eat the bread of others' tables, to climb up strangers' stairs, but he got closer to the heart of the mystery of life than anyone had ever done and he gave us the significance of life on the curtain of eternity.

Both Longfellow and Lowell in this country, and ever so many others in European countries, have compared Dante to a Gothic cathedral. Longfellow's Sonnets, written to precede his translation of the three divisions of Dante's *Divine Comedy,* are well known and have given many a Dante lover a thrill and many a Dante student his first impulse to take up the study of the divine poet. Lowell's comparison with a cathedral is one of the most eloquent passages in that greatest of studies of Dante, Lowell's essay. In the days when Gothic architecture was considered barbarous — and even the first edition of the *Encyclopaedia Britannica* find no better epithet for it than that — Dante of course could not be properly appreciated. Now that the great Gothic churches are rising all over the country and Gothic architectural lines are finding their way into all sorts of buildings, no wonder that 2,500 books have been written about Dante in this twentieth century. The Gothic cathedral and the *Divine Comedy,* with the universities wherewith they are so intimately connected, are the supremely great gifts of the Middle Ages to humanity.

XVII

THE FIRST GENERATION OF PRINTING

THE last generation of the medieval period, during the first half of the fifteenth century, gradually perfected the art of printing, first with wooden blocks and then with movable metal types, so that the invention must be credited to the Middle Ages. The Latin grammar of Donatus was probably printed before 1450. Shortly after the middle of the century printed books began to appear regularly. Gutenberg was already at work on his first great triumph of printing, the Bible called by his name, before the fall of Constantinople (1453), which is usually set down as the end of the medieval period. Soon printed books began to multiply in ever increasing numbers. Manifestly this generation, born immediately before the close of the Middle Ages, comprising the scholars who had been educated by the last groups of medieval teachers, was deeply interested in the acquisition and diffusion of knowledge. Above all the men of this time were intent on the reproduction of works of enduring influence by the new method which meant so much for the rapid multiplication of books. For those not familiar with the facts it is a great surprise to learn how many printed books this generation of the second half of the fifteenth century bought at the high prices necessarily current, because printing was as yet such a time-taking and laborious art.

The books printed by this first generation that enjoyed

the benefit of printing, down to 1501, are called *incunabula,* that is "cradle" books of the art of printing. Almost needless to say they are considered very precious, not only because of their distinction as rare examples of early printing, but above all because they represent some of the best specimens of the printing art ever issued. Incredible almost as it may seem, some of the earliest printed books were also among the most beautiful books ever printed.

As a result of their preciousness, few except collectors know very much about the books printed at this time, for they are usually stowed away carefully in reserve departments of libraries, or kept in fireproof compartments or safes because many of them are now worth much more than their weight in gold.

In recent years numerous studies of the incunabula have been made, and above all catalogues of them have been published. It is comparatively easy, therefore, to secure information with regard to these books, through which the initiative imparted by the last generation of the Middle Ages was carried onward by the first generation of modern times. Increase of knowledge with regard to them has proved a matter for profound astonishment because of the number as well as the character of the books printed in this incunabula period.

A valuable article on "Incunabula" appeared in the fourteenth edition of the *Encyclopaedia Britannica.* It was written by Pollard, who for many years was Keeper of Printed Books in the British Museum, which contains the largest collection of printed books in the world and where also more incunabula are gathered than in any other place. The writer makes an estimate as to the number of different works and the number of separate volumes that were printed at that time. Mr. Pollard probably has a better right to the formulation of an opinion on this subject than anyone else in our day. Besides he is in possession of more data than could possibly be gathered with regard to this subject until these past few years.

He calls particular attention to the gradual increase in the estimates of the number of books printed before 1501.

Gutenberg's Bible, often called the first book, was issued in 1455–56. At the highest estimate less than a dozen other books (the number is usually set down as seven) were believed to have been issued by the end of 1460. During the next decade, as it was thought, several scores of books came from the press. Then, in the succeeding decade, there were several hundreds. Several thousand, according to the general impression, may have appeared from the presses of Europe in the last decade of the century down to 1501. That was considered a liberal guess. Most people, even among educated booklovers in this country, were inclined to think that when the Vollbehr collection of 3,000 incunabula was acquired for the Congressional Library at Washington, at a cost of $1,500,000, the purchase was well worth while, since with this addition to its store of early printed books the Library of Congress must surely be in possession of nearly a complete collection of incunabula.

Even a little more than half a century ago competent bibliophiles were inclined to think that twelve to fifteen thousand volumes represented the highest possible estimate of the number of different works printed before 1501. Gradually, however, as the result of patient research, the number of *catalogued incunabula* has gone up, not only by addition but by multiplication. Hain succeeded in listing, though he did not live to finish his catalogue, some 13,000 different works. Coppinger, a few years later, raised the number to a little over 20,000, and then Reichling brought it up to nearly 25,000. As research went on, further additions were constantly made. Now German bibliophilic experts are engaged in making a *Gesammt Katalog,* a complete catalogue of the incunabula, and the editors are reasonably confident that they will be able to list well above 35,000 separate items issued from the printing press before 1501. The comparatively recent cataloguing of the Vatican Library has added some 700 previously unknown volumes to the estimate of Pollard.

At least 40,000 items, that is, different works, were printed before 1501. A few of these were insignificant broadsides, single sheets, circulars, or booklets, but the vast majority of them were real books in the fullest sense of that term. Not a few of the books indeed were huge tomes, like the Bible which Gutenberg issued in two large volumes, or Vincent of Beauvais' *Triple Mirror* in three large volumes, or Durandus' *Rationale,* and the *Catholicon* of Balbus, both folio volumes. All these were printed during this less than half a century at the close of the Middle Ages and the beginning of the modern period.

Pollard estimates the number of separate volumes printed by computing the average number of copies in an edition. In the earliest days of printing there were a little over 200 in each edition, and then the type was distributed. The number gradually rose until, in the last decade of the fifteenth century, 700 and sometimes 1,000 or more were printed as a rule in an edition. Pollard thinks it only fair to calculate that the average number in an edition of incunabula would be some 500 or more, and that surely this figure does not represent any exaggeration in the matter. If 40,000 separate works were printed in average editions of 500, then this first generation that was given the opportunity to take advantage of printing absorbed altogether something like 20,000,000 books. This was high tribute to the new art that had come into existence as the result of a climax of medieval inventiveness, but it represents a still higher tribute to the book-mindedness of that generation and the scholarly urge for reading that must have existed among them. Most of them had been born and educated before the Middle Ages came to an end, so that they represent a very interesting exemplification of the intense longing of that group in history for printed books.

It is now some twenty years since Pollard ventured to make that estimate. At first bibliophiles, especially those in possession of reasonably large collections of incunabula, were not willing to accept it. As time has gone on bibliophilic scholars have found more and more reason to credit the figures, and there is question now whether even more books may not have been printed in the incunabula period. Clemens Loeffler, the librarian of the University of Cologne, who has been particularly interested in incunabula, declared at first that the estimate was entirely too high. Cologne was an important center of the printing art in that first generation of printing so that his opinion carried weight, but subsequent studies have led him to the declaration that the figures should not be considered excessive. The average of 500 copies for an edition, as not being too high, has been amply established by recent investigations, so that now there would seem to be no doubt of the truth of that astounding figure of 20,000,000 separate works, not a few of them large tomes and many of them consisting of several volumes.[1] Vincent of Beauvais' *Triple Mirror* consists of three volumes, but they are said to be the equivalent of some sixty volumes octavo in our day.

The greatest surprise is to find how beautifully many of these books of the early days of printing were actually printed. Of course the printers had before them as a rule the illuminated editions which had been made at the cost

---

[1] This enthusiasm for printing continued to grow for the next generation in spite of the fact that a great many printers did not make money and not a few of them failed in business. Father Lenhart has estimated that in the next twenty years, after the beginning of the sixteenth century, there were about 35,000 separate works printed. Since the number in an edition had gone up to 1,000 and even more on the average by this time, he believes that some 35,000,000 books found their way into the hands of readers during that period. This was before the Reformation began to make itself felt. Manifestly there was not only the most complete liberty but also the greatest encouragement of the practice of the printing art. It certainly flourished most happily in Italy, and was particularly patronized by the pope and Church dignitaries and the scholarly ecclesiastics of various ranks who were attached to the Roman schools and colleges and to those of Italy generally. Printers were deeply intent on supplying the reading public with the great works of the olden times and especially the writings of the men who for centuries had been looked upon as the leaders of Christian thought and the bulwarks of Christianity against infidelity.

of so much labor and patience, and these served as models for their printing setup. Miss Stillwell in her *Incunabula Americana*[2] has reproduced a page of the superb Roman type employed by Sweynheim and Pannartz in their volume of *Strabo's Geography,* which they issued at Rome in 1469. She says that, "No books have surpassed these and the volumes issued by Jensen in Venice, and few have equaled them." Miss Stillwell is the librarian of the Annmary Brown Memorial Library, at Providence, where they are very proud to have a collection of examples of practically all the early printers. She would then be in a position to know this subject from wide actual experience and to have such intimate familiarity with all these books as should make her opinion with regard to them of very great value.

The latter half of the fifteenth century was not a period particularly productive in original thought. Scholars were much more intent on securing copies of authors whose works had lived for centuries rather than those of the current day. The master printer of the early days soon realized that the demand was for the great works that had been written during the Middle Ages and especially during the thirteenth century when Scholastic philosophy was at a climax of its development. Manuscript copies of these great medieval works had been preciously preserved in the libraries and had been multiplied by the slow process of handwriting in the monasteries, in spite of the time and labor and almost infinite patience demanded for this purpose. Such books were too precious to be handed about much and special valuable pledges had to be given to secure their circulation. Librarians did their best to satisfy the demands of readers and it is surprising how much they succeeded in doing with the limited means at their command. The new art of printing opened up great new resources for study and these were grasped at eagerly by the scholars of the time who were

---

[2] Columbia University Press, 1931.

anxious to devote themselves to the classics, Christian and pagan, which the new art made so readily available.

The hunger of the time for examples of the great writers of the past accounts for the readiness of men during the first years after the invention of printing to pay the prices that had to be demanded for these early printed books. The new art, though representing such a great improvement over handwriting, was still very slow and expensive. All the work had to be done by hand, the setting of the type was extremely slow, and the hand presses in which each sheet had to be set by itself and then brought firmly down upon the inked type by the slow movement of a handscrew, made the prices that had to be paid for printed books very high. Indeed it has often been said that had it not been for the women, who patronized the printing press wholeheartedly and without complaint of the cost of books, it would have been extremely difficult for the publishers to have gone on and gradually developed the art of printing until it reached what it has become at the present time.

As a rule it had become impossible to obtain manuscript copies of the important works of philosophers and theologians unless they were borrowed through the university or monastic library or were secured by direct connection with the *scriptorium* of a monastery. The reproduction in comparatively large numbers of the old books by the new process brought a great many seekers after books into the market at once. As a result an immense number of volumes were published in the very first generation of printing and were put to ardent and almost constant use immediately. They were studied very sedulously by scholars everywhere. It is not surprising, then, that a great many of these books, indeed the vast proportion of them, disappeared from view in the course of a few generations as the result of the constant use to which they were subjected. The loss of others must be accounted for by the vicissitudes of time and fire and war to which they were exposed. This is what had made the problem of the actual number of incunabula printed rather difficult to solve. Fortunately, enough of these precious old books remain, indeed have been preserved in their entirety, while a large number of others have become known to us in fragmentary form and in references, so that we might make bold to declare that this generation at the end of the fifteenth century was indeed a generation of bookworms. They paid good round sums for solid old books and they took such care of those that a great many of them, many more than could be hoped for from our generation, have lasted for centuries and have come down to us.

Pollard has emphasized the fact that the books printed in the early days of printing were those for which printers felt that there would surely be a demand. Indeed with regard to most of them so many demands had already been made by seekers after knowledge that there was no doubt of the success of the venture of printing them. In a preface written for Professor Osler's *Incunabula Medica*, the former keeper of the printed books in the British Museum, said:

"The real incunables, the books printed before the close of the year 1480, have a spirit of their own for those who take this larger view of bibliography, because these are the books which keen men of business thought it best worth while to spend their money on multiplying when printing became available. The great majority of them represent the work which students already knew by use or hearsay but which [though many of them had been generously multiplied in manuscript] had been difficult or costly to obtain. The amount of original writing [printed at this time] was comparatively small. It was as though the world of letters was taking stock of what it possessed before the new start visible in the markedly different output of the sixteenth century."

The religious books printed during the incunabula period represent three fourths of all that were printed. This is the Renaissance time and many would be inclined to think that a large proportion of the early printing must have been devoted to the reproduction of editions of the classics and works with regard to them. Many would feel that it was this new occupation for intellectual energies which brought about the religious revolt in Germany called the Reformation. As a matter of fact, less than one in five of the printed books were in any way connected with the Renaissance. Some 10 per cent of the publications consisted of works written by humanists, while less than 10 per cent were editions of the Latin and Greek classics. What the clients of the new art of printing called for above all were the great books of the older time, the Fathers and Doctors of the Church, and the philosophers and theologians of the thirteenth and fourteenth centuries. It was these works with which the printers proceeded to supply their customers, and which represent by far the greater majority of the books accorded the privilege of print at this time. The controversial religious books which sowed the seeds of the religious revolt throughout Europe were printed not before but after Luther began his movement. That movement was mainly political rather than religious.

Some of the beautiful manuscript volumes that were made from the twelfth to the fifteenth centuries formed the models from which the printed books of the incunabula period were taken. In order to appreciate the beauty of these manuscript books they must be seen. Words fail adequately to convey an idea of the charming perfection with which they were done. A visit to the Spencer room, with its collection of manuscript books on display at the New York Public Library will enable one to understand in the course of a few minutes better than any amount of description could do, what marvels of precious beauty these books are. There is, for instance, a Latin Vulgate Bible of the thirteenth century done in small type on vellum, handy, so that it was literally a manual and could actually be read from the hand. It has a series of rubrications and miniatures that are charmingly attractive. There is a little Latin Bible of the thirteenth century, with numerous miniatures, initials, and decorations in the best style of that period, which is one of the world's treasures of bookmaking. There is a collection of histories from the Bible, with lives of the saints, that belongs to the earliest French manuscript period and is illustrated with over 800 miniatures whose colors retain all their original freshness. It is in three volumes on vellum and quite, as the descriptive card proclaims, "a compendium of medieval art and imagination." There is a series of volumes of Offices of the Blessed Virgin Mary, *Horae Beatae Mariae Virginis,* each one apparently more beautiful than the other, depending on the one you happened to look at first.

All these beautifully written and decorated books serve to exemplify the fact that time and labor meant nothing to these artists, who were intent on making beautiful things under religious inspiration and with the deepest religious motives. These bookmakers of the later Middle Ages certainly made it very clear that they had taken to heart the thought contained in that precious maxim, "A thing of beauty is a joy forever." These missals and office books, delicately handled by those who appreciated their artistic quality, remain as an illustration of the charming work done by the men of that day. Most of these works were actually used, at least on festival days, for the purpose of participation in the office of the Blessed Virgin as chanted in religious houses.

The kind of books that were printed during that first generation of printing during the incunabula period will be best appreciated from the statistics of the printing presses of that time, as they have gradually become available. There are over 300 editions of Aquinas' various works among the incunabula and it is very clear that practically every printing press that was founded wanted to have the prestige of issuing something written by this prince of Scholastic philosophers and theologians who had illuminated so many other important human interests besides philosophy and theology.

Surely these early printers must have been rather good business men, with a flair for what the public wanted, or they would not have been able to continue their combined publishing and printing trades for long. They knew what was likely to sell and above all what was being called for in the world of scholarship of that time. Hence the run on Aquinas' books, practically all of which are represented in the list of early volumes printed, and some of them many times. One can easily imagine the joy of the ardent student who had been anxious for a look at certain of Aquinas' books, but had not been able to secure them, and now suddenly found that the new art made them readily available. Then there were others who had secured possession of hand-written copies, but for all too short a time to study them as they would have liked, because there were other anxious students who wanted the opportunity to consult and refer to the great master of Scholasticism in his own words. All of these now had a chance to secure the easily readable copies of the printed editions of the Angelic Doctor.

He was a Doctor of the Church, the most sought after authority so far as philosophy and theology were concerned, but also it must not be forgotten, a writer of mystical and practical treatises, quite equal in value to his better known works. It is not surprising, then, that he was a best seller in the incunabula period, nor that we have so many copies of his works among the very early printed books which now command such good prices whenever they come on the market, though more and more they are being stored away in libraries that consider them their specially precious treasures.

After Aquinas in number of publications at this time came St. Augustine, bishop of Hippo, the great Latin Father of the Church. His *De Civitate Dei,* usually considered his most important work, or at least the one with which every scholar with any pretensions to learning in Church history felt that he ought to have some definite familiarity, was one of the very earliest books printed after the Bible. There is an undated edition of the *De Civitate Dei* which was probably issued in 1467, and then another dated edition of that year. Besides there was a further edition in 1468, and an edition in Rome, and a fifth in Venice in 1470, and so on. Altogether 33 editions of the *De Civitate Dei* were published in the incunabula period. Practically all of the cities of Europe that had printing presses, and there were a great many, wanted to have the prestige of issuing an edition of Augustine as well as of Aquinas. The great bishop of Hippo was looked up to as the supreme Christian philosopher, and the scholars of that day were interested in his opinions with regard to all the important questions concerning man and his relations to God and to the universe. He was the most read theologian and more heretics claimed to found their doctrines on him than on any other.

The next popular author in those early years of printing was Cicero, the Roman orator and philosopher. More than 300 editions of his various works were published before 1501. Probably no one would have been more pleased than Augustine himself to know that he and Cicero were rivals in the scholarly attention which they attracted one thousand and fifteen hundred years respectively after their departure from the worldly scene.

Following Cicero came Aristotle with something like 250 editions to his credit. Surely, a wonderful quartet: Aquinas, Augustine, Aristotle, and Cicero, and they still continue to be among the world's greatest authors, whose works remain a valued treasure for scholars. The generation that made best sellers of these authors in the very first period of the art of printing honored themselves by the fine tribute which they paid such writers. Surely the generation deserves the highest recognition for their anxiety to secure the books of these authors so that edition after edition of their works poured from the presses everywhere throughout Europe. The readers of that day were practically all educated in the Middle Ages, that is, before the fall of Constantinople (1453). The picture of scholarly interest which their book buying affords us is, therefore, very different from the long prevalent delusion which actually regarded that generation as uneducated.

After the four great authors mentioned came another distinguished scholar with an A at the beginning of his name. This was Albertus Magnus, the only man ever to have the adjective "Great" attached to his name because of his scholarship. He had written very learnedly on philosophy and theology, he had published a great many observations on natural theology, he had discussed many problems of psychology and indeed was considered the most universal genius of the Middle Ages, the *Doctor Universalis*. No wonder that under such circumstances there were something over 250 editions of the various works of Albertus Magnus that issued from the printing presses of Europe at this time.

The works of the Fathers of the Church naturally attracted the special attention of the early printers. As practical, hard-headed men of business, they were confident that these works would sell. All the monastic libraries, and there were literally many thousands of monasteries in Europe at that time would want to have copies of the works of the Fathers. Accordingly we have, after Augustine's 300 editions, Chrysostom in some 40 editions; Basil the Great with 30; Ambrose, the Latin Father of the Church and Archbishop of Milan, with 24; Athanasius, with 10. The other Fathers of the Church likewise were represented in a number of editions. Many of these books reveal now that they must have been often consulted in the early days, and yet they have been so lovingly cared for during the centuries ever since that we are still able to secure an excellent idea of their original appearance. As a rule, almost without exception, they were books of dignity and nearly always of beauty. Quite needless to say the printing was excellent, the paper is well preserved, and is quite ready to last another five hundred years with any reasonable care. In a great many cases the original bindings still remain, and it was these that touched the heart of William Morris and set him to imitating their appearance for the libraries in the homes he was designing.

Certain other books were called for in rather surprisingly large numbers and the supply was regulated by the demand. For instance, of Balbus' *Catholicon* (in reality an encyclopedia of all matters relating to the Latin language, written originally in the thirteenth century) some 30 incunabula editions were printed. The *Catholicon* was first given to the press about 1459 and is the fourth of the dated books, the first extensive work of profane learning. As it is nearly the size of an unabridged dictionary one would imagine that at most two or three — let us say a maximum of half a dozen — editions would have been the most that could possibly have been sold at this time. Yet, as we have said, there are some 30 incunabula editions of the *Catholicon*. After the *editio princeps* almost each successive year during the latter half of the fifteenth century saw the appearance of a new edition of Balbus. Latin was the language not only of the Church but also of education and science. Hence the widespread interest in Balbus as soon as the work appeared in print.

Certain other books besides those of special ecclesiastical interest were issued in a number of editions at this time, though none of them rivaled in any way Aquinas or Augustine or Aristotle or Albertus Magnus. Law was a very interesting subject because it regulated men's rights as to their worldly possessions, so it was not surprising to find that there were some 200 editions of the various works of Bartolus de Saxoferrato. He was a distinguished professor of law in Bologna, born about the middle of the fourteenth century, who died well on in the fifteenth. In point of time he therefore barely anticipated the comparatively few writers who were contemporaries of this period of printing and had the honor of appearing in a large number of editions.

The most important contemporary of the printing press, however, so far as the number of editions of his various works were concerned, was St. Antoninus, the distinguished

Dominican, afterward the Archbishop of Florence. He was one of the most scholarly men of the fifteenth century but lived only until 1459. He must have heard much of printing and he may have seen some printed books but that is rather doubtful. Printing was not done in Italy until after his time.

St. Antoninus achieved a world-wide reputation in his day for his great work on moral theology. In this he lays down and applies certain fundamental principles with regard to the rights of property and the rights of workmen, the living wage as well as the just price, and other important social questions that are still occupying mankind and never more so than during these past few years. By the general public he was best known for his *History of the World*. This is of great value for a proper understanding, from the viewpoint of a contemporary, of the happenings in Italy during the beginning of the Renaissance period. His reputation as a man of wide information, combined with his leadership in theology, made the early printers (especially after printing presses were established in various parts of Italy) realize that his works would have an extensive sale. As a result of this confidence some 220 editions of his various books were published in the incunabula period during the forty years after his death. The confidence of the booksellers was justified and edition followed edition, bought not only by his own order and monasteries generally but by scholars everywhere, because it was recognized that here was a great scholar, philosopher, theologian whose works would be classics.

A small number of writers, actual contemporaries of the incunabula period, received the honor of print in a number of editions. A typical example among these, an author evidently much sought by the book world of his time, was Battista Mantuanus, Baptista of Mantua, who was considered one of the very clever writers of that period. He was born in 1436 and died early in the sixteenth century. His books are mainly literary and critical and altogether more than 120 editions of his various works were issued before 1501. This is all the more astonishing in view of the fact that only thirty editions of the various works of Dante were issued at this time. Admiration for Dante, however, was in abeyance to a considerable extent during the Renaissance, and it was only later that the supreme greatness of Dante as a poet came to be recognized once more. Mantuanus had the advantage of not requiring so much thoughtfulness for satisfactory reading as Dante and therefore he had a much wider audience and was a far better seller. Best sellers, except during the incunabula period, have usually not been serious books and very seldom books that were to attract attention for prolonged periods after their own time.

The generation which had been educated mainly during the Middle Ages was athirst for information on all the world around them at that time, so we are not surprised that the various encyclopedists, the compilers of information who had been popular during the earlier and later Middle Ages, such as Isidore of Seville, Bartholomew the Englishman, and Vincent of Beauvais, were now in demand among printers and readers. In brief the list of incunabula would illustrate very well Matthew Arnold's definition of literature as the best that had been said and thought.

XVIII

ST. FRANCIS, MEDIEVAL AND MODERN

IN THE concluding chapter of this book on medieval culture we can perhaps do no better than to present in the life of St. Francis of Assisi the key which better than any other unlocks the mystery of the Middle Ages, especially that latter half of them which we have just been considering. It brings us, moreover, directly into touch with the deep spirituality of the Middle Ages.

The growth of sympathetic understanding of this period in modern times is probably more due to the growth of interest in "the little poor man of God," as he liked to call himself, than to any other single factor. The faith, the poetry, the painting, the architecture, the beautiful arts and crafts of that time; the intense resolution to make everything that was used in the service of the Lord beautiful as well as useful, are all marvelously illustrated in the career of St. Francis and in the tributes of those who wanted to do him honor. Taine, the French critic and litterateur, said that the great Gothic church of San Francesco at Assisi "is the most beautiful thing in the world." It is probably the greatest monument ever built to a man. To understand the period in which it was erected, one must devote time to the study of the charming things that are contained in it. It is a paramount educational factor in the period and demonstrates the influence that St. Francis and the early Franciscans exerted over the mental development of their time.

To begin with, it is worth while to know some of the more

important details at least of Francis' life, so full of meaning for his time, but also so full of significance for our own day. Scores of lives, longer and shorter, of St. Francis have been written in the twentieth century, and not a few of them have been among the best-selling nonfiction books of their day. Our money-making, money-loving generation has paradoxically taken to its heart this lover of holy poverty who gave up everything in order that he might be free to cultivate his mind and heart and soul by putting off all physical cares.

Francis was the son of a prosperous cloth merchant of Assisi. His father was wealthy enough to supply him with fine clothes so that for a time he was the glass of fashion for the youth of Assisi, a stalking horse in fine apparel, as it were, to advertise his father's business. According to his own confession, he actually sowed some wild oats, though it is extremely difficult to think, from what we know of his gentle, lovable, saintly character, that these were of any very sturdy variety. Like many a young man of our generation Francis' first experience of life came through service in the army. There was a little war on between Perugia and Assisi, cities of the hill country, a dozen miles apart. Francis, with youthful patriotic spirit, volunteered for service. He was taken prisoner in one of the early battles and his imprisonment afforded him an opportunity to do some rather serious thinking about the emptiness of earthly glory.

Not long after his return from this military experience he was quite ill for a time and had a rather prolonged convalescence. A physician would suspect that he might have suffered from typhoid fever, that companion of armies which until our generation always carried off more soldiers than the enemy killed. Francis seems to have come rather close to the boundary line of life and death.

Life looks very different when viewed through the lens of death, and Francis, as the result of his illness, came to the conclusion that life was not worth living for merely worldly things. So it was that he finally worked out a viewpoint dominated entirely by other-worldly considerations. Even at that time, more than seven hundred years ago, there was a feeling in the minds of chosen spirits, who thought in their hearts as well as their minds, that "things are too much with us," early and late. They found indeed that only too often "things are in the saddle and ride mankind," while thoughts get all too scant a chance to lead men to legitimate conclusions on the purpose of their existence.

Stripping himself of all worldly goods, and in particular casting off his fine clothes as a sign that he would incur no further obligations from his father who sought to deter him from carrying out his resolutions, Francis entered on his new life. He wanted henceforth to have nothing that he could call his own, for he understood the tyranny of things and resolved to be rid of it. Wandering through the little hill towns of the Umbrian country he spoke to men of God and their true home in another world than this. But most people were occupied with the round of their daily affairs, little inclined to give time for serious occupation with the hereafter.

To a great many people, and particularly those who knew his father and his relatives, Francis must have seemed a harmless, innocent sort of fellow, their words implying something of contempt. Friends, doubtless, blamed him for failing to occupy himself with business affairs, accumulating property, and becoming a substantial citizen. Human nature has not changed since Francis' time in this regard and we all know how our generation would be likely to express itself in the presence of events of this kind.

Yet strange enough as it may seem, it was but a short space before other young men came and asked the privilege of following Francis' way of life and of being accepted as companions to him in his prayers and wanderings. Perhaps it will help us to understand his popularity, even in our own sordid day, when we learn that the first who made application to join St. Francis was a rich man of Assisi. He had been watching Francis and had come to appreciate the fact that he was ever so much happier in his new way of life than those around him. Francis was willing to have a companion, but the rich man's possessions stood in the way. Yet this difficulty was after all not insuperable. After a night spent in prayer together the two friends traveled forth into the streets of Assisi, sold all the precious things, and gave the money to the poor, the widows and orphans, to prisoners who were in need, and to pilgrims whom they met along the road, until it all had disappeared. Then they went on their way rejoicing, feeling just like brothers and wearing in their new-found freedom a look of light-hearted happiness that very soon drew others to inquire how they had secured it.

Soon a third postulant asked the privilege of joining them. He had the reputation in Assisi of being a miser. His life had been given to making money, and he liked to have it in gold that he might handle it and gloat over its possession. He had never done any good with it but kept it only to himself. To have the privilege of joining Francis he had now to give away his accumulated treasure and begin the task of doing good for others, forgetful of himself. After the magic number three had been reached, many others, especially of the younger generation, asked the privilege of joining St. Francis. As a result he was now obliged to make out a set of directions for them. He would have preferred to let all have the freedom of the children of God, but he worked out a rule of life that would help them to preserve their liberty amid the worldliness around them.

Then a still more surprising thing happened. One of the girls of Assisi, named Clare, as yet only seventeen years of age and a daughter of one of the best known families of the town, conceived the idea that young women too ought to have the privilege of being followers of St. Francis, or at least imitators of him in this new way of life. She ran away from home to accomplish her purpose and the Saint could not find it in his heart to refuse her appeal. He sent her to a convent where she might be prepared for the new life. Next he refitted for her an abandoned church and some buildings, and so the Franciscans of the Second Order, the Poor Clares, as they have since come to be called in honor of their founder, were established.

Clare's family considered itself disgraced, and when the younger sister too joined St. Clare — as she now is known to us — they stormed the convent and violently dragged her back to her former home. But the girl remained steadfast in her resolve to be a Franciscan, and so eventually they relented and allowed her to rejoin her sister. Not long after this, their mother came to share the happiness of the Franciscan life. Since then, how many thousands of Poor Clares have heroically entered on this way of life!

But the very heart of the mystery of St. Francis is to be found in the admiration he has evoked in our time, some seven hundred years after his death. We have been so much preoccupied during most of the twentieth century with worldly affairs of all kinds, with the building and rebuilding of cities, with wars and the making of money, that it would seem as though the life of St. Francis could have little interest for us. Poverty, with him, was a cardinal virtue so that his mystical marriage to her was the heart of his life. Other-worldliness is anything but the keynote of existence in our day, and yet the life of St. Francis has become of the highest possible interest. Probably over a hundred lives of the "little poor man of God" have been written in the present generation, some of them among the world's best sellers.

What is further surprising is to note the very different classes of people whom Francis affected deeply, not only in his own time but in ours. Men of the most diverse disposition and character have found a common bond of brotherhood in him where it would be least expected. They have found their own deepest aspirations after what is best and highest in life reflected in Francis' all-embracing attitude of mind toward the Creator and His creatures. It is almost astounding to realize the chasms of understanding that had to be crossed to bring together such very different men in admiration of a medieval saint. Professor Kuhns, for many years professor of literature at Wesleyan College,[1] himself a descendant of the rather literal-minded Pennsylvania Dutch yet with deep admiration and reverence for the German mystics, has expressed something of the astonishment that inevitably comes over the lover of St. Francis at the multitudinous and multiphase literature that has gathered round St. Francis. Professor Kuhns said:

"But in his character, far more than in these legendary outward things, did he resemble his Master. All men who have studied his life — rationalist historians like Renan, learned German theologians like Ritschl, enthusiastic specialists like Sabatier — are agreed that no man ever came more near to the character of Christ than Saint Francis. His gentleness, his serenity and sweetness of spirit, his perfect tact, his deep compassion for all suffering humanity, his need of prayer, his discouragement, his yearning for communion with God from time to time, his practical application of religion, his mingling with the crowds in the market-place, and his simple appeals to the hearts of the people — all these things and many more make the life of Saint Francis a true imitation of Jesus Christ."

Those who are inclined to think that the men of the Middle Ages had very little of that deep love of nature which is characteristic of modern times surely do not know their St. Francis. The "little poor man of God" was deeply in love with nature around him, as is so well illustrated by his hymn of the Creatures, *Il Cantico del Sole,* "The Song of the Sun." One of the rubrics in the *Speculum Perfectionis,* by Fra Leone, tells us of "the singular love St. Francis had for water and stones and trees and flowers." For him they were all creatures, animate and inanimate, who had come from God and compelled reverence for that reason. In their own humble way they reflected the beauty and glory and strength of their

---

[1] Middletown, Conn.

Creator. It was thus that Francis spoke and thought of them.

The only creatures with whom Francis was not quite in sympathy were the ants, as Fra Egidio tells us, "because of their excess of prudence in gathering and laying away stores of grain." There was the Scriptural recommendation, "Go to the ant, thou sluggard, and learn wisdom." That was well and good for the sluggard. Francis was no less busy in his own way, but so far as temporal goods were concerned he felt that somehow the Lord would provide. It was a New Englander who said that surely Francis cannot be blamed much for this atttitude of mind "for frugality and thrift are useful qualities but one could hardly call them lovable."

His famous sermon to the birds is after all a revelation of his love of nature and a corresponding revelation of his own heart and his attitude toward the Creator as well as the creature. The incident is said to have occurred one day when St. Clare found him somewhat depressed and encouraged him to go on with his work in spite of the neglect of men. Under that impulse he started out with renewed courage and joy. Coming upon a flock of birds near Bevagna in the hill country he thus preached to them:

"Little birds, ye are much beholden toward God your Creator, and in every place you ought to praise Him. You should thank Him for your warm covering, and for the air which He has given you to live in; that, neither sowing nor reaping, you are fed by Him; that He gives you the mountains and the valleys for your refuge, and the high trees to build your nests in, and the rivers and fountains to drink in. Wherefore, little sister birds, since God loves you so much, beware of the sin of ingratitude and forget not to praise Him."

A number of the stories about St. Francis seem so childish that it would seem as though they could not possibly have interested any except very young people, and them only in a very unsophisticated time. There is the story of Brother Angelo, the rich nobleman's son, who came to ask to be received among the Franciscans, and whom Francis was very glad to receive. He warned him, however, that it would be hard for a young man brought up as he had been in comfort and plenty to bear all the hard things that the Friars Minor had to face in their work. But Brother Angelo met the test and in due course became the guardian or superior of one of the houses in which the Friars Minor lived. One day it happened that three robbers came and demanded food. Brother Angelo refused to have anything to do with them and told them quite frankly what he thought of them.

When Francis heard about the robbers. and how they had been driven away when they demanded food, he refused to eat what was offered him. Instead he required that Brother Angelo should go and find the robbers and give them at least this bread and wine from him. After a long search Brother Angelo found them. Kneeling down, he begged them to forgive the hard words he had spoken to them and offered them the bread and wine which Francis sent. This softened their hearts and they came back to ask Francis to forgive them. He told them to ask God to forgive them, and so these robbers became converted in heart and after proper trials were permitted to enter the community of the Friars Minor, showing themselves very worthy members of the Franciscan family.

This story, like that of the wolf of Gubbio, the marauder who had been working such havoc among the flocks that the shepherds were intent on his destruction, would seem to be little more than a fable. The wolf, after having listened to St. Francis' admonition that he must not slay the little lambs any more, became so changed in heart that he actually seems to have taken the place of the regular sheep-dog guardian of the flock.

It would be easy to think that any man about whom such stories were told would not be taken seriously, and yet surely if anybody has been taken seriously, it is Francis. During the seven hundred and more years that have elapsed since his death there have been throughout the world a million or more of men and women who rejoiced in the privilege of being called Franciscans, because they were trying to shape their lives after that of their father, St. Francis. Some of them lived in the world as Franciscan tertiaries, but all of them in spirit at least were trying to follow in the footsteps of this glorious little poor man of God, who wandered through the hill country round Assisi, insisting that the real purpose of life was to be found not in this world but in another world that comes after it.

Soon the poor man of Assisi realized what an attraction for the hearts of a great many his ideal of holy poverty was, and how it made men happy by freeing them from all solicitude about earthly things. He had foretold it when he said:

"I have seen a great multitude of men coming to us desiring to put on the habit of our holy vocation and to live under the rule of our blessed religious order and their sound is in my ears as they come and go under the orders of holy obedience. I have seen the roads from all the nations full of men coming into these parts: the French are coming, the Spaniards are hastening, the Germans and the English run, and great is the crowd of them who hurry along speaking other tongues."

This might possibly seem to be the language of enthusiasm sweeping sober truth away with it, but we know from definite records that by the middle of the thirteenth century, scarcely twenty years after Francis' death, there were more than 25,000 Franciscans in the world. As early as 1217 there was a house of Franciscans in Jerusalem which has continued to exist there ever since, and the sons of St. Francis still watch over the holy places, while more than 2,000 martyred friars testify to the tenacity with which they have held their posts. The Franciscans were in England, at the other end of Europe, as early as 1224, and were probably in Ireland even before that date.

Francis himself sought martyrdom among the Moslems, but he won their hearts instead and they granted him a safe conduct through Jerusalem in order that he might visit the tomb of the Saviour. In 1220 five Franciscans went to Morocco; they were martyred. It was not long, however, before others followed, evangelizing northern Africa from Morocco to Egypt, whence they descended into Abyssinia and Ethiopia.

Shortly after the middle of the thirteenth century, counting the First, Second, and Third Orders of St. Francis, there were probably 300,000 Franciscans in the world. To a great many people it would seem that Franciscanism, the following of the dear poor little man of Assisi, was a typical medieval procedure, but that it would lack appeal in modern times. As a matter of fact at the present moment there are well above 40,000 members of the First Order of Franciscan friars, comprising some 25,000 Friars Minor, and 4,500 Conventuals and over 13,000 Capuchins. There are 14,000 Poor Clares of the Second Order of St. Francis throughout the world and probably more than 3,100,000 members of the Third Order of St. Francis, not including some 83,000 Brothers and Sisters who live in convents and are proud to be counted among the spiritual daughters of St. Francis and of St. Clare.

It has been suggested that Francis was really a pre-Reformation reformer with ever so much more sympathy with the individualism of Protestantism than with the community spirit of the Catholic Church. Renan dreamed of writing a life of St. Francis in which the little poor man of God would have been the Saint of Nature, in revolt against the Church, an individualist in piety, a forerunner of Luther. Under the inspiration of this French rationalist, Paul Sabatier wrote a life of St. Francis from that standpoint, but as pointed out by Reverend Father James in his little volume on the Franciscans,[2] Sabatier lived to retract his error and with an admirable intellectual honesty proclaimed the fact. Opening a series of lectures on St. Francis before a Protestant audience,

---

[2] London, 1930.

in December, 1914, M. Sabatier found no more fitting theme than that suggested by the significant strophes of the Catholic liturgy:

> *Franciscus vir catholicus,*
> *Et totus apostolicus,*
> *Ecclesiae teneri*
> *Fidem Romanae docuit,*
> *Presbyterosque monuit*
> *Prae cunctis revereri.*[3]

M. Sabatier declared that this antiphon, which emphasizes the doctrinal side of the Saint's life, is the expression of strict historical truth.

How much less profoundly Sabatier understood Francis than those who have been immersed in his spirit for a lifetime is well illustrated by a paragraph from Father James' book *The Franciscans.* The modern son of St. Francis emphasizes the fact that Francis was a true mystic, a "God-intoxicated man," who finds God everywhere:

"Francis did not start from Nature. He set out from God and found Him everywhere. To start with Nature, it would seem, is to start at the wrong end. True, from Nature to Nature's God is a logical passage for the human mind. Indeed man has never been satisfied to remain at the sense level. For a truly aesthetic appreciation of Nature it is necessary to see it flooded with the light of the invisible. Paganism created a dryad for every tree, a naiad for every spring — so true is it that the eye is not filled with seeing, nor the ear with hearing. Yet, historically, the results were not always happy. It is characteristic of Nature's most brilliant activities that, though vaguely suggesting the infinite, they attract attention to themselves and clothe themselves with divine attributes."

It is St. Francis' intoxication with the Deity that explains for us the mystery of the intense influence which he exercised over men and the immense following he secured within a

---

[3] "Francis, a man Catholic and entirely apostolic, taught fidelity to the Roman Church, and recommended the veneration of priests above all other men."

very few years. Nothing illustrates so well how incurably religious man is than the readiness which develops in men and women to follow after religious leaders. It would be easy to think that the followers of St. Francis, who was himself not a man of great intellectual parts, were almost without exception men of no mental acumen. It might even be thought that many of them were the predestined failures among mankind, who found in the novelty of this new mystical doctrine an attraction that gave them an opportunity to be different from other people and therefore minimize the feelings of intellectual inferiority by which they were obsessed.

As a matter of fact, however, Francis attracted to himself some of the most distinguished thinkers of his day. Many books have been written about them. So far from being dead, they are now, seven hundred years after their bodily death, more alive in the influence they exert than ever. Their gentle sister, the death of the body, to use St. Francis' sympathetic phrase, took away what was mortal of them and now they have entered upon immortality as greater vital forces in the the world than when they were living mortals.

The appeal of Francis has been to the greatest souls down the ages. In the century after Francis, Dante was proud to be a member of the Third Order and to be buried in its habit. According to the old tradition the exiled Italian poet, weary with wandering, knocked one evening at the door of a lonely monastery of Franciscans in the Apennines. To the question, what did he wish, he replied in a single word, "Peace." That was what Francis meant to a disturbed world of his time more than anything else. He had given his sons as the words of greeting that they were to pass on to all those whom they met, "Peace be to you," and when they would enter any dwelling, "Peace be to this house."

Ever since, all down the ages, St. Francis has brought peace to many a disturbed soul. He has touched most deeply those who were themselves most intelligent. Cardinal Mercier, of whom the whole world came to think so much during the

Great War, once said, "One cannot help regretting that so much time is wasted in seeking elsewhere the lessons of spirituality when it would have been so easy to learn them from St. Francis in contemplation of Christ crucified."

There are many other distinguished Franciscans who look up to their great founder as one of the most wonderful men in the world. Among them are such distinguished scholars as St. Bonaventure, a leader of thought in his day; Alexander of Hales, philosopher and teacher; Duns Scotus, one of the subtlest of human minds; to say nothing for the moment of many others. Jean Gerson, chancellor of the University of Paris, did not hesitate to proclaim St. Bonaventure in his day as the surest master of the spiritual life. The Franciscan Alexander of Hales was looked upon by the great Dominican theologian, St. Thomas Aquinas, as "master of those who know in the realm of theology."

These were among the early Franciscans. Father Cuthbert, in his volume on the Capuchins, has pointed out that the Capuchin humanists of the sixteenth and seventeenth centuries were the great leaders in a real reform movement within the Church. Father Cuthbert was not less surprised and bewildered by the wealth of their wisdom than the great French literary man and member of the French Academy, Henri Brémond, by their literary and poetic abilities. Father Cuthbert's chapter in *The Capuchins* (Vol. 1), with the title "The Capuchins Make Literature," reads like a romance.

So little did these early Franciscans care for worldly prestige or recognition during their lifetime, so like were they to their father, St. Francis, in the matter of avoiding personal prestige, that it has occasioned in our day a difficult problem to ascertain their authorship in the case of even important literary works. Not infrequently some of their great hymns have been attributed for centuries to others than the real authors because of this fact. A typical example is to be found in the *Dies Irae,* declared to be one of the supreme hymns of all time, which was for centuries attributed to Pope

Innocent III; its author was really Thomas of Celano, one of the intimate friends of St. Francis. The same thing is true of the *Stabat Mater Dolorosa*, ascribed for many years to other writers, until Luke Wadding, the Franciscan historical writer in the seventeenth century, restored it to Jacopone. There are more than forty English translations of this wonderful religious poem and there are many hundreds of translations into other languages. Of the *Dies Irae* there are said to be more than a thousand translations of poetic merit. Music for these hymns has been written by all the great masters of church music and by many of the writers of secular music. Franciscan hymns proved the stimulus for great composers to endow Church music with some of the most inspiring of religious melodies.

Several years ago I had the privilege of a long hour's talk with Jörgensen, the Danish poet, whose life of St. Francis attracted so much attention in our generation and was translated into most of the modern languages. For a time Jörgensen was attracted to St. Francis mainly because of the poetic genius of *il poverello*, but also because they had in common such an intense love of nature. Jörgensen soon came to realize that Francis' way of life meant ever so much more than the prayerful attitude of mind in the presence of the setting sun or the splendor of the starlit night. It was not his love of nature but his love of nature's God that was the secret of Francis' influence over men and the attraction which he exerted over them. A great many in all generations have shared Francis' quest of the meaning of life. Jörgensen's discovery of the real St. Francis led to his conversion to the Church of which St. Francis is such a glorious representative, and it further resulted in the writing of the life of St. Francis, which has given the Danish poet a distinguished place among the followers of the little poor man of God.

Jörgensen's life of St. Francis has further won for him the honorary citizenship of St. Francis' beloved city of Assisi. To have been brought even a little into intimate touch with the

Danish poet is to appreciate very thoroughly how the attraction which St. Francis exerted seven hundred years ago in that little hill town of Umbria for chosen spirits, is still weaving its web as of yore. It has been said that St. Francis is the most perfect Christian who ever lived. He incarnates the life of Christ so profoundly that he exerts an enduring attraction for the souls of men of good will. Mankind will have to become something very different from what it is at the present time before the attraction of Francis will cease to exert its influence. He is still a living spirit, walking the narrow crooked streets of his native city, and almost inevitably visitors will come under the spell of the influence exerted by that spirit, even though their stay may be but brief. It is an unforgettable experience to have walked in the paths and along the roads once trod by Francis himself, the ardent follower of Christ.

The more one knows about St. Francis the harder it becomes to understand the strong devotion in our day of all sorts of people to *il poverello di Dio*, "the little poor man of God." The basis of St. Francis' life is Christ's precept, "Give up all thou hast and follow Me." If there is anything in the world that this generation is not ready to do it is follow that counsel of Christ to the rich young man, on whom the Master looked and whom He loved, yet who turned away because the counsel seemed too hard to him. Though it was a counsel only and not a precept, yet there are those who say that this was *il gran rifiuto*, "the great refusal," of which Dante speaks.

Probably the best explanation we have of the modern devotion to St. Francis is that given in *The True St. Francis*:

"What is the cause of the present widespread homage to St. Francis? It is, of course, far too wide a question to allow the present writer to do more than make a few suggestions. First and foremost, we must ever reckon with the perennial charm of the Saint's personality, which seems to wield an ineffable influence over the hearts of men — drawing and holding those of the most different habits of mind, with a sense of personal sympathy. Perhaps no other man, unless it be St. Paul, ever had such wide-reaching, all-embracing sympathy; and it may have been wider than St. Paul's, for we find no evidence in the great apostle of a love for nature and of animals. This exquisite Franciscan spirit, as it is called, which is the very perfume of religion— this spirit at once so humble, so tender, so devout, so akin to the 'good odor of Christ' — passed out in the whole world and has become a permanent source of inspiration. A character at once so exalted and so purified as St. Francis was sure to keep alive an ideal; and so he does. From this one can easily understand St. Francis' dominance among a small but earnest band of enthusiasts now pointing the world back to the reign of the spirit. It was this same gentle idealism of St. Francis which inspired the art of the Umbrian people; it was this which was translated into the paintings of the greatest artists. No school of painting has ever been penetrated with such pure idealism as the Umbrian; and this inspiration, at once religious and artistic, came from the tomb of the *poverello,* above which Giotto had painted his mystical frescoes. The earnest quasi-religious study of the medieval beginnings of Western art has therefore rightly been set down as another cause for some of the latter-day pilgrimages to Assisi. In like manner, the scientific treatment of the Romance literature leads naturally to St. Francis as to the humble upper waters of a mighty stream; at the beginning of the thirteenth century is St. Francis, at the end is Dante. It was Matthew Arnold, we believe, who first held up the poor man of Assisi as a literary type — a type as distinct and formal as the author of the *Divine Comedy.* 'Prose,' he says, 'could not easily satisfy the saint's ardent soul, and so he made poetry.' 'It was,' writes Ozanam, 'the first cry of a nascent poetry which has grown and made itself heard through the world.' "

St. Francis seems typically medieval to a great many people in our day, and that is exactly what he is, yet he is so modern in his appeal that more lives of him have been written in our generation than of almost anyone else. Seven hundred years ago he attracted young men to follow him by the thousands, but he is attracting them no less at the present time. Thousands on thousands of Franciscans are working over all the world, proud to think of him as their father in Christ. He was the subject of intense interest to men of all kinds in his own century, to painters, poets, sculptors, architects, but so is he in the twentieth century. His appeal is just as strong and the depth of his attraction shows how little man has changed in the interval. It is not surprising to have him come back into the love and reverence of mankind so strikingly, since all the contemporary interests of mankind of that time have come back in very much the same way. Gothic architecture and Gothic art, Gothic literature and Gothic crafts, have all been brought to a focus of attention in the present generation. They represent the triumphs of medieval power of achievement, but not the least of these was Francis who proved to be one of the greatest factors for the awakening of the human spirit.